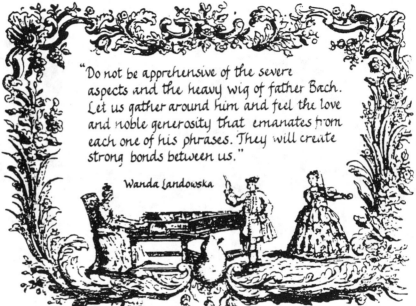

"Do not be apprehensive of the severe aspects and the heavy wig of father Bach. Let us gather around him and feel the love and noble generosity that emanates from each one of his phrases. They will create strong bonds between us."

Wanda Landowska

Johann Sebastian Bach

Johann Sebastian Bach

As His World Knew Him

❧

Otto L. Bettmann

Foreword by Martin Bookspan

A BIRCH LANE PRESS BOOK
Published by Carol Publishing Group

A Birch Lane Press Book
Published by Carol Publishing Group
Birch Lane Press is a registered trademark of Carol Communications, Inc.
Editorial Offices: 600 Madison Avenue, New York, N.Y. 10022
Sales and Distribution Offices: 120 Enterprise Avenue,
Secaucus, N.J. 07094
In Canada: Canadian Manda Group, One Atlantic Avenue, Suite 105,
Toronto, Ontario M6K 3E7
Queries regarding rights and permissions should be addressed to
Carol Publishing Group, 600 Madison Avenue, New York, N.Y. 10022

Carol Publishing Group books are available at special discounts for bulk purchases,
sales promotions, fund raising, or educational purposes. Special editions can be
created to specifications. For details, contact Special Sales Department, Carol
Publishing Group, 120 Enterprise Avenue, Secaucus, N.J. 07094

Manufactured in the United States of America
10 9 8 7 6 5 4 3 2 1

Frontispiece courtesy of Archiv für
Kunst and Geschichte, Berlin.

Border on the title page is a decoration from Bach's Clavier Übung IV,
the *Goldberg Variations*, 1742.

*All illustrations not otherwise credited
are from the author's collection.*

Library of Congress Cataloging-in-Publication Data

Bettman, Otto.
Johann Sebastian Bach as his world knew him / by Otto L. Bettmann;
foreword by Martin Bookspan.
p.   cm.
"A Birch Lane Press book."
Includes bibliographical references.
ISBN 1-55972-279-7 (hardcover)
1. Bach, Johann Sebastian, 1685-1750—Encyclopedias.   I. Title.
ML410.B1B3938 1995
780'.92—dc20
[B]   94-41052
                                                                        CIP
                                                                        MN

For Dianne Skafte
with whom I have enjoyed a long friendship
in the Bachian spirit

In the editorial development of this book, I have had the invaluable assistance of Melvin Kalfus, a friend and historian of high standing. (His psychobiography of the great American landscape architect Frederick Law Olmsted [New York: New York University Press 1990], has become an authoritative source in the field.) Dr. Kalfus and his wife Alma have worked tirelessly on my manuscript, far beyond the call of duty. They have contributed greatly to its final shaping, and I will always be deeply indebted to them.

Contents

Foreword

For more than a century, the name of Johann Sebastian Bach has been firmly established in the pantheon of composers—as the creator of such complex and protean works as the *Well-Tempered Clavier*, the *Brandenberg Concertos*, the *Goldberg Variations*, the *Art of the Fugue*, and countless other masterworks. Indeed, so august has been his stature that it is hard for us to visualize behind the image of "the Holy Cantor" the very human individual who had to deal with the frustrations and conflicts and heartaches that life holds for us all.

It may also be hard for us to conceive of the fact that for several generations after his death Bach had been all but forgotten by the music-loving populace, and that what remained of his vast number of creations mostly gathered dust in remote archives or private collections. It remained for Felix Mendelssohn, but twenty years old, to bring about a revival of interest in Bach's works with his 1829 performance of the *St. Matthew Passion*. By 1850, publication of the Bach *Gesamt-Ausgabe* (complete edition) had begun—which was to have an enormous influence on late-Romantic composers.

By the early years of the twentieth century, two monumental biographies had been published, the first written by the pioneer music historian Philipp Spitta, the second by the great organist and humanitarian Albert Schweitzer. The Spitta biography is exhaustive in its scholarship on Bach's life and works. The Schweitzer book is a masterpiece of insight into Bach's creative genius, the kind of book that could only have been produced by one who was not only a great writer and scholar, but also a great musician. Both these works continue to be regarded as classics even in the face of the enormous advances in Bach research during the many decades since their appearance. Both of them, however, may have contributed to the persistent image of Bach as the bewigged "Holy Cantor," an image that—together with the sheer bulk of these two mighty biographies—may have made Bach the man seem unapproachable to modern-day music-lovers.

In the time since their publication, we have seen the growth of a veritable cottage industry of Bach scholarship, varying from numerous biographies to specialized studies of individual works or episodes in Bach's life. These studies tend to be musicological in spirit and often exceedingly technical in their detail, written by scholars mainly for the edification of other scholars. Individually and collectively, they contribute greatly to an understanding of Bach's works and a re-creation of his times, but they too are often intimidating to the average music-lover who might otherwise wish to know more about the Leipzig master.

Thanks to the electronic revolution of our time, the great works of Bach are now available in almost innumerable recordings and interpretations made by the leading musicians and conductors of the twentieth century. Little did the Leipzig cantor know that the music he composed for a few hundred congregants in his town's churches would one day be the passion of a growing number of music-lovers throughout the world—millions of people of many different beliefs and nationalities. But we may hazard a guess that very few among this vast audience know very much about Bach the man and his times. With this fascinating and remarkable book—*Johann Sebastian Bach: As His World Knew Him*—even the casual music-lover has an opportunity to learn more about the man behind the great masterworks.

Otto Bettmann, the author of this new approach to Bach biography, has some unique credentials for undertaking a work such as this. In 1909, only a year after the German edition of Schweitzer's massive biography of Bach had been published, his father, Dr. Hans Bettmann, an orthopedic surgeon, established his Leipzig clinic and his home in the heart of "Bach country." Only six years old at the time, Otto would spend his formative years perhaps five hundred feet from the Thomaskirche, the church for which Bach had been the cantor for twenty-seven years (1723–1750).

As he notes in his delightful illustrated autobiography, *Bettmann, The Picture Man*, Otto and his brother, as they walked to school each day, would pass by the Thomaskirche courtyard, with its imposing Bach monument. The calendar of his childhood years was marked with two Bach highlights: the annual Good Friday performance of the *St. Matthew Passion* in the Thomaskirche, and a New Year's Eve performance of Bach chorales from a tower directly across from the Bettmann residence.

At ten, Otto was recruited, along with several other Jewish boys, to sing in the Auxiliary Boys' Choir which performed on the second

Sunday of each month in the Thomaskirche. To go to synagogue on Friday night and sing in a church on Sunday, Otto Bettmann notes, did not then seem odd to the children of a cultured German-Jewish family. As was also traditional in such families, young Otto was put in the care of a certain Fräulein Schütze, a stern piano teacher who soon had her student mastering, among other works, "the simple gavottes, minuets, and marches Bach had written for his young sons."

Three decades later, the situation in Germany would change drastically with the emergence of Adolf Hitler as Reichschancellor in 1933 and the onset of the Nazi nightmare in Germany. In 1935, when American cousins persuaded Otto to be the first of his family to flee from Nazism, he took with him only two treasures—the trunkful of photographic negatives that would in the United States become his livelihood, and a deep and abiding love of Johann Sebastian Bach and his music.

Long before those dark days, Otto received a doctorate at the University of Leipzig, then served a short stint as a junior editor in the Leipzig music-publishing house of C. F. Peters. Next, Otto became a librarian in the Prussian State Art Library in Berlin. It was here that he developed his strong interest in iconography—"history told in pictures"—and began to photograph and collect artwork depicting the vast scope of human activities across the centuries. And it was here that he experienced one of the great periods of avant-garde creativity in history, Berlin in the 1920s and '30s, prior to the rise of Hitler—the Berlin of Bertolt Brecht, Arnold Schönberg, Josef von Sternberg, Max Reinhardt, and countless others, many of whom enriched American culture as émigrés in the decades during and after the Second World War.

When he too joined the emigrant outpouring to America, Otto found himself residing in New York City during America's Great Depression. In 1936, making good use of the photographic treasures he brought with him from Germany, he founded the Bettmann Archive. At one time housed in a converted coal cellar, the Archive is today an enterprise known worldwide among editors, authors, art directors, and film producers as a source of illustrations for articles, books, advertisements, and television programs.

Although well known as the "Picture Man," Otto Bettmann could also be called the "Book Man." A self-confessed "workaholic," he managed—despite his responsibilities as director of the Archive—to author or coauthor almost a dozen books, among them the *Pictorial*

History of Music and a perennial favorite, *The Good Old Days—They Were Terrible*, surely one of the more irreverent history books ever written.

In 1981, approaching eighty years of age, Otto Bettmann sold the Bettmann Archive to the Kraus-Thomson Publishing Group and "retired" to Boca Raton, Florida, where he had spent part of each winter for the prior several years. When he recounts this part of his life story, Otto always has a twinkle in his eye, for the word *retirement* hardly describes his regimen since becoming a full-time citizen of southern Florida's Gold Coast. Building on a relationship he had established as a part-time resident, Otto now became the curator of rare manuscripts for Florida Atlantic University. And he continued to produce books: *The Delights of Reading*, which was launched with a program at the Library of Congress in 1987, and his illustrated autobiography, which was published in 1992 (in his ninetieth year).

Otto Bettmann also took with him into "retirement" his enduring love of Bach. As he notes in *The Picture Man*, Otto ends each day "taking refuge" in the "unfathomable works" of his patron saint. Playing on an earphone-equipped Yamaha (to spare his neighbors), he immerses himself in the music of the *Well-Tempered Clavier*: "I leave for a few precious moments the disorderly world with its myriad unsolved problems and enter one where serenity and order prevail."

It has long been Otto's hope to produce a new kind of Bach biography. Through the decades of his fascination with Bach—man, musician, and composer—he assembled a rather comprehensive Bach library and developed what he called his Bach "Organon"—a collection of hundreds of entries filed under every conceivable aspect of Bach's life and work. The result of his lifelong obsession is the present book: *Johann Sebastian Bach: As His World Knew Him.*

Otto describes his book as a "Bach Lexicon"—both a reference work and a collection of personal essays on Bach's life and Bach's music, arranged alphabetically by subject. None is more than a few pages long, and all are fascinating and accessible. The standard biography of any artist is usually produced as a year-by-year chronological work, exhaustive in detail. It normally takes a dedicated enthusiast to wade through the hundreds of pages of such a work, often a daunting task. How refreshingly different is this book! According to your preference, you can start with the first essay, *Abendmusik* (Evening Concerts), and read consecutively to the last, *Zeitgeist*, sitting down to an entry, or two or three, whenever you have a half-hour or an hour to spare for relaxation and edification. Or you can pick out the subjects that appeal to you the most and work your way here and there through the book, returning for more whenever you find the time. Since the essays are arranged alphabetically, and not chronologically, Otto Bettmann has thoughtfully provided a brief introductory chronology to serve as a handy guide to the years and locations of various events in Bach's life, and to his age at the time. As one might expect from the "Picture Man," the book is filled with marvelous illustrations.

I have long considered myself quite knowledgeable about Bach's life and works—but I confess that I have learned much by browsing through Otto Bettmann's fascinating book. You have a treat in store!

—MARTIN BOOKSPAN

The Thomaskirche *(left)*,
center of Bach's activities
during his Leipzig years
(1723–1750). View seen
from the balcony of the
house where the author
grew up, in the midst of
"Bach country."

Chronology

1685–1695
To Age 10
Eisenach

Johann Sebastian Bach was born March 21, 1685, the youngest (eighth) child of Johann Ambrosius Bach, town musician of Eisenach in the Thuringian forest. His father gave Sebastian his first musical instruction, on the violin. The youngest Bach attended the Eisenach Gymnasium, irregularly, receiving an early education in the classics. Sebastian's mother died in 1694. His father, who had remarried, died a year later.

1695–1700
Age 10–15
Ohrdruf

An orphan at ten, young Sebastian found refuge in the home of his older brother, Johann Christoph, organist in neighboring Ohrdruf and a pupil of Johann Pachelbel. The young boy attended the Lyceum—a school of considerable repute in the humanities. He received his first instruction in keyboard-playing from his brother and began his lifelong practice of copying the manuscript scores of other composers, for self-instruction.

1700–1703
Age 15–18
Lüneburg

With his brother's family responsibilities increasing, fifteen-year-old Sebastian was forced to fend for himself. He hiked more than two hundred miles north to Lüneburg, where he was given a scholarship as a member of the choir at the Michaelisschule. The school provided him with a thaler-a-month income and training in music and the humanities. Just after he turned seventeen, and without finishing school, Bach accepted his first professional post as violinist and lackey in the court orchestra of Duke Johann Ernst of Weimar. Bach had by this time established a reputation as a highly accomplished organist. He was at Weimar only a few months when he was invited to test and inaugurate the new organ at the Neuekirche in Arnstadt, close to his hometown of Eisenach.

1703–1707
Age 18–22
Arnstadt

Young Bach so impressed the Arnstadt consistory with his organ-playing that he was offered the post of organist and choirmaster of the town's Neuekirche. His Arnstadt tenure, however, did not prove a happy one—as Bach neglected his cantorial duty of training singers and often was at odds with the church and town leaders.

Late in 1705, Bach (now twenty) was given a one-month leave to visit the Hanseatic city of Lübeck in north Germany, to become acquainted with the evening concerts (*Abendmusiken*) of Dietrich Buxtehude, the famed Danish organist. Much to the dismay of the Arnstadt town fathers, Bach remained for four months in Lübeck—apparently under the spell of Buxtehude's concerts. Returning from this artistically inspiring venture, Bach was taken to task by his Arnstadt superiors for overstaying his leave, then was severely criticized for playing "daring variations with many strange sounds"—no doubt inspired by his Lübeck venture.

1707–1708
Age 22–23
Mühlhausen

In June 1707, Bach secured the job of organist of the Blasiuskirche in Mühlhausen (some forty miles northwest of Arnstadt). Though his stay was brief, it was marked by two significant events. On October 17, 1707, he married a distant cousin, Maria Barbara Bach—with whom he would have seven children. Also, he began to establish himself as a notable composer of church music, especially for the organ. A few months after his marriage saw the performance of his first cantata, *Gott ist mein König* (God Is My King). Printed at the expense of the Town Council, this was the only one of Bach's estimated three hundred cantatas to be published during his lifetime. But increasing Pietist opposition to the use of music in church services spurred Bach to move on.

1708–1717
Age 23–32
Weimar

Bach significantly improved his station in life when, on July 14, 1708, he was appointed court organist to Duke Wilhelm Ernst of Saxe-Weimar, a highly cultivated, if somewhat dour and self-willed ruler. In 1714, Bach was given the additional appointment of concertmaster of the court's orchestra. Encouraged by the duke's obvious pleasure in his performances and compositions, Bach wrote most of his important organ works in Weimar. It was here too that Bach first became acquainted with the great masters of the Italian school—especially Antonio Vivaldi. He also began to travel frequently to neighboring towns as a consultant on the construction of organs.

The Weimar years were notable for the birth of six Bach children, four of whom survived to adulthood. These included two sons of exceptional musical talent: Wilhelm Friedemann (1710) and Carl Philipp Emanuel (1714).

Passed over for the position of capellmeister of Duke Wilhelm Ernst's court orchestra in 1712, Bach chafed under the absolutist rule of the duke and finally sought a new position elsewhere. In 1717, he was offered the capellmeister post by a visiting nobleman, Prince Leopold of Anhalt-Cöthen. Accepting immediately, Bach was prevented from leaving Weimar by the obstinate duke, who had his now-famous organist imprisoned for a month before giving him a grudging dismissal.

1718–1723
Age 33–38
Anhalt-Cöthen

As capellmeister to Prince Leopold, at Cöthen, Bach was to spend six of the happiest and most productive years of his career—except for the sudden death in 1720 of his wife, Maria Barbara, after twelve years of marriage. But Bach was to make a most fortunate second marriage, in 1721, to Anna Magdalena Wülcken—a gifted professional singer who was twelve years his junior.

Bach's Cöthen years were devoted almost entirely to instrumental music—particularly keyboard works, concertos, and chamber music, including the first volume of the *Well-Tempered Clavier* (1722). But Prince Leopold, after his second marriage, began to lose interest in his orchestra, prompting Bach to once again seek a new position. One effort in this direction was the composition of a gift for the Margrave Christian Ludwig of Brandenburg-Prussia—the six Brandenburg Concertos (1721). Had Bach composed nothing more after Cöthen, his reputation would have been secure with the many treasures he had created at Prince Leopold's court.

Nevertheless, Bach's immortal gift to the Brandenburg margrave did not secure a new position for him, so in 1723 he accepted, after some hesitation, the post of cantor of the Thomaskirche in the important commercial town of

Leipzig. Though this was a prestigious position, Bach left Cöthen with considerable regret and some feeling that surrendering the title of capellmeister (orchestra leader) at the court of Prince Leopold for a position as the Leipzig cantor (director of church music) represented a significant reduction in status.

1723–1730
Age 38–45
Leipzig: The
Early Years

As Leipzig's cantor and music director, Bach was responsible for the supervision of many areas of music-making for the Thomaskirche and its school, for the town itself, and for the town's historic university. Unfortunately, these diverse responsibilities also meant that Bach would be called upon to serve many masters, very few of whom could appreciate his artistic genius and creative achievements. This resulted in unending quarrels: with the church Consistory and the rector of the school, with the Town Council, and with the university leaders. While these squabbles added to Bach's burdens, he defended his rights tenaciously and delegated as many of his onerous responsibilities as he could—devoting his genius to the creation of "a compleat church music."

At the outset of his Leipzig career, Bach produced a veritable avalanche of cantatas, which often poured forth at the astonishing rate of one a week. Undoubtedly inspired by the rising popularity of opera in Europe, Bach provided the soloists and choir with much greater instrumental support than was traditional for the cantata form. Indeed, what he created for the weekly Sunday services in Leipzig was a new musical genre which he preferred to call *Hauptmusik* (principal music).

Shortly after his arrival in Leipzig in 1723, Bach had completed and performed the three-hour-long *St. John Passion*. And this continuing flood of church music was crowned, in 1729, by the *St. Matthew Passion*—a majestic and complex four-hour work. But his efforts remained on the whole unappreciated by the church leaders and town officials.

Bach's great Leipzig works had to be almost always performed with inferior vocal and instrumental resources. After seven years of bickering with the penny-pinching town fathers, Bach let loose a cannonade of complaints in his *Short but Most Necessary Draft for a Well-Appointed Church Music*, submitted to the Town Council in August 1730. In this memorandum, Bach argued that to provide the town with a proper and inspiring church service would require an orchestra of eighteen to twenty accomplished instrumentalists and a chorus of twelve to sixteen talented singers, some of whom would serve as soloists.

The town's leaders ignored his complaints and his request for additional financial support. Instead, the members unleashed their own torrent of complaints about their music director—especially about his stubbornness and high-handedness. Thus rebuffed, Bach wrote an old friend—the diplomat Georg Erdmann—of his frustrations, noting that his income was inadequate and that his position had become one of "almost constant vexation, envy, and harassment." He told Erdmann that he felt compelled to seek his fortune elsewhere, asking the diplomat's help in finding a suitable new post. He was fated, however, to spend the rest of his days in Leipzig.

1731–1740
Age 46–55
Leipzig: The
Middle Years

Frustrated in his cantorial duties and apparently unable to locate a suitable position elsewhere, Bach seemed to turn away from the composition of church music during his middle years, concentrating on more worldly works which he performed at the town's Collegium Musicum. This group of instrumentalists was at one time headed by Bach's famed contemporary, Georg Philipp Telemann. It held forth in Zimmermann's Coffeehouse, a gathering place for Leipzig's merchant class, stressing a secular sort of musical fare—lighter than the music offered in the town's churches. (The Collegium Musicum, modest as the group was in Bach's time, would evolve into the famed Leipzig Gewandhaus Orchestra.) One of the secular cantatas Bach produced in this period was undoubtedly written for the Collegium and first performed at Zimmermann's—the *Kaffee Kantate*, his stab at what we might today call an operetta.

As he approached the age of fifty, Bach created one of his most profound sacred works—ironically, not written for his Protestant employers. This was the *Kyrie* and *Gloria* of the Catholic Mass (the *B Minor Mass*), composed for the new Catholic elector of Saxony recently installed in Dresden. It was clearly presented to the elector in the hope of securing an appointment to the royal court.

In the meantime, the cantor's family was growing, and the next generation of Bachs began to take its place in Germany's music world. Bach's oldest son, Wilhelm Friedemann, was appointed organist of the Sophienkirche in Dresden in 1733. His second son, Carl Philipp Emanuel, became, in 1738, harpsichordist to Crown Prince Frederick of Prussia. But most of Bach's parental concern in this decade was devoted to his third son, also musically gifted— Gottfried Bernhard. Bach interceded personally both to obtain posts for this troubled young man and to pay off the debts that Bernhard had incurred. Bernhard died in 1739 at the age of twenty-four.

When Bach was fifty, yet another son, Johann Christian, was born. Christian—like his older brother, Carl Philipp Emanuel—would later achieve considerable international renown in the emerging Art Galant style of music. Wilhelm Friedemann, the oldest and reputedly the most gifted of all the cantor's progeny, would dissipate his talent with drink and irresponsible behavior.

1741–1750
Age 56–65
Leipzig: The
Final Years

Working assiduously, often at night by candlelight, Bach was increasingly plagued by eye troubles. As he reached his late fifties, Bach detached himself more and more from his Leipzig duties, both sacred and secular. Turning progressively inward, he now set out to create the three great works that mark his final decade and have become exemplars of the Baroque style—of which Bach was undeniably the greatest practitioner.

Bach's efforts in this direction were initiated in 1741–42 by a work of stupendous power—recognized today as the unquestioned high point of eighteenth-century clavier music. This masterwork was, of course, the celebrated *Goldberg Variations*, whose daring and depth brought keyboard music to a level not to be reached again until the appearance of Beethoven's *Hammerklavier Sonata* in 1818.

The popular title of this majestic work immortalizes not the aristocratic patron for whom it was said to have been created, Count Hermann Carl von Keyserlingk, but rather the count's employee, the legendary keyboard artist and prodigy, Johann Theophilus Goldberg. The young virtuoso was said to have played the *Variations* to while away the painful hours during the count's frequent attacks of insomnia.

The second of Bach's final masterworks was also written for a music-loving nobleman—Frederick II, king of Prussia, known to posterity as Frederick the Great. In 1747, at the rather advanced age of sixty-two, Bach undertook an arduous two-hundred-mile trip to Berlin to visit his son Carl Philipp Emanuel, who was the principal harpsichordist at the court of the Prussian king. It must have been particularly tempting for the aging cantor to seek a connection with a court that could boast of a fine orchestra and was ruled by a highly cultured monarch who passionately loved music. The king was an accomplished flute-player, and had himself written over one hundred concertos for this instrument.

King Frederick II had heard of Bach's fabled skill as an improviser and, during the master's visit to the court with his son, the king went to one of his harpsichords and intoned a theme, asking his guest to use it as the basis for a fugue. Bach began, but as he improvised, he found that his theme was not quite suitable to serve as the basis for a six-part fugue. Hence, he replaced the "Royal Theme" with one of his own invention, which he developed into a three-part fugue.

Unhappy at failing to meet the king's specific request, Bach, after returning home to Leipzig, used the "Royal Theme" as a springboard for the composition of one of the great masterworks of keyboard music, which we know now as the *Musical Offering*.

Bach was still working on the last of his three "summation works"—the *Art of the Fugue*—when he died in 1750. In this final masterwork, he displayed the full potential of the style of music he had spent a lifetime perfecting. His final creation was a chorale that he—blind and on his deathbed—dictated to his son-in-law and star pupil, J. C. Altnikol. This valedictory chorale, touchingly appropriate, was "Before Thy Throne O Lord I Stand."

Postmortem: Oblivion and Revival

Bach had received a fairly comfortable income during the last decade of life, leaving an estate valued at about three hundred thalers (almost three hundred thousand dollars in today's money). However, much of this estate went to his adult sons—Wilhelm Friedemann, Carl Philipp Emanuel, and Johann Christian. The older two also took possession of most of Bach's manuscripts, which were not included in the valuation of his estate. Bach's devoted wife and her three unmarried daughters were reduced to a life of poverty, living off scant handouts by the town of Leipzig that Bach had served so faithfully for twenty-three years. It was none other than Ludwig van Beethoven who, together with his Vienna circle, established a fund that sustained Bach's youngest daughter, Regina Susanna, until her death in 1809, at the age of sixty-seven.

Abruptly—almost timed to the year of Bach's death—the fugal style of composing that the Leipzig cantor had perfected went into decline. Its once highly esteemed practitioners were consigned to oblivion, with Bach leading the parade. For more than seven decades, Bach's music was largely forgotten by a culture that had turned to the simpler, more melodious works of the Art Galant style. Finally, in 1829, the Romantic composer and virtuoso Felix Mendelssohn sparked a Bach revival by staging the first performance of the *St. Matthew Passion* in the hundred years since its premier. In 1850, publication began of the Bach *Gesamt-Ausgabe* (complete works). By century's end, Johann Sebastian Bach had finally and firmly taken his place among the giants of Western music.

Glossary

A Capella   Choral music performed without instrumental accompaniment. Bach's six known motets are *a capella* compositions.

Aria   Song that responds to, and comments emotionally upon, the preceding action in operas, cantatas, and Passions. In Bach's *oeuvre*, arias usually express biblical texts and themes. A typically joyful aria reflects upon the birth of Christ; distraught in mood are those arias that meditate upon His crucifixion. Arias for one or two voices are basic elements in Bach's sacred and secular cantatas.

Bourrée   A dance of French or Spanish origin composed in a rapid, upbeat tempo. It is a basic element in all of Bach's instrumental suites.

Canon   A multivoiced composition in which each voice sings or plays the same melody but enters at different times. "*Frère Jacques*" exemplifies a popular canonic song. In his *Goldberg Variations*, Bach used the canonic form after every two variations in the conventional fugue form.

Cantata   A church concert by soloists, choir, and orchestra based on the gospel text assigned to each Sunday of the Protestant calendar. Performed before the sermon, it marked the high point of the congregation's Sunday service. Nearly two hundred of Bach's church cantatas have been preserved. It has been estimated that Bach composed another one hundred cantatas that must be considered lost.

Capellmeister   Music director of a princely residence, essentially charged with composing and conducting music for the entertainment of the court.

Chorale	A hymn tune intoned by the congregation. In contrast to the rest of the Sunday service—which in Bach's time was still conducted in Latin—the chorale, at Luther's initiative, was sung in the vernacular. Chorale themes varied widely: from gratitude for God's mercy to songs of solace and encouragement in despair. Fewer than thirty of the known two hundred Bach cantatas lack the unifying element of the chorale.
Chorale Prelude	Organ variations on the hymn tune assigned in Protestant ritual to each Sunday of the church year. These were employed to apprise the members of the congregation of the pitch, speed, and rhythm of the chorale in whose singing they were subsequently to join. Bach wrote over three hundred chorale preludes for organ.
Concerto	Orchestral piece which in Bach's time was dominated by one or two solo instruments, usually the violin. The harpsichord initially played a subservient role, essentially charged with stressing the bass part. Under Bach's aegis, the harpsichord assumed a more prominent role—becoming the solo instrument in many of his concertos.
Continuo	The bass part in Baroque music, assigned to the harpsichord or organ. It provided the rhythmic beat that held the performance together and gave it unity.
Da Capo	To repeat—literally to go back again to the "head" or beginning of a piece. Most of the arias Bach wrote for his cantatas and passions are da capo arias repeating at the end their initial theme, thus providing a satisfying conclusiveness to the presentation.
Dynamics	The varying and constrasting degrees of intensity or loudness in musical tones. One of the difficulties Bach suffered was the inability of the cembalo (harpsichord)—the prevailing keyboard instrument of his time—to produce dynamic gradations. Only the invention of the fortepiano toward the end of the eighteenth century created the potential to produce passages with varying gradations of tonal strength.

Extemporizing	To perform spontaneously, improvising on a given theme. Both Bach and his son Wilhelm Friedemann were unsurpassed masters of this art.
Fugue	A quintessential element of Bach's style in which a theme (called the subject) is stated by one voice and modified by another one (in imitation: usually a fifth higher)—yet both voices, intoned at different intervals, add up to a harmonious whole. In Bach's definition, a fugue is a conversation between two or more voices talking about the same subject in different ways, but in the end always uniting in a final harmonious concord.
Hymn	Poem sung in praise of God—transformed and expanded by Luther into a chant sung by the congregation in the vernacular. (See *Chorale*)
Invention	A short piece in free contrapuntal style, developing one theme in an impromptu fashion. Inventions were part of Bach's *Clavier Übung*—his first venture into publishing under his own imprint.
Liturgy	Basic rites and prayers of the Christian church. In Bach's time, Protestant liturgy required a service that lasted from early morning to the noon vespers. Bach, giving instrumental support to his chorales and cantatas, tried to imbue the liturgy with renewed life and musical uplift.
Motet	A sacred vocal composition in contrapuntal style, usually for voices alone. In contrast to the hundreds of cantatas Bach wrote for chorus and instruments, only eight *a capella* motets have come down to us—an indication of Bach's strong leanings toward the orchestral medium that was coming to the fore in his time.
Oratorio	A dramatic composition for chorus and soloists accompanied by orchestra and organ. Bach wrote only one work in this form—the *Christmas Oratorio* (1734), a composite of six of his cantatas. The oratorio form reached its peak with Handel's *Messiah*, which premiered in Dublin in 1742, the year Bach published the *Goldberg Variations*.

Parodying	One composer copying or freely adapting the melody of another composer (or even of one of his own earlier works). This method of good-natured melody-stealing was widely practiced and morally acceptable in Bach's time. The term *parody* was then quite devoid of the sense of travesty that we associate with it today.
Passion	A musical retelling of the events leading to the crucifixion and resurrection of Christ, as told in one of four gospels: St. Matthew, St. Mark, St. Luke, and St. John. In the Catholic service, this was originally sung by a priest. Bach and some of his predecessors expanded the Passion form into a "music drama" with choir, orchestra, and soloists. Though Bach wrote Passions based on four different Gospels, only two of them—the *St. John Passion* and the *St. Matthew Passion*—are known to us in their completed version.
Recitativo	Vocal part of cantatas, Passions, or oratorios reporting events in a declamatory style (in contrast to the more emotional arias). Bach's recitativos are predominantly based upon biblical texts. They represent the emotional heights of the *St. Matthew Passion*—wherein Christ's pronouncements are accompanied by a "halo" of instruments that give them great dramatic power.
Suite	A composition consisting of a series of dances in the same or a related key, mostly of French origin: *bourrée*, *gavotte*, *minuet*, *passepied*, and ending with a *gigue*. Bach wrote suites for almost all the instruments of his time: harpsichord, violin, cello (viola da gamba), flute, trumpet, etc.

Johann Sebastian Bach

Abendmusik

In the summer of 1705, young Johann Sebastian Bach had already landed a solid job as organist and choirmaster of the Neuekirche in Arnstadt, a small sylvan town close to his birthplace of Eisenach. Considering his age—just turned twenty—the pay was good (84 thalers a year, about $7,000 in today's money). Still, he was not happy.

Possessed by a burning ambition, Bach was stymied in Arnstadt, a restless striver cooped up in provincial surroundings. As he himself expressed it, he wished *"eins und anderes seiner Kunst zu begreifen"*—"to comprehend one and another thing about his art." His hope was to expand his musical horizons through a visit to the prosperous Hanseatic town of Lübeck. There Dietrich Buxtehude, a fine organist and distinguished composer of Danish descent, had gained fame through the *Abendmusiken* (evening concerts) that he staged in the town's Marienkirche.

Lübeck's *Abendmusiken* had been inaugurated in 1660, eight years before Buxtehude's arrival on the scene.

View of Lübeck, which in Bach's time was a prosperous member of the Hanseatic League, which controlled European trade with the East. The League is symbolized by the putto with mercurial staff. In the double-towered Marienkirche (*right of center*), the famed organist Dietrich Buxtehude presented evening concerts (*Abendmusiken*) for the enjoyment of the town's prosperous merchant class.

3

Woodcut showing instrumentalists in rehearsal, from the title page of Michael Praetorius's *Syntagma Musicum* (Basics of Music), Vol. II (1618), which describes the types of and quality of instruments available to contemporary composers such as Buxtehude and Bach.

The town itself was one of a group of commercial cities in northern Germany that in medieval times formed the Hansa, a cooperative league controlling a major part of the trade entering and leaving Europe during the Middle Ages. ("Hansa" means "company," a word that is best known to Americans today as part of Lufthansa.) The wealthy burghers of Lübeck—descendants of the Hanseatic merchant class—sponsored the evening concerts, which apparently provided them with a relaxing interlude after a busy day in the counting house. This powerful patriarchical class was to survive in Germany until the late nineteenth century, when it would undergo the decline that later would be so well chronicled by Thomas Mann in *Buddenbrooks* (1901).

While Buxtehude offered traditional chorale and sacred works as part of his *Abendmusik*, he seems to have gained considerable approval (and financing) by featuring secular instrumental music, employing seventeen professional players to supplement his thirty choristers. Buxtehude clearly attached great importance to orchestral music, and he received funds from the town to buy instruments and hire capable performers. Once, he boasted, he had bought two fine trumpets "such as hitherto not seen in any prince's band."

Until the introduction of Buxtehude's instrumentally oriented concerts, Germany had lagged behind France and Italy, where both opera and instrumental music had been flourishing for more than a century. By the time Bach had secured his Arnstadt post in 1703, Arcangelo Corelli (1653–1713) had developed his sonatas for violin as a new art form, while Antonio Vivaldi (1678–1741) would soon be pioneering in concert music (*The Seasons* would debut in 1725). The warm response of the burghers of Lübeck to Buxtehude's *Abendmusik* seemed to be an omen that the future was to belong to instrumental rather than choral music.

Young organist Bach, isolated in provincial Arnstadt, apparently had heard of the innovative musical life in Lübeck and was eager to learn more about it. Hence, in the fall of 1705 he wrangled permission from the Consistory (his Arnstadt masters) for a month's furlough to visit Lübeck, some two hundred miles to the north. Bold in all his ventures, Bach must have decided to walk the considerable distance. He left Arnstadt in November 1705, arriving in Lübeck just prior to Advent season, when *Abendmusik* was at its height.

Bach had perhaps participated in instrumental music a few years earlier, when as a student in Lüneburg he had visited the nearby court of Celle. Nevertheless, Buxtehude's *Abendmusik*—employing instrumentalists who were fine artists, "not mere town pipers"—must have opened up for the young Bach a new world of sound, one which he eagerly absorbed. Obviously fascinated by what he heard, he forgot all about his job in Arnstadt—stretching his one month leave of absence into a four-month sojourn. When he finally returned to his post in Arnstadt in February 1706, he found the town fathers fuming. They lost no time in raking their wandering young organist over the coals.

It is possible that Bach was more than a listener at Buxtehude's *Abendmusik*. To finance his trip from Arnstadt, he may well have taken part in the concerts as a paid performer. It has also been suggested that Bach journeyed to Lübeck in the vain hope of becoming Buxtehude's successor. But this seems a rather unlikely scenario, particularly since it has been alleged that the great organist (then nearly seventy), would only award the post to a candidate willing to marry his thirty-year-old daughter, Anna Margaretha. Handel supposedly had also turned the post down because he felt that Buxtehude's precondition was too high a price to pay.

In any event, once Bach returned to Arnstadt, the impact of Buxtehude's *Abendmusik* must have been apparent in his organ-playing, as he ventured into swirling new melodies derivative of those he had heard in Lübeck. Bach was severely criticized by the Consistory for playing "daring variations with many strange sounds which totally confounded the congregation." As Alice Meynell, the late-nineteenth-century poetess and Bach-lover, observed in an essay, "We feel the quick obstinacy and scorn, which—as later incidents in his life also demonstrate—was one of Bach's characteristics." Bach, filled with a new consciousness of his own powers, must have looked now upon his Arnstadt masters as graybeards who were far behind the times. Certainly, following his visit to Lübeck, we note the young organist's ever-growing interest in instrumental music—powerfully stirred by Buxtehude's *Abendmusik*—even though vocal works would always loom large in Bach's creative output.

During the ensuing decades of the eighteenth century, instrumental music would come ever more strongly to the fore, rising in a mighty crescendo as the symphonic age burst upon Europe in the music of Haydn, Mozart, and Beethoven. It was a trend that would raise to prominence two of Bach's sons—Carl Philipp Emanuel and Johann Christian—while the world forgot their father (see *Art Galant*). Only at the beginning of the nineteenth century, at the dawn of the Romantic era, was the greatest of all Bachs to be rediscovered (see *Revival*)—the unequaled master of both sacred and instrumental music.

Acclaim

Few artists are lucky enough to gain critical recognition in their own time, fewer still to experience the approving roar of the crowd. But to be denied all recognition for the vast creative output an artist has amassed through decades of ceaseless toil—to feel that one has been speaking into a void—is to invite a case of melancholia. Bach was to know both the fulfillment of wide acclaim and the haunting frustration of near-universal neglect.

It was as a performing artist that Bach achieved acclaim; he was highly regarded, even apotheosized, as a virtuoso on both harpsichord and organ. But he suffered almost total neglect, if not ignominy, in the area that was eventually to make him immortal—as a composer.

The world around him raved about the works of Vivaldi and Telemann and went wild about the operatic productions of Alessandro Scarlatti and Handel. These favorites of the public had no trouble getting their works published. Most of Bach's immense output had to wait for more than a century to be discovered and to appear in print.

While Bach was alive, only a few cognoscenti praised his wizardry in fugal writing. Others—such as the music critic Johann Adolph Scheibe (see *Detractors*)—condemned him for his habit of putting "fugal themes on the torture rack...devising mechanical futilities." Few of his contemporaries apprehended the true measure of his greatness. Johann Christoph Gottsched, of Leipzig University, is said to have written a poem in praise of German music in which he mentioned only Telemann and Handel, notwithstanding the fact that Bach was practically his next-door neighbor.

Of the nearly one thousand Bach compositions listed in the *Bach-Werke-Verzeichnis* (BWV)—an index of works that requires 750 tightly printed pages—hardly a dozen were published in Bach's lifetime. A few of them he had printed at his own expense. Masterworks like the *Well-Tempered Clavier* first appeared in printed form fifty years after his death. The cantatas, and with them a prodigious number of other treasures, lay dormant for a century. Many of them were lost to posterity through the carelessness of his heirs. The Bach works that survived were published in the monumental Bach *Gesamt-Ausgabe* (see entry) beginning in 1850, to mark the centennial of the composer's death.

When Bach died in 1750, a few friends and some of his admiring students tried to preserve in handwritten copies the corpus of immortal works he had left behind. But in the remaining years of the eighteenth century, when there was talk about a musician by the name of Bach, it probably referred to one of the master's sons. Carl Philipp Emanuel gained acclaim as a representative of Art Galant (see entry), while his younger brother, Johann Christoph, gathered laurels in London as a composer of operas, a highly popular genre. Telemann penned a memorial sonnet that praised the senior Bach as both a virtuoso and a composer, but suggested that Bach's posthumous renown would be as the father of illustrious sons. It was not until a later generation—after Mendelssohn's Bach revival of 1829 (see *Revival*)—that Johann Sebastian Bach was rediscovered in his true greatness.

Acoustician

The acoustics of orchestra halls have remained a problem from Bach's time to our own. Music lovers may remember the difficulties that the designers of Avery Fisher Hall in New York's Lincoln Center had to face when they attempted to replicate in the New York Philharmonic's new home the ideal acoustic conditions which prevailed in Carnegie Hall.

Without the sophisticated devices and architectural aids available to the acousticians of today, Bach dealt with similar difficulties when he

A Sunday service in Nikolaikirche, one of the Leipzig churches whose musical service was supervised by Bach. Vast Gothic spaces created echoes that marred musical performances. Bach studied these effects and tried to counteract them.

assumed his post as music director of Leipzig's churches in 1723. His principal center of activity was the Thomaskirche, which was originally a Gothic cathedral. As such, it was one of the monuments to the Age of Faith. And indeed, the considerable expanse of the Thomaskirche was probably quite adequate for the singing of the rhythmically and textually simple Gregorian chants with which this erstwhile cathedral had reverberated. But such vast spaces were far less adapted to music that was complex in structure and text, marring its majestic effects with unwelcome echoes.

Complicating the acoustical problem prevailing in the Thomaskirche at Bach's time was the fact that Sunday attendance, as in most Protestant churches, was in decline. Today, it is a matter of common knowledge that a "full house" (or a well-attended church) is apt to yield better acoustics than an empty one. In the eighteenth century, this fact may have been less evident. Handel, for example, seems to have been ignorant of the phenomenon. Accustomed to overflow audiences, he once entered an empty hall with a group of musicians. Noticing their hesitation, he encouraged them by the remark: "The music will sound all the better."

Leipzig's Thomaskirche, in its original Gothic incarnation, was built to accommodate at least one thousand people, but statistics indicate that in Bach's time the church's Sunday service attracted at best only some three hundred congregants. In contrast with the highly focused liturgy of the Catholic church, the texts of Bach's music were far more complex and many-faceted, at times even verbally over-loaded. To counter the echo effects that resulted from the multivoiced Lutheran cantatas and chorales, an effort had been under way even before Bach's arrival to install wooden walls, pews, and side galleries, which collectively would have the effect of deadening unwanted reverberations. Acutely sensitive to the effect produced by his music, Bach continued to plead for further improvements along these lines.

When Bach came to Leipzig in 1723, he was already recognized

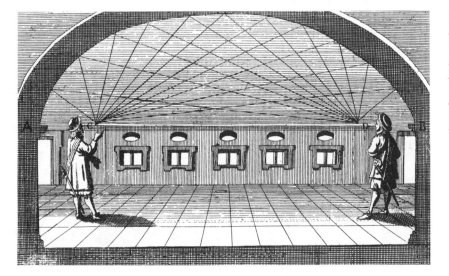

Echo chamber experiment: an illustration from Athanasius Kircher's *Musurgia Universalis* (Rome, 1650), a treatise on acoustics with which Bach seems to have been familiar.

as an outstanding expert in the field of organ acoustics. He had been widely consulted on the sound and mechanical problems of newly built instruments. Quite a number of Bach's reports on new organs amaze us to this day by their display of astute technical and acoustical insights. These also stood him in good stead as a star performer on this instrument, helping to make him an organist of great boldness (see *Organist Supreme*).

Equally competent was Bach's evaluation of acoustical effects when he was called upon to conduct a group of instrumentalists. He made a speedy and competent judgment not only of the piece to be performed, but of the special spatial conditions in which it could be performed to best effect. In the notes he contributed to the biography of his father (1753), Carl Philipp Emanuel observed: "The placing of an orchestra he understood perfectly. He made good use of any space and grasped the sound property of any piece."

During his 1747 trip to Berlin—and after a momentous encounter with Frederick the Great (see entry)—Bach and his son had an opportunity to visit Potsdam's great opera house. As they entered the large, grandiose vestibule, Bach was quick to notice that the architect had accomplished a remarkable acoustical feat, perhaps without intending to do so. "Namely," his astonished son later reported, "that if someone went to one corner of the oblong-shaped hall and whispered a few words very softly upwards...a person standing in the corner of the other diagonally opposite with his face to the wall would quite clearly hear it...a feat very rare and much admired."

The acuteness of Bach's hearing stood him in good stead in other areas of musical sound production, showing, for example, great fussiness in matters of tuning. "No one could tune his instruments to his complete satisfaction," Carl Philipp Emanuel remarked, "so he did this mostly by himself." At times Bach was called upon to tune the musical instruments of his various princely masters, charging their treasuries but a thaler for his ministrations—the bargain of the century if there ever was one. Who wouldn't be happy to pay Johann Sebastian a few dollars to come to the house and tune that old baby grand?

Anhalt-Cöthen:
The Ideal Post

In 1717, while still in the employ of the stern Duke Wilhelm Ernst of Weimar, Bach, then thirty-two, was offered the position of capellmeister at the court of Prince Leopold of Anhalt-Cöthen. Once free of the duke's imperious supervision (see *Imprisonment*), Bach hurried to Cöthen with his family to join the household of the twenty-three-year-old prince—already a highly skilled musician, a gifted player of the viola da gamba.

Prince Leopold of Anhalt-Cöthen, who made his court an important musical center. Bach spent six happy and extremely productive years (1717–1723) as capellmeister in the court of this young prince "who not only knew but loved music." *Courtesy of Archiv für Kunst und Geschichte, Berlin*

By all accounts, Prince Leopold was of a lively and cheerful disposition, devoted to artistic genius, which he had readily recognized in Bach. The "Cöthen connection" was the most fortunate turn of fate in Bach's career. He and the prince formed a warm personal attachment, and Bach's stay in Cöthen would bring forth a myriad of masterworks to the world's great music: concertos for a variety of instruments, including the *Brandenburgs*; inventions, sonatas, and suites for the violin, viola, flute, and oboe; and, last but not least, the first volume of *The Well-Tempered Clavier* (1722), as well as other harpsichord works that have since become classics.

It is noteworthy that the corpus of Bach works produced at Cöthen is almost devoid of sacred compositions. The prince's court was in a Calvinist region of Germany—hence, music was barred from the local churches. Bach's work in Cöthen, therefore, was almost exclusively for Prince Leopold's household capelle (or band) of eighteen musicians of the highest caliber and was almost exclusively devoted to instrumental music (with a sparse number of cantatas and serenades for solo singers).

From his trips to Italy, Leopold often brought back copies of the

Prince Leopold was a master on the viola da gamba (forerunner to today's cello). He sometimes joined with his fine court orchestra, while Bach conducted. *Courtesy of Archiv für Kunst und Geschichte*

VIOLA DI GAMBA.

latest masterworks of Italian music. Always anxious to enhance his compositional skills, Bach drew fresh inspiration from these "finds" of his cosmopolitan employer and friend. The youthful Leopold was a man of advanced tastes for his age, forever looking for fresh musical excitement. Bach was inspired to continually provide it.

His relationship to his aristocratic master was not confined to matters of music. The prince expressed his personal interest in Bach and his family by becoming the godfather of one of the capellmeister's children, the last of the three sons and four daughters that Bach's first wife, Maria Barbara, had contributed to the Bach dynasty before her untimely, shocking death in 1720 (see *Helpmate*).

Trapped later in a rather disappointing Leipzig post, Bach looked back nostalgically to his Cöthen days. In the famed Erdmann letter of 1730 (see *Leipzig Ordeal*), he praised his former master, Prince Leopold, as a true friend and man who "loved and understood music"—a comment that was quite possibly also meant as a dig at his Leipzig masters, who had no feeling for music. When Leopold died suddenly in 1728, Bach, though burdened with heavy responsibilities in Leipzig, found the time to compose a cantata in memory of his princely friend.

Leopold's second wife, Frederica, did not share her spouse's interest in music. Bach called her "an *amusa*"—involved in trivial pursuits. She prompted her husband to lose interest in his orchestra, and eventually he disbanded it.

Even if Bach had created nothing else in the twenty-seven years of life remaining to him when he left Cöthen in 1723, his name would still rank among the immortals of music because of the works he produced during these five miracle years—works that were expressive of the friendly artistic spirit that prevailed at the court of Prince Leopold. "There is an exuberance and optimism in this music," biographer Karl Geiringer has observed, "that only a genius aware of his newly achieved mastery could call forth."

Like all good things, Bach's idyllic Cöthen days had to come to an end—though much earlier than he might have wished. Leopold's interest in his court orchestra had markedly declined after his marriage in 1720 to his second wife—a princess of Brandenburg with a taste for worldly pleasures and decidedly uninterested in her new husband's musical ventures. Bach called her an *amusa*, that is, one who had no feeling for things of the aesthetic realm—especially music. But the smitten Leopold followed her whims completely and neglected—then finally disbanded—his fine orchestra. In 1723, approaching forty and with an ever-expanding family, Bach was ready to move on.

Art Galant

Bach brought the fugal style to its ultimate perfection. In the *Art of the Fugue* (1747–1750), he displayed the full potential of the style of music he had spent a lifetime perfecting. But this great work also serves as an epitaph both for the fugal style and for Bach himself. Abruptly—almost timed to the year of Bach's death—this style of composing went into decline. Its once highly esteemed practitioners were consigned to oblivion, with Bach leading the parade.

This dramatic turn of events was largely due to cultural changes that had been in the air since Bach's birth in 1685. At the time, the church was still the primary influence in man's life—a cultural dominance that was reflected in the solemnity and formal discipline of the fugal style. By the time of Bach's death, however, the Age of Enlightenment had shone forth in its full glory (see *Zeitgeist*)—bringing with it the celebration of individualism and the pursuit of secular pleasure. In the realm of music, this trend had led to a growing yearning for lighter, more sensual fare. The musical style of choice during the Age of Reason was Art Galant.

A musical soirée with amateur instrumentalists during the reign of Art Galant.

As the church's influence began to wane, the complex contrapuntal style that Bach had practiced was to give way to the free flight of melody: "cheer music" was to take the place of "creed music"; "music to play by" gained the upper hand over "music to pray by," which had been the traditional form of music since early medieval times. In 1759, nine years after Bach's death, Haydn had produced his first, highly melodious string quartets. More than seventy were to follow during Haydn's lifetime. If we compare the lighthearted, pleasing style of these early quartets with the somewhat heavy-handed technique of Bach's *Art of the Fugue*, we can well gauge the abyss that was to separate the two styles and the radical change in musical taste which left Bach behind.

Even Bach himself, deeply immersed though he was in complex counterpoint, seemed to be well aware of the change that was taking place around him. In an angry manifesto to his Leipzig bosses (see *Leipzig Ordeal*)—"*Draft for a Well-Appointed Church Music*" (1730)— he astutely observed that "our gusto [taste] has changed decidedly and the former style of music no longer seems to please our ear." Interestingly, Bach used the growing popularity of the new style as a way of prodding his superiors to grant him, among other things, a greater number of instrumentalists (most of whom were already conversant with the Art Galant style, for which skilled instrumentalists were essential).

Moreover, Bach also seems to have taken up the new melodic style himself. Lorenz Christoph Mizler (1711–1778)—a Bach student, music critic, and founder of the prestigious Society of the Musical Sciences—declared in 1739: "The Master can compose perfectly in accordance with the newest taste." However that may be, Bach remained fundamentally committed to the fugal art, continuing to compose his great "summation works" (see entry), *Art of the Fugue*, as he was dying. With his passing, fugalism quickly faded from public taste and memory. The cantata form, which Bach had cultivated from the inception of his career, became obsolete.

Even Bach's sons, whom the master had trained with the utmost care in the fugal art, pointedly neglected this priceless heritage (see *Heirs*). No record exists that any of them ever presented one of their father's cantatas. Indeed, Carl Philipp Emanuel—ranked among Europe's leading musician-composers after his father's death—became an important and fertile practitioner of Art Galant.

The masters of Art Galant produced a prodigious amount of music for the aristocratic salons of the Age of Enlightenment—salons which had replaced the churches as the focal points of artistic development. But, in the end, what did it all amount to? Arnold Schönberg summed it up well when he observed: "The early [adherents of Art Galant] thought Bach's music outmoded. . . . Today much of their music is outmoded while Bach's survives eternal."

B-A-C-H

Bach, it seems, was born with just the right name—short and
memorable, like an acronym. Myriad in number are the works
and written documents carrying this signature. Still, his family name,
while aptly lapidary, has always been somewhat puzzling. Since the
German word *Bach* connotes "a little brook," Beethoven suggested
that it was somewhat inappropriate for so gigantic a figure. Rather than
a little rivulet, he noted, Bach's prodigality would be better symbolized
as a mighty ocean.

Though Beethoven's comment has been endlessly repeated, the
origin of the clan's name actually had little to do with the watery
element. Etymologically, its origin was considerably more prosaic.
The Bach name seems to have derived from an ancestor's professional
involvement with milling and the baking trade. According to the brief
family chronicle Bach himself wrote in 1735, his great-great-grand-
father, Veit Bach, was both a miller and the first Bach with an interest
in music. In time, Veit extended his interest to the more prosperous
baking trade. Hence, the deduction is tenable that the Bach name
derives from this forebear's bread-making vocation (the German word
for "bake" is *backen*).

Since music was at the core of the Bach family, it was only
natural that one of its members would translate the letters B-A-C-H
into musical terms. Nicholas Bach, town musician of Arnstadt, is
usually credited with this nifty innovation. It was, however, the
greatest of the tribe who proved it eminently suitable for fugal
elaboration. When this motif appears in one of Bach's compositions, a
certain finality is achieved. In the same way that a painter, after much
labor, puts his signature to one of his creations, so too did Bach

The name of Bach spelled out in German musical nomenclature. This motif recurs frequently in Bach's compositions and those of other composers.

employ at times the B-A-C-H theme as his proud assertion of authorship.

Bach used his signature in the fugal flights of the *Musical Offering*, as well as in some of his chorale variations. He even worked it, perhaps with somewhat puckish intent, into a canon that he submitted when he was invited to join Lorenz Mizler's Society of Musical Science in 1747 (see *Numerology*).

At the very end of Bach's life—during the creation of his last monumental (and unfinished) masterpiece, the *Art of the Fugue*—the B-A-C-H motif once more appears, conveying an almost mystic sense of closure. Bach's son, Carl Philipp Emanuel Bach, observed: "While at work on this fugue, where the [theme] B A C H is brought into the countersubject, the composer died." Thus, the countersubject of this sublime triple fugue turned out to be the master's epitaph—the final musical signature of Johann Sebastian Bach, the world's unsurpassed composer of fugues.

Long after his death, Bach's signature was to reappear, in the writings of both Classical and Romantic composers. Beethoven, in the early 1820s, wanted to write an overture on the B-A-C-H theme, but nothing came of it. Both Schumann and Mendelssohn made it the basis of piano variations. More recent composers such as Busoni, Stravinsky, Schönberg, and Berg, as well as many practitioners of both jazz and rock and roll, have woven—often humorously—the B-A-C-H theme into their compositions. This seems both a cryptic greeting to the master across the centuries and a touching symbolic tribute from today's innovators to that supreme creator of fugues—intoned as if to say: "Here is the man to whom we owe it all."

Banter

Mention the name of Bach and the picture of a serious, staunch churchman appears before our mind's eye. We envision the composer of *musica sacra*, the supreme cantor proclaiming—in his chorales, cantatas, and passions—the Gospel's message of the redemption of man.

Yet this traditional picture of Bach has lately undergone a revision, and the image of a "smiling Bach" has become visible, freed

Hie sichst du gegen
Harmsen Bachen.
Wenn du es hörst so
mustu lachen.
Er geigt gleichwol
nach seiner art,
Vnnd tregt ain hipschen
Hanns Bach zu Bart.

Hans Bach, an early ancestor, became well known in the region as a musical funster. A popular ditty paid tribute to his antics: "Hans Bach the fiddler has a style that when you hear him you must smile. He is indeed quite droll and weird with his pointed Hans Bach beard."

Baroque organ in the Protestant palace chapel of Altenburg, in the vicinity of Leipzig. Bach played on this instrument, built by Gottfried Trost, in September 1739. *Photo by Werner Reinhold*

of the somber, Teutonic drapery in which he had all but suffocated. In truth, the somber cantor's garb swathed a very dynamic personality—a man with his feet planted solidly on this earth, animated by a decided zest for life. There dwelt in him a free spirit, hemmed in as it was by duties, worries, and frustrations. Even his contemporaries noted that the "holy cantor" was not averse to "joining pleasantly in trivial amusement with his fellow men."

In many of Bach's compositions, a joyous mood of banter prevails. A typical example is the opening movement of the first *Brandenburg Concerto*. Here Bach intones a strong and simple theme, then reverses and transposes it with obvious abandon. The theme reappears time and again, ingeniously transformed. Bach seems to be having fun—exhibiting his fugal wizardry.

This love of musical banter is typical of many of Bach's works (see *Quodlibet*). Even his strictly sacred pieces at times exhibit this tendency. As Johann Nikolaus Forkel, Bach's first biographer, observes: "In spite of his genius for the sublime, he sometimes composes something gay and even jocose. His cheerfulness and joking were that of a sage."

This Bachian spirit remains alive to this day. During a celebration of Bach's three-hundredth birthday at Lincoln Center in 1985, the conductor Christopher Hogwood was asked what Bach had wanted to convey when he applied the heading "Badinerie" to the flute movement in his second *Orchestral Suite*. Hogwood quipped, "Play a little whoopie." Unexpectedly, in the midst of this reverential memorial, the concert hall echoed with laughter—a tribute to the frolicking Bach.

The music historian Roland Gelatt said it best: "Bach's music gives him away. In the incredible legacy he has left us, he smiles again and again. No composer has ever expressed more winningly the mood of clamorous jubilation, of quiet gladness, of vigorous merriment."

Baroque

Textbooks of musical history tend to present Johann Sebastian Bach as the ultimate representative of the Baroque Age. In some aspects, he deserves this title; in others, he seems far removed from the ideas and ideals that this term connotes.

As a rule, we think of the Baroque style as characterized by flamboyance—often expressive of extreme emotions. Rubens's enormous canvas *The Massacre of the Innocents* and Louis XIV's extraordinary palace at Versailles come to mind. But it was not only the art and architecture of the times that tended toward the extravagant. The lifestyles of the powerful and the affluent—and of many of the artists themselves—were as flamboyant as the great works of the Baroque period. It has been said that Rubens and Bernini "lived like lords." Indeed, Rubens was unsurpassed in his expansive way of living— courtier, European traveler, and diplomat. Extravagance, grandeur, pomp seemed to be the mainstays of the period's art—and of its art of living, at least among the mighty.

On first sight, we can detect few of these Baroque characteristics in Bach. Indeed, the cosmopolitan Handel seems a far more typical musical representative of the Baroque Age. Handel, who unlike Bach was to die a wealthy man, was well traveled, at home in Germany, Italy, and England—an artist whose expressive power ranged from dramatic opera music and majestic compositions for royal patrons to the spiritual grandeur of his oratorio *Messiah*. (See *Handel*.)

Bach's career, on the other hand, was confined to the rather provincial backwaters of Thuringia and Saxony. His trip to the court of Frederick the Great in Berlin (see entry), some two hundred miles distant, was perhaps his most extravagant adventure. Bach lived a soundly bourgeois life (unless one considers his child-producing record, twenty offspring, to be extreme). The bizarre, the overstated, and world-conquering ambition were foreign to his character. Such impulses are also absent from most of his music, scores that, for all their intricacy, are extremely disciplined, well ordered, and finely balanced.

Bach's obvious serenity (only occasionally interrupted by a show of temper), his almost simplistic Lutheran faith, do not seem to qualify him as a typical Baroque man. To all outward appearances, he was a man who strove for fulfillment in a job and an honest living, rather than one who would devote himself to heroically unattainable goals. Then how was it possible that this dyed-in-the-wool provincial should at the same time catch the spirit of gigantism and overreaching that ruled the Baroque art world?

It is the miracle of the Bach phenomenon that the Leipzig cantor became in time a consummate practitioner of one of Baroque art's major characteristics: the creation of gigantic "superworks." This Baroque characteristic comes most powerfully to the fore in Bach's organ works (see *Organist Supreme*). In his mighty organ preludes, fugues, and toccatas, Bach builds structures that at times affect the listener as truly cosmic. They are, in power and grandeur, akin to the greatest Baroque masterworks of art and architecture. They inform us that, despite all outward appearances, Bach possessed an inner self of heroic proportions.

This striving for the ultimate is also evident in Bach's "summation works" (see entry). In the *St. Matthew Passion* (sixty-eight sections, performance time of four hours; three choruses, two orchestras, five soloists), Bach proved himself an overreacher in the true Baroque spirit. And he later crowned his opus with the monumental *Art of the Fugue*, a masterwork which, true to fate's ever-tragic dictates, he was unable to finish. "Herculean" is perhaps the proper term to sum up these and other truly Baroque efforts that crown his career.

In this context, it is perhaps no accident that Bach had a distinct admiration for Hercules (also the subject of one of Handel's oratorios). The secular cantata subtitled *Hercules at the Crossroads* (BWV 213) comments on the cosmic quest of this overreaching ancient strongman. "Where will I bring to fulfillment my unquenchable strivings?" the hero asks in one of the cantata's recitatives. It is a question very much in the Baroque vein—one to which Bach himself searched all his life for an answer.

Bach is considered a master of the Baroque contrapuntal style—a style which, in its elementary form, features two voices moving in opposite directions to meet at the end in a harmonious resolution. Might we not argue then that Bach's own persona was, in this sense, contrapuntal? He was at once both the humble, pietistic believer *and* a true Baroque superman, striving in his art for ultimate pronouncements. These apparently contradictory elements were so fused in Bach's nature as to produce a man who seems to us at peace with himself and secure in his creative powers.

Biographers
Spitta and Schweitzer

The shelves of our libraries groan under the weight of books about Bach's life and music. Among these, two works published decades ago stand out as classics—the biographies written by Philipp Spitta and Albert Schweitzer.

The original German edition of Spitta's *Johann Sebastian Bach*, in two volumes, was published between 1873 and 1880, and is still popular in its three-volume English edition and Dover reprint. Overwhelming in its documentation and detail, Spitta's enormous biography has remained the basic reference work in any Bach library—despite more than a century of progress in Bach research and criticism that has been produced since the book's first appearance.

Spitta's vast panorama—close to two thousand pages—is a monument to dedicated scholarship and is replete with insights into the Bachian phenomenon. Its very bulk, however, may be an obstacle to seeing its hero clearly. One critic, Rutland Boughton, put it succinctly: "The enormous frame gobbles up the picture. Spitta's Bach weighs down on the reader like a most expensive cemetery memorial."

Albert Schweitzer's two-volume Bach biography is of another spirit. It was first published in 1905 in a French edition, later to be greatly expanded in a German edition (1907). This work is somewhat less weighty than Spitta's, but penetrates more deeply to reveal the scope of its subject's genius. In contrast to Spitta, an admirably tireless scholar and documentarian, Schweitzer was as close to a "universal

Albert Schweitzer at the organ. From time to time he made concert tours in Europe and America to raise funds for his medical mission in Lambaréné, Africa.

man" as one could imagine. He made his mark not only as a Bach scholar and an eminent organist, but gained worldwide fame as a theologian, a philosopher, and a medical missionary—a rich life crowned by the Nobel Peace Prize in 1952. Diverse and wide-ranging as Schweitzer's life was, the music of Bach resounds through it as an ever-recurring *leitmotif*.

Schweitzer came from an Alsatian background that was both religious and musical: his father was a preacher; his mother, a singer. His early career, at the dawn of the twentieth century, was as a theology professor and preacher at the University of Strasburg. But he soon began the medical studies that would eventually make him a physician heading a missionary hospital in Central Africa—a role that consumed the second half of his life. With all this, Schweitzer still found the time during these early years to become an outstanding organist and an expert in the construction of organs.

His friend and mentor, Charles Widor, a world-renowned organist, once expressed to Schweitzer his regret at the lack of knowledge of Bach among his students. Widor asked Schweitzer to fill the gap by preparing a brief introductory essay on the Leipzig master. This essay was so favorably received that Schweitzer expanded it into a full-fledged biography, an enterprise that was greatly helped when an English lady offered him her forty-six-volume collection of Bach's works (see *Gesamt-Ausgabe*) at the bargain prize of £12.

Schweitzer's career as a doctor and missionary took a dramatic turn when he left Europe in 1913 to establish a hospital to fight leprosy and other illnesses, at Lambaréné, a jungle settlement in French Equatorial Africa. Shortly before his departure to Africa, the Missionary Society of Paris presented him with a zinc-lined piano with pedal attachment, specially built for use in the tropics. Thus, as he toiled through his endless days of charitable and medical ministration, Dr. Schweitzer found relief each evening by turning to the music of Bach, which he played—slowly—but with virtuoso skill. In the succeeding years, he interrupted his missionary work only for occasional concert trips to Europe. On these occasions, his Bach recitals and recordings provided welcome funds for his Lambaréné mission.

Schweitzer died in 1965, at the age of ninety, after a life filled with intellectual, musical, and humanitarian accomplishments inured with the spirit of Bach. He once was asked to sum up the phenomenon of his master, and declared: "His immense consciousness was like the forces of nature and for this reason it is as cosmic and copious as nature itself."

Blindness

From early youth, Bach was possessed by a burning ambition—he was in fact a workaholic. Contemporary observers commented on his "unheard-of zeal in studying, and his indefatigable diligence." His first biographer, Forkel, reported that the young Bach copied music nocturnally "by the light of the moon." Later witnesses also attested to this penchant (or perhaps necessity) for composing into the late hours of the night (see *Composing*).

This obsessive zeal brought forth in the course of Bach's life an

Increasingly blind in his final years, Bach is led to the organ by a choirboy.

unfathomable harvest of music. But his nocturnal work habits may well have contributed to the eye troubles of his later years and thereby hastened his death—albeit only after several miraculously productive decades of good health.

Fortunately, Bach was a naturally robust man, remaining quite vigorous even in his later years. He was sixty-two years old—an old man by the standards of the time—when, in 1747, he ventured out to visit Frederick the Great of Prussia. It was a two-hundred-mile journey from Leipzig to Berlin, a grueling trip. In the same year, he wrote his *Musical Offering*, then took upon himself the considerable task of having printed copies of the work ready for the Leipzig Fair in the fall of that same year (see *Music Publisher*).

But as the great physician William Osler once observed: "Nature, while patient, never fails to send her bill." Two years hence, there were indications that Bach's eyesight was on the wane. By the end of 1749, when Bach was approaching sixty-five, this affliction had reached a critical stage. He was unable to finish in his own hand the last section of his mighty "summation work"—the *Art of the Fugue*. Alfred Einstein—one of the twentieth century's foremost music scholars and, like his cousin Albert, a refugee from Nazism—observed that one can detect the deterioration of Bach's eyesight in his last years through "the ever diminishing size of his writing," as he bent "lower and lower over his music paper." Soon he must have been unable to write at all. In 1748, Anna Magdalena, his ever-helpful second wife, had to pen a recommendation that a student had requested—signing it with Bach's simulated signature.

Some Freudian-oriented medical practitioners have, in recent years, provided a psychosomatic explanation for this fading away of Bach's eyesight. This interpretation takes note of the fact that, as the mid eighteenth century approached, Bach's work had been completed and gloriously summarized. His contrapuntal style of composition had become outmoded and was at times ridiculed by the upstarts of Art Galant (see entry). Hence, Bach's physical decline can be interpreted as a merciful and logical closing of his life's cycle.

Still, Bach was of sturdy stock and could perhaps have lived on for some years if he hadn't fallen victim to the ministrations of a quack who proffered a cure for the master's failing vision. When the state of his eyesight had become critical, Bach and his family engaged the services of a London "physician" of great repute—the Chevalier John Taylor, who was the court oculist to King George II of England. The traveling chevalier specialized in "cataract couching," a procedure

Chevalier John Taylor, court oculist to King George II of England. He was actually a quack, whose dangerous method of treating cataracts proved fatal to both Bach and Handel.

that consisted of pressing down the clouded lens into the eye's lower recesses. Quite often this yielded, in the initial postoperative stages, rather startling results—for traces of vision seemed to return after the fogged lens was pushed downward. Unfortunately, Dr. Taylor had "couched" Bach's cataract—as was his habit—with a lancet that was the inadvertent breeding ground of bacteria (the age of Lister was still a century away).

Bach and his family rejoiced, as Forkel reports, when it seemed at first that a miracle had been wrought and a semblance of the master's sight had been restored. However, the recovery was of short duration (Dr. Taylor was at pains to make a fast getaway). Septicemia followed quickly upon the heels of the "miracle cure," which resulted first in the patient's loss of sight and then in a poisoning of his circulatory system. This in turn brought on two strokes. After spending six months in total blindness with his vital powers ebbing, Bach died on July 30, 1750. He was sixty-five.

A few years later, the irrepressible Dr. Taylor performed unsuccessful cataract surgery upon Georg Frideric Handel, in London. Bach's great contemporary was virtually blind during the final years of his life—dying in 1759 at the age of seventy-four. These misadventures of Chevalier Taylor led Edward MacDowell, the *fin de siècle* American composer, to make the ironic observation: "Bach and Handel were in every way quite different, except that both were born in the same year and killed by the same doctor."

Bookman

Although Bach had limited formal education, he became an avid reader and collector of books, assembling a library of over eighty volumes. This was an impressive accumulation, especially when one

Bach assembled a considerable library of books and music during his lifetime. One of his Bibles, notated in his script, found its way to America and is now preserved in the Concordia Seminary, St. Louis. *Courtesy of* Oxford Companion to Music, © *Oxford University Press*

considers that his large family presented a perpetual strain upon his financial resources.

A complete appraisal of Bach's library was made after his death. It included various works of Martin Luther; the writings of the fourteenth-century German mystic Meister Eckhart and his disciple Johannes Tauler (the pantheistic writings of Eckhart were condemned by Pope John XXII in 1329); a copy of Josephus's *History of the Jewish War*; and various Pietist pamphlets.

The Pietist tracts probably stirred mixed feelings in their owner. The Pietist wing of Lutheranism cultivated the "inner light" and sought direct contact with God through silent prayer—an orientation which was akin to Bach's religious beliefs. But the Pietists were also somewhat puritanical in religious practice and held that music created a "sensuous interference" with the attempt to converse with God. They believed, therefore, that music should be banned from divine service—a view that Bach, of course, vehemently rejected.

Cantor Bach, busy as he was, even seems to have once sneaked away to a book auction. When the library of a Leipzig theologian, Andreas Winckler, went under the hammer, Bach was one of the bidders—acquiring his ten-volume Luther edition. The transaction, involving 10 thalers, is recorded in a receipt still extant and signed by Bach in September 1742.

After his death, the master's library was dispersed among his heirs. But, miraculously, one of Bach's Bible sets has come down to us, after an amazing odyssey. In the summer of 1934, a synod of churchmen was held near Detroit, Michigan. One of its participants, the Reverend C. G. Riedel, lodging with his cousin, a farmer, casually roamed through his host's library. Just by chance, Dr. Riedel took the third volume of an edition of the Bible from his cousin's shelves. The volume contained not only the conventional text, but also an extensive commentary by the orthodox Lutheran theologian Abraham Calovius (1612–1686).

Looking at the previous owner's signature—in a fine calligraphic entry, identical in each volume—Dr. Riedel suspected that he had made an epochal discovery. Further research by German Bach experts (including carbon dating of the comments and underlinings in the

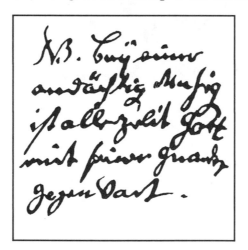

"If devotional music is played, God in his mercy is present." Note made by Bach in the Calovius Bible. *Courtesy of Concordia Seminary, St. Louis*

text) established its authenticity, leaving no doubt that this was Bach's own working Bible. Virtually all of Bach's sacred works—the motets, chorales, and cantatas—are based on biblical texts. For all these works, the *Calovius Bible* must have served Bach as what today we would call "an indispensable reference tool."

In his Bible studies, one verse from the twenty-fifth chapter of the first book of Chronicles seems to have caught Bach's special attention. It reports that King David, to embellish his religious service, recruited "two hundred four score and eight singers and instrumentalists." Near this passage, Bach had penned: "This is the basis of all God-pleasing church music." There are no less than sixty-one markings and underlinings in the set—even corrections of the printed text—all made by Bach, who was by repute a Bible expert *par excellence.*

Bach's three-volume *Calovius Bible* is now in the possession of the Concordia Theological Seminary in St. Louis, Missouri. The comments and underlinings in the Bible's text have yielded invaluable insights not only into the workings of Bach's mind, but also into the depths of his piety, and what he perceived as his mission as a church musician.

Calligrapher

B ach was a many-sided genius. Those of his contemporaries who recognized his greatness marveled at his many talents—composer, conductor, and organ virtuoso with unsurpassed powers of improvisation.

One would expect the *oeuvre* of such a titan to have Olympian qualities—imposing but remote. Yet Bach's creations, overwhelming in their number, exude a rare intimacy. Most of what he wrote reveals the warmth and radiance of his personality. Even his style of writing exemplifies his genius for clarity, order, balance and, at times, a playful whimsy. This holds true even for his compositional sketches, hastily set down to meet a deadline. (See *Composing*.)

Bach's calligraphic talent was already evident as he prepared the manuscripts of his first cantata, which has been preserved in his own handwriting. The title of this early work—*Aus der Tiefen rufe ich, Herr, zu Dir* (Out of the Depths I Cry, oh Lord, to You) is a harbinger of things to come. This cantata was written during Bach's stay in Mühlhausen (1707–1708) when he was in his early twenties. Robert L. Marshall, an acknowledged authority on Bach manuscripts and the composer's creative processes, has observed: "Bach succeeded in penning a score that rivals a printed edition in the regularity of its layout—surpassing print in elegance and character."

After his stay in Mühlhausen, the twenty-three-year old Bach entered a new phase in his profession, as court organist in Weimar, and his script began to take on a marked assertiveness and daring. This is noticeable in his works for the organ, an instrument he cultivated with untiring zeal during these Weimar years (1708–1717). The might of the instrument seemed to be reflected in the powerful calligraphy of the works he created during this assignment—the undulating strokes of his pen reproducing the up-and-down oscillations of his mind. A similar graphic imagery is evident in the manuscripts of his emotion-packed sonatas and suites for solo violin (see *Violinist*). On the other hand, when writing for an upbeat occasion such as the arrival of the new year, Bach, obviously in a joyous mood, accompanies the celebratory words of welcome with what has been called "a merry ballet of notes."

In his later years, Bach took pride in preserving what he considered his greatest achievements. Among these summation works, the *St. Matthew Passion* must have ranked supreme in his mind, and deservedly so. In this masterwork, as Paul Henry Lang has observed, Bach carried musically the central biblical drama "to its ultimate and unsurpassable height." Long after its first performance in 1729, Bach continued to work on the *St. Matthew Passion*. (See *Radiant Masterwork*.)

Bach's attachment to this work inspired him to create a version whose calligraphic beauty would reflect its importance. It was probably in the late 1730s that Bach took the time to create such a version of the *St. Matthew Passion*. Using ruler and compass, he spared no effort to put together a work of impressive calligraphy. (For the Gospel's words, he used red ink.) What is today considered to be Bach's finest manuscript was the result—a prized possession of the Deutsche Staatsbibliothek in Berlin. Even when studied in one of the various facsimile editions, this manuscript makes one appreciate why it has been said, justifiably, that Bach wrote *Augenmusik*—music for the eye.

Cantor or Capellmeister?

Like Goethe's Faust—who confessed "two souls, alas, dwell in my breast"—Bach's aspirations pulled him in two opposite directions. Which was he to be: a cantor—the choral director of a Lutheran church; or a capellmeister—the orchestra leader in a princely court?

Bach's early training and his deeply religious nature clearly gave the Lutheran church a strong claim upon his loyalty. His commitment to Protestantism remained unflagging throughout his life. (The historian Will Durant calls him the "Luther of Music.") But the instrumental music that was increasingly coming to the fore at the time exerted a strong pull in another direction. When a career change appeared in the offing, Bach was clearly attracted by what today we would call "employment opportunities" at one of the aristocratic courts where secular music flourished.

Hardly twenty years old, Bach aroused the ire of the Arnstadt church authorities, where he was employed as an organist, by his overlong stay in Lübeck. In Lübeck, he was an acolyte of Dietrich Buxtehude, whose *Abendmusiken* (see *Abendmusik*), with their accomplished instrumental performances, had a strong attraction for Bach. His later post in Weimar (1708–1717) proved to be a more productive

A church cantor (choirmaster) instructs his young singers in sacred song.

one, because it involved both sacred and worldly music. The pietistic Duke Wilhelm Ernst of Saxe-Weimar favored the inspirational powers of music over its entertainment values, though he was a highly civilized man, not only enamored of music, but also of poetry and the fine arts.

Hired as court organist, Bach prospered in this environment. The austere duke seems also to have recognized Bach's violinistic talent, making him, in 1714, the concertmaster of his court orchestra. But this title and assignment in no way seemed to satisfy Bach. Now approaching thirty, he remained in Duke Wilhelm's employ at the court of Weimar for another two years before being offered the position of capellmeister at the court of Prince Leopold of Anhalt-Cöthen (see *Anhalt-Cöthen*). The six years (1717–1723) he spent at Leopold's court, where a worldly atmosphere prevailed, turned out to be the happiest period of his life.

When Prince Leopold later lost his interest in music, it was time again for Bach to move on. He did so with obvious regret. Still, a cantorial assignment in Leipzig offered decided temptations. After all, Bach had so far labored in the provincial backwaters of Germany. In contrast, Leipzig was an important town in Saxony, with a three-hundred-year-old university that could, in future years, provide first-rate academic training for his growing sons (a training he himself had missed). Nevertheless, leaving the court of Cöthen for a position as a director of church music must have seemed a reduction in status. As Bach confessed: "It did not seem at all proper to me to exchange my post as Capellmeister for that of a Cantor. It is for this reason that I postponed my decision to accept the Leipzig offer for a quarter of a year."

His apprehensions proved justified. Bach had been hardly a year in Leipzig when trouble started, and it followed him like a shadow during his twenty-seven-year stay as cantor of the Thomaskirche (see

Capellmeister (orchestra leader) of a princely court in fashionable garb and wig. He indicates tempo with rolled-up music sheets serving as his "baton."

Leipzig Ordeal). These endless parochial disputes fed his yearning for a more worldly assignment. Time and again he tried to escape, applying for jobs in other towns. But his hope for a court position, where he would be less hampered by a narrow-minded bureaucracy, remained unfulfilled.

Both his worldly ambitions and his continuing dissatisfaction with his Leipzig post can be sensed graphologically. Bach's signatures during these years stressed his "noble connections," even if these were but honorary. When Bach published his *Clavier-Übung II* (the *Italian Concerto*) in 1735, he still felt the need to identify himself as "Johann Sebastian Bach, Capellmeister to his Highness the Prince of Anhalt-Cöthen"—twelve years after he had left Cöthen and its court *capelle* had long since been disbanded.

During Bach's last years, the inner conflict between Bach the cantor and Bach the capellmeister seems to have remained unresolved. In this light, Bach's visit to Frederick the Great in 1747—three years before his death—can be seen as a final attempt to escape from Leipzig's unpleasantness to an imagined courtly paradise. (See *Frederick the Great*.)

But if Cantor Bach was unhappy in Leipzig, so were the members of the Consistory. Almost from the time they had hired him, these burghers continued to carp that they had hired a cantor but had been stuck with a capellmeister. If they only could have known what a *rara avis* they had caught!

Catholicism

Wasn't it somewhat paradoxical, perhaps even slightly heretical, that in the early 1730s the Protestant Cantor Bach of Leipzig's Thomaskirche tried to offer his services to the Catholic King Friedrich August II of Poland? After all, Bach's career was to flourish only two centuries after Martin Luther had nailed his ninety-five theses to the church doors in Wittenberg, a town on the border of Saxony, northeast of Leipzig. The religious strife thus inaugurated was to occupy the next 150 years, culminating in the barbarities of the Thirty Years War (1618–1648).

The Peace of Westphalia (1648), ending the slaughter, had left the German lands a patchwork of religious enclaves. In Bach's time, regions favoring Lutheranism, Calvinism, and Roman Catholicism existed cheek by jowl, at times with considerable apprehension and mutual distrust.

We might expect that, as a staunch Protestant, Bach might have hesitated to seek an assignment at a Catholic court. But then he had never expressed any hostility toward the Catholic faith or its rituals.

Friedrich August II, elector of Saxony. In quest of a Dresden court appointment, Bach composed and submitted to the elector in 1733 the *Kyrie* and *Sanctus* that were to become a part of the *B Minor Mass.*

Indeed, Luther himself had incorporated parts of the Catholic mass into the Protestant liturgy. And moreover, as a practitioner of the Baroque style of music (see *Baroque*), Bach must have felt a friendly kinship with his Catholic colleagues. One might well say that Bach's style was as deeply rooted in the work of Palestrina, Carissimi, and Frescobaldi as in that of his Protestant predecessors Heinrich Schütz, Johann Pachelbel, and Georg Böhm.

Nor is it likely that Elector Friedrich August II would have felt uncomfortable in accepting a Lutheran composer into his circle. The ruler's father, Friedrich August I (August the Strong), was a Protestant who had accepted Roman Catholicism as the price of being elected king of Poland by that country's nobility. The Polish monarchy was not hereditary, but upon the death of August the Strong (1732), his son Friedrich August II was elected king of Poland. Soon afterward, Bach—either to boost his standing in Leipzig by way of a court title or to secure a better position—petitioned the new king, asking for a chance to prove his "indefatigable diligence in composing church music," and to devote his "whole powers to your Majesty's service." The petitioner sent along a *Sanctus* and a *Kyrie*—mainstays of the Catholic mass—as a sampling of his competence.

The royal answer was long in coming. Finally in 1736, after a wait of three years, Bach's appointment as court composer was confirmed. He worked on completing and perfecting the mass throughout his life. The resulting work is known as the *Mass in B Minor*, though most of it is written in the key of D major.

We have no indication that the entire *B Minor Mass* was ever performed in Bach's lifetime. But it stands to this day as a glowing example of Bachian piety and perfection. Too Catholic to enter the Protestant liturgy, too Protestant to be accepted by Catholics, it transcends all denominations and movingly expresses a universal human creed.

Collegium Musicum

Toward 1728, after five years as the cantor of Leipzig's Thomaskirche, Bach's frustration with his post seems to have reached a critical stage. Up until this time, he had worked with unflagging industry in the face of the antagonism and the discouraging apathy shown him by the town burghers he had wished to please.

Bach had every reason to be disgruntled. Prior to taking the Leipzig post, he had spent six years in the court of Prince Leopold of Anhalt-Cöthen (see *Anhalt-Cöthen*), years which he later considered to be the happiest and most productive of his life.

By 1728, at forty-three, Bach must have realized that he had failed to bring to fruition his grandiose plan as Leipzig's cantor: to produce "a compleat church music." He was in the grip of what Hindemith once called, in a Bach memorial, a "crisis of creativity." The avalanche of cantatas—which during his early period had often poured forth at the rate of one a week—now dwindled markedly. As a composer, Bach began to turn his attention to secular music and pedagogic works designed for his students and the growing group of musical dilettantes. As a practicing artist, he made a similar shift of interest from church to secular music—a new direction marked by his involvement in Leipzig's Collegium Musicum.

This group of instrumentalists was at one time headed by Georg Philipp Telemann (see *Telemann*)—its core of musically gifted stu-

dents from Leipzig University reinforced at times by accomplished professionals. Telemann himself had a facile way of reflecting the newest trends in musical taste. Thus, the group he gathered provided secular fare of a type lighter than the music offered in the town's churches.

The performances of the Collegium Musicum were held in Leipzig's popular Zimmermann's Coffeehouse, giving the town's burghers a chance to relax, drink beer, smoke, and listen to pleasant music. The group was most active during Leipzig's spring and fall fairs, when it entertained the foreign merchants visiting the town. A former cantor of the Thomaskirche, Johann Kuhnau, had put it well when he defined the *Collegium's* purpose as "establishing side by side a pleasing harmony of sounds and meeting of the minds."

Bach accepted the conductorship of this group in 1729. Whereas he had to struggle endlessly as a cantor to secure competent instrumentalists, he found such performers—both students and professionals—happily assembled in the Collegium Musicum. Quite obviously, Bach was inspired to compose for this group music of a less solemn nature than that demanded by his church work. In the chronological list of Bach works, secular cantatas and instrumental concertos now begin to take on greater prominence.

Early secular Collegium Musicum consisting of instrumentalists and singers. Such groups came together not for religious reasons but for the love of music: Their motto: *"Musica noster amor."*

The group also assumed the duty of providing music for the town's festive occasions (see *Pageantry*). Bach's sons and Bach himself appeared in the Collegium's concerts as soloists, as on occasion did celebrated visiting musicians. Carl Philipp Emanuel (Bach's second son) reports: "It was seldom that musical masters passed through town without getting to know my father and to play for him," undoubtedly referring to their performances as soloists with the Collegium's ensemble.

Bach remained the guiding spirit of the Collegium Musicum until 1739, when his creative powers became engaged in the composition of his summation works (see entry)—the *Goldberg Variations*, the *Musical Offering* and the mighty *Art of the Fugue*.

It should be noted that secular concerts by groups like the Collegium Musicum were by no means confined to Leipzig. Similar groups had sprung up even before Bach's time in other towns. In historical perspective, the kind of music-making practiced by these secular-oriented ensembles paved the way for the rise of concert orchestras which were to dominate the music world of the nineteenth century.

Leipzig's Collegium Musicum disbanded after the death of its host, Gottfried Zimmermann, in 1744. But the concerts were revived by a group of instrumentalists under the name Neue Konzerte. The group performed in the market hall of the Saxon linen merchants, a fact which gave the group the name under which it would become world-renowned—Gewandhaus Orchestra (*Gewand* connotes "dress"), later led by such luminaries as Felix Mendelssohn and Bruno Walter and Wilhelm Furtwängler. When I was a young apprentice in a Leipzig bookshop, I received special permission to attend the Thursday morning rehearsals of this fine orchestra, which had evolved out of Bach's modest but pioneering Collegium Musicum.

Composing

Bach's productive prowess is overwhelmingly attested to by the forty-six tightly packed volumes of the first *Gesamt-Ausgabe* (see entry)—his *Complete Works*. But it is not only Bach's productivity that is awe-inspiring. Equally impressive is the high quality evident throughout his vast corpus. As Debussy once noted: "We shall seek in vain for one fault in taste in all that amount of work."

Though Bach undoubtedly had his moments of frustration, few of his manuscripts reflect the struggle, strain, or frenzy that characterized the creative processes of a Beethoven or Chopin. The easy flow is all the more impressive in his cantata writing, which he undertook in the face of crushing deadlines. Once the main theme had been established, his musical notations seemed to leap and fly across the page.

Ideas apparently came to him, in the words of William Hazlitt, the English essayist, "on the gusts of genius," so speedily that his pen could scarcely follow his inspirational flights. At times, one can see evidence of Bach's impatience as he waited for the ink to dry before turning over the page. Anxious not to lose his thunderous train of thought, he would scribble the succeeding passage along the margins in his own musical shorthand.

Bach wrote "with a rapid creative impetus," and rarely does he seem to have agonized over details or encountered "writer's block." He always knew where he was going, untroubled, as are modern composers, by a need to find a structure for his work. Once his theme had been developed, he simply embarked upon the prescribed fugal round-trip. Yet Bach was a tireless corrector of his work, ever trying to improve even the smallest details.

A boundless energy moved him throughout his life, until he was felled by his last sickness. As a young musician, Bach had set himself an exalted task: the creation of "a well-regulated church music to exalt God's glory." Indeed, he belongs to the class of persons described by Gide as "ever prone to take on overwhelming burdens." For him, the day was not long enough to complete his assignments, and the demands of an ever-growing family increased his load. Hence, Bach was forced to work long into the night. To this habit his contemporaries ascribed the blindness that descended like a cloud upon his final years (see *Blindness*).

Bach seemingly had developed this habit of working at night when, during his tenth through fifteenth years, he lived with his brother Johann Christoph. The young boy worked by the light of the moon to copy music that he was anxious to study, but which Johann Christoph, in an apparent case of fraternal jealousy, was intent upon keeping out of his grasp (see *Education*).

Later in life, as one of his students observed, the master "felt the need to use the night in order to perfect what he had written (or perhaps just sketched) during the day." One may also venture a more metaphysical explanation for Bach's nocturnal creativity. It was said of El Greco that he preferred to paint at night because the brightness of the day interfered with the "inner light" that guided his brush. This might with equal validity be applied to Bach. When the sun went down, his luminous soul began to shine.

Copying

B ach's work was far from over when he had finished his "composing scores" and put down the last note of his latest project, be it a Sunday cantata, a Mass, or a concerto. Next, the composition at hand had to be readied for performance. Every note, every voice or orchestral part, had to be "copied out" so it could be given to the performers. This was a deadening chore for a mind as fertile as Bach's. What he wouldn't have given for a Xerox copier!

The first task was to prepare the paper—each sheet needing to be lined by hand. A "rastrum"—a five-point pen—offered some help, but it was apt to malfunction. As Telemann, Bach's contemporary, complained, he had to write

with ink whose flow is much too thick
for quill pens—soft and apt to stick.

As a youth, Bach zealously (and secretly) copied works of master musicians, ancient and contemporary, from his brother's library— working by the light of the moon. A lifetime of copying manuscripts by poor light may have led to the blindness of his later years.

It was relatively easy to create the finished manuscript for a work based on a one-voiced melody. But what an enormous chore of coordination Bach had to face when he had to copy the score for one of his gigantic Passions or Masses—requiring perhaps sixteen staves for the choral part and double orchestra (each stave—the five parallel lines on which music is notated—was devoted to a different instrumental or choral group).

Luckily, Bach was very handy with the pen and was, it seems, a copyist of lightning speed. At times, he was a bit too hasty, turning out scores that were rather sketchy. On other occasions, he went beyond the routine chore of copying, transforming one of his compositions into a work of fine calligraphy (see entry).

Bach's account books indicate that—in Weimar and Cöthen at least—he received contributions for the purchase of paper (expensive stuff at the time and used in ream quantities by Bach). But there is no indication that he received funds for copying help. In his work-filled Leipzig years (see *Leipzig Ordeal*), Bach enlisted the services of his students. Also, his two young sons, Wilhelm Friedemann and Carl Philipp Emanuel, and his second wife, Anna Magdalena, assisted him in the seemingly endless task. (See *Delegator.*)

But to prepare his scores for performance was only a part of Bach's copying chore. From his early youth, he was engaged in a life-long self-education process—copying the works of other composers, both his predecessors and his contemporaries. His primary motivation for this task, which he pursued to the end of his life, was a constant search for new techniques to add to the Bach canon (see *Education*). As his first biographer, Forkel, noted, "He taught himself chiefly by observing the work of the most famous and proficient composers of the day and his own reflections upon them."

Though a traditionalist by nature, Bach was always interested in current musical trends. While he was the court organist for Duke Wilhelm Ernst of Weimar (1708–1717), he benefited from the travels of the court's sickly young prince, Johann Ernst (who would die in 1715 at the age of nineteen). After journeying to Italy for his health, the prince usually returned with a new hoard of Italian masterworks, which Bach proceeded to copy, possessed by an intense zeal to encounter and to absorb new musical ideas, copying with special abandon the works of Albinoni, Corelli, and Vivaldi.

In Bach's continual search for "new input," he was often surprisingly uncritical when selecting examples to copy. Even after he had clearly established his superiority over composers such as Antonio

Caldera, Nicolas de Gigny, and Johann Kaspar Kerll—mostly forgotten today—Bach continued to copy their works. Similarly, his friend Telemann (see entry) was an amazingly prolific composer—purportedly writing more music than Bach and Handel put together—but he was in no way in Bach's class. Yet Bach humbly continued to study the new works of his renowned colleague as they were published. Bach's willingness to learn from even the least gifted of his associates stood in stark contrast to Beethoven, who was said to have avoided exposure to other composers in order to preserve his own originality.

Whether copying the works of the greatest or the least of his predecessors and contemporaries, Bach's purpose was, as the famed pianist and harpsichordist Wanda Landowska so aptly observed, to "quench his thirst by extracting from them the substance he needed to assert his own power." The young, would-be composers of our own day who seek to master the complexities of musical composition could do no better than to be inspired by the ceaseless application with which Bach pursued the secrets of his art.

The Dance

Since the preponderance of Bach's musical works are of a sacred nature, it might seem paradoxical that the staid "Holy Cantor" should have shown a decided interest in the world of the dance. Of course, as a devoted student of the Bible, Bach must have been well aware of the association that the Scriptures have established between religious ecstasy and the dance. Exodus tells us that after the Children of Israel escaped from Egyptian bondage, Moses' sister Miriam "took a timbrel in her hand, and all the women went out after her with timbrels and with dances." The markings and underlinings which Bach had made in his copy of the rare Calovius Bible (see *Bookman*) reveal that the master took pleasure in King David's use of music and dance as a form of devout religious expression.

Clearly, however, it was secular dance music that had gripped the populace during Bach's lifetime and claimed an increasing share of his attention. As so often in cultural matters, France led Europe in the growing popularity of dance music, particularly in the form of theatrical dance. This was largely a result of the operatic ballets

The dance music of France provided themes for Bach's suites and partitas—composed for nearly every solo instrument of the time. Nor was the master averse to making use of dance themes in his sacred music. He based the final movement of the *St. Matthew Passion* on a sarabande, a slow dance.

I. I. Nilson Sculp.

created by Jean-Baptiste Lully (1632–1687), who ruled at Versailles under Louis XIV as music's absolute dictator. Lully, a high-strung, talented musician and composer, met with a tragic end. He had the habit of conducting the court orchestra by beating time on the floor with his walking stick. Probably enraged by a disappointing performance, he accidently smashed the stick into his big toe, causing his death by blood-poisoning.

A generation later, Bach's contemporary, François Couperin (1668–1773), a master of the harpsichord, composed dance suites appropriately called *ordres*. Widely admired for their clarity, precision, and charm, these suites earned him the sobriquet "Couperin the Great." The French master's influence is clearly evident in Bach's own dance suites for the clavier.

Bach must have been well aware of the burgeoning market for dance and instrumental music in the towns and courts of his native land. Nearly forty Bach suites and partitas have come down to us, written for practically all the solo instruments popular during his time: harpsichord, lute, violin, cello, and flute—even trumpet. With Bach's awareness of scriptural precedent, and his innate spirituality, he had no trouble in adapting brisk and joyful dance forms—music that some might have considered to be frivolous—for use in his sacred works. Clearly, in Bach's thinking the two genres of music—secular and religious—were not irreconcilable.

The final chorus of the *St. Matthew Passion* is based on a sarabande Bach had previously used in a dance suite for solo lute. He based the introduction of Cantata 29, *We Thank Thee, God, We Thank Thee*, on the prelude of the E Major Partita for violin solo. In the motet *Sing Unto the Lord a New Song* (BWV 190A), ecstatic dancing is invoked by the line "Praise the Lord in dancelike procession."

Alfred Einstein has described the six partitas combined in Bach's *Clavier-Übung I* (see *Music Publisher*) as the summit of all Bach's dance suites, surpassing all that had preceded them, even those "which in themselves seem unsurpassable."

Bach wrote his suites and partitas principally "to uplift the spirits" (*Gemüts Ergötzung*)—absolute music designed to heighten spiritual enjoyment: to move souls, not necessarily to move feet. In the *Goldberg Variations* (see entry), for example, the strict formalism of the music seems to be far removed from the corporeal exuberance of the dance. Yet choreographer Jerome Robbins staged this work in a highly successful ballet, which was first presented by the New York City Ballet in 1971 and has been a staple offering of the company's repertory ever since. The company's famed director, George Balanchine, recommended that one should listen to a recording of this work before seeing a performance of the *Goldberg Variations* ballet. "In any case," he added, "what you see and what you hear will be marvelous."

Perhaps this simply offers further evidence that the protean music of Bach captures the whole scale of human feeling, from meditative doubt to life-affirming joy.

"Bach recognized the universal power of the dance to lift man's spirit to extravagant and joyful realms of selfidentity."

Jan Chiapusso

Daughters

During Bach's inordinately busy life, he was called upon to play many roles—composer, conductor, virtuoso, teacher, and, last but not least, the father of an ever-expanding family. He sired twenty children with two wives—seven by Maria Barbara and thirteen by Anna Magdalena. Nine of his children were daughters, only four of whom were still alive at the time of their father's death.

Whenever Bach's letters discuss his children, his sons take the limelight, with his daughters mentioned only in passing. Bach's prejudices in this respect were very much in keeping with the social mores of his times, when "the weaker sex" was vastly suppressed, if not actually abused. *Kirche, Küche, Kinder* (church, kitchen, children)—these, in popular opinion, were the only proper concerns for women.

Only once did Bach pay a compliment to a daughter—and a rather restrained one at that. In the 1730 letter to Georg Erdmann—in which Bach sought his old friend's help in securing a better job—he

described musical performances held in his own home, featuring members of his family in vocal and instrumental roles, noting, "My wife sings a good clear soprano and my eldest daughter too joins in not badly."

Of the four Bach daughters who lived to adulthood, Elisabeth Juliana Friderika was the only one who married. Johann Christoph Altnikol—one of her father's gifted students and later a composer of some rank—became her husband on January 20, 1749, at a time when Bach was already approaching blindness (see entry). Undoubtedly delighted to have his favorite student as his son-in-law, Bach had made every effort to secure a good position for the groom. Proceeding with some secrecy, he had succeeded in securing for Altnikol a post as organist in the neighboring town of Naumburg. Bach presented the young couple with a certificate of this appointment as a wedding gift. A boy was born to the Altnikols in October 1750. They named him Johann Sebastian after his grandfather, who had died the previous July. Unfortunately, the child survived for only two weeks, as was the rule rather than the exception in those "good old days."

During Bach's life, it was his sons who benefited from his parental zeal to provide for their future. Indeed, after Bach's death, four of them went on to notable careers (see *Paternal Devotion*). On the other hand,

A nineteenth-century illustration envisioning a Sunday afternoon in the Bach home, with Father Bach at the harpsichord as dinner is readied. His grown daughters act as domestic help, the role they were confined to in Bach's time.

his daughters suffered almost total neglect, taking on the not-uncommon role of household servants in their father's home. After Bach's death (1750), the three unmarried daughters who survived him—like his widow, Anna Magdalena—were reduced to poverty.

Bach's youngest daughter, Regina Susanna (born 1742), was the only one of the family's children to live to see the nineteenth century. Fifty-eight years old in 1800, she was discovered to be close to starvation by Friedrich Rochlitz, the editor of Leipzig's principal music magazine. Rochlitz initiated a collection to help the last child of the man who was, in Beethoven's words, "the greatest master harmonist of the centuries." Rochlitz's appeal had at first somewhat meager results, collecting a total sum of only 96 thalers (about $10,000 in current money). When Beethoven heard of this, he planned on composing a piece for Susanna's benefit—but nothing came of it (see B-A-C-H). However, he and his Vienna circle started a new collection which established a fund of 256 thalers (nearly $30,000), which sustained Regina until her death in 1809, at the age of sixty-seven.

Sadly, the man who left a priceless heritage for music-lovers, to be enjoyed by generations to come, had been unable to provide an adequate inheritance for his daughters, the most helpless of his children.

Death and Transfiguration

Many of Bach's cantatas are profound soliloquies on the ever-enigmatic theme of death—the fear that the grim reaper inspires in the sinner, and the hope of redemption promised to the steadfast believer. In his chorales, Bach frequently explored this subject in all of its perplexities, based upon his own intensive study of the Bible. This resulted in a body of cantatas dealing with the theme of mortality—works that can still provide consolation in our own notoriously secular age. His musical interpretation of human fears and hopes offers us a moving thematic context for contemporary speculations on "the art of dying."

For the believers of Bach's time, the major concern was that of salvation. The Lutheran creed held that salvation (immortal life) could be earned through faith alone. As Luther himself stated: "God has taken salvation out of the control of my own will, and put it under the control of His, and promised to save me, not according to my work or running, but according to His own grace." Thus, a devout Lutheran like Bach could not place his own hope of salvation on his earthly works, but only upon the strength of his own faith in God's mercy.

According to the doctrine in which Bach was schooled, then, death should hold no fear for the faithful, but rather be welcomed as a relief from earthly burdens and as the portal to eternal bliss. This article of faith is expressed in the titles and liturgy of many of Bach's cantatas. Fundamental Lutheran attitudes toward death are the thematic basis of Cantata 95, whose first tenor aria intones the theme, *"With joy and happy heart will I from here be going,"* a hymn of liberation from the squalor and narrowness of earthly life. Equally poignant is Cantata 156 with the *leitmotif* "And when it comes my time to go, withhold not Thine affection. With helping hand my care dispel, for all is well that ends well."

Memento Mori (Man, Remember You Must Die). Charcoal drawing by Albrecht Dürer. Many Bach cantatas dealt with the theme of human mortality—and the hope for salvation after death.

Bach's power—compounded of artistic genius and a tranquil Christian faith—to endow the grim theme of death with a special profundity, and to turn existential fear into spiritual solace, was deepened no doubt by his own personal encounters with death. He was hardly ten years old when he lost both parents and was thrust out into the world, the ward of an older (and not too kindly) brother. In 1720, his first wife, Maria Barbara, died unexpectedly while he was on a trip to the spa of Carlsbad with his patron, Prince Leopold of Anhalt-Cöthen. Of the twenty children he sired, only nine survived him—some dying in infancy, as was all too common in premodern societies. Professionally, he was often called upon to compose funeral music, with the frailty of human life as the dominant theme. And he created many works designed to bring solace to the dying.

The fragility of man's life and the desperate yearning of his spirit are themes that link one of his earliest masterpieces, *Aus der Tiefen rufe ich, Herr, zu Dir* (Out of the Depths I Cry, oh Lord, to You), with the last work of his life, the chorale *Vor deinem Thron tret' ich* (Before Thy Throne I Stand). In effect, this later work was Bach's farewell to the world, to which he gave voice when he was already blind and unable to hold a pen. He dictated it to his son-in-law, Johann Christian Altnikol. Revealingly, it is a reworking of an earlier melody, *Wenn wir in Höchsten Nöten sein* (When We Are in Our Direst Need).

In these, as in so many of his works, Bach seems to acknowledge the dominion of death while at the same time assuring the believer that its awful finality could be overcome through unflagging faith. In the *St. Matthew Passion*, Bach addressed this theme—through the crucifixion of Christ—in an unparalleled music drama (see *Radiant Masterwork*). And in the *Resurrexit* of the *B Minor Mass*, the impassioned fortissimo of the trumpets announces the ultimate triumph over death—the resurrection of Jesus which promises immortality to all of His faithful followers.

The subject of death and immortality engaged Bach throughout his life not only as a religious man, but also as the quintessential artist, who reaches out through his art beyond temporal themes to express the eternal verities. As an artist, Bach had an evident craving for immortality, an intense desire to create works worthy to be passed on to future generations. Clearly, Bach tended to see himself as a conscientious laborer in the field of music ("I worked hard"). But there is little doubt that his genius strove to imbue his creations with the high art that made him immortal. As André Malraux once observed, "Art escapes death."

Defending His Domain

In May 1723, Bach began his assignment as cantor for Leipzig's two principal churches, one of them the Thomaskirche, with which he has been most closely linked in music history. Paramount among his many duties and responsibilities was the provision that he write cantatas for each Sunday and feast day throughout the year, as well as oratorios, masses, and other works required for the church year's special occasions. In the face of these heavy commitments, we may wonder how the master ever found the time to tend to his more mundane duties, let alone to his personal and family needs.

Moreover, the supremely spiritual nature of his Leipzig church music suggests an artist imbued with an inner serenity, his mind preoccupied with metaphysical challenges beyond the reach of everyday life. Consider that in his first few years at Leipzig, Bach also produced two magnificent oratorios: the *St. John Passion* (1724) and the *St. Matthew Passion* (1729). In these great works, Bach evoked the immensity of human emotions, expressed vocally and instrumentally—anxiety and aspiration, suffering and transcendence, abysmal despair and sublime faith.

It is hard to imagine that the artist who urged his listeners on to celestial spirituality could at the same time have had his feet so firmly anchored upon the earth. But the fact is that the genius who produced these works was at the same time the hard-nosed professional who was quite mindful of the practical aspects of the job that provided sustenance to him and his continually expanding family. Not only was Bach ever ambitious to expand the scope and status of his position at Leipzig, but he would react with true Teutonic ferocity to the attempts of other professionals to impinge upon his territory.

A telling example of Bach's boldness and tenacity in defending his domain was the four-year battle he waged to retain the position traditionally held by Leipzig's cantors—that of director of music for the Paulinerkirche, Leipzig University's church. When Bach came to Leipzig in 1723, he must have thought this post was his. But the university authorities elected to give this responsibility to a hack organist named Johann Gottlieb Görner, who had the grandiose notion of thinking himself Bach's equal. Bach raised a furious row over this usurpation of a position he felt should have been his, along with the annual stipend that went with it.

In the course of the battle royal, Bach had nerve enough to appeal directly to the highest authority in the land: he put his complaint before his sovereign, King Friedrich August (the Strong), elector of Saxony and king of Poland. His first letter to the monarch, dated March 11, 1725 (when Bach was forty), received a surprisingly prompt reply. Perhaps startled by Bach's boldness, the king—who had been expending a fortune in making his Dresden residence a second Versailles—patiently lent his ear to a dispute over a mere 12 thalers,

August the Strong, elector of Saxony, who spent millions of thalers on beautifying his capital city of Dresden. Bach was stubborn enough to seek the help of this mighty potentate in trying to save a job that paid all of twelve thalers per year.

the stipend to which Bach laid claim. The king and elector promised that the matter would be decided once the university had presented its side of the argument.

But Bach was not one to let matters rest. Afraid that the university might misrepresent his claim, he wrote again to the king-elector, requesting a copy of the university's arguments and warning the monarch to withhold his decision in the matter until Bach had the chance to refute any misstatements. Bach's *chutzpah* paid off, and August the Strong sent along a copy of the university's version of its quarrel with the cantor.

Once he had all the evidence in hand, Bach wasted no time in launching a counterattack. In a bristling letter to the king-elector dated New Year's Day, 1726, he lashed out against his adversaries. As Bach biographers Sydney and Eva Mary Grew note: "Bach replied to [the University document] in an analytical statement that a solicitor preparing a brief could not improve upon. . . . He proved that the university had fabricated untruths and was guilty of inconsistencies in their argument."

The four tightly written pages of labyrinthine prose must have impressed the king-elector, but won Bach only a partial victory. August the Strong decreed that the Herr Cantor Bach must be paid the traditional 12 thalers, retroactive to the beginning of the dispute. But the monarch also reasserted the university's right to appoint whomever it chose for its musical needs.

Unable to admit even partial defeat, the fuming Bach refused to sign a formal pledge complying with this latter proviso (a humiliating document that was composed by Görner himself). As a result of Bach's stubborn recalcitrance, his relations with the university remained cool throughout his Leipzig years. Nevertheless, he was occasionally called upon to write festive music at the request of the student body, which apparently had a much higher regard for Bach's genius than did their small-minded elders.

Bach had a similar dispute with the new, young rector of the Thomaskirche school, Johann August Ernesti. In 1738, the feud reached its climax when the rector appointed as prefect for the church choir a dissolute and incompetent student. When Bach dismissed him, the situation erupted into an unseemly public quarrel between rector and cantor, with the two even confronting each other in front of the church choir. Bach now appealed to the new king-elector (the son of August the Strong—see *Catholicism*) in defense of his prerogatives, a strategic move that seemed to bring about a truce between the parties.

These rather petty quarrels stamp Bach as a dedicated practitioner of what, in sociobiological terms, has been called "the territorial imperative." His pen, protesting intrusions into his domain, moved at a furious pace, and his sharp argumentative mind was not apt to make concessions. Moreover, he had shrewd political instincts and would not hesitate, when it could help his position, to take advantage of rivalries between the church Consistory and the Town Council, or the council and the ruling body of the university, each of which jealously guarded its own traditional prerogatives.

Thus, when we consider the beatific spirituality of Bach's cantatas, we should remember that in contrast to the spirit of his church music he also had a highly combative side, which Schweitzer referred to when he called Bach a "mighty thunderer." Bach the artist was never so lost in the clouds of creativity that he could not spare a little thunder for his earthly adversaries.

Delegator

Bach was an inveterate and highly organized "delegator." His ability to free himself from routine chores is at times reminiscent of a modern executive responsible for a vast array of business matters, one who efficiently accomplishes his tasks through the support of a well-trained staff. Similarly, Bach shrewdly organized his affairs so that he could free himself from duties imposed upon him by his employers, which he felt would interfere with the creative needs to which he gave the highest priority. Arnold Schering, a leading Leipzig Bach scholar, has observed, "He was utterly parsimonious with his time, chary of getting involved with a chore he disliked and he could pass on to others."

In order to devote himself primarily to composing, Bach often assigned the training of his young choristers to gifted older students.

His Leipzig years (1723–1750) give clear evidence of the means by which Bach achieved these ends, especially in connection with his cantorial teaching responsibilities in the Thomasschule. Indeed, teaching a class in Latin (of which Bach had a surprisingly fine command, considering his spotty education) was one of the duties spelled out in his Leipzig contract of 1723. It was also a chore that Bach quite obviously hated. Hence, one of the first things he did after settling in Leipzig was to hire a substitute Latin teacher, Carl Friedrich Pezold, to whom Bach paid 40 thalers a year out of his own pocket, in order to free himself for more inspiring activities.

Ambitious and strongly driven to start his Leipzig incumbency in a burst of glorious creativity—smarting perhaps from the knowledge that he had not been considered one of the leading candidates for this position by the town fathers—Bach for a time composed a new cantata each week (one a month would have been a miracle). Expending the creative energy to accomplish such a staggering output (not in numbers alone, but also in the supreme quality of the work) seems beyond our comprehension.

But complicating Bach's superambitious program even further was the need to prepare each new cantata for the performance itself. This latter burden alone—usually assumed by the cantor—would have overwhelmed Bach with tedious detail. He was astute enough to delegate such tasks to his very capable second wife, Anna Magdalena, who headed a "scriptorium," freeing the master's time for more creative tasks (see *Copying*).

To train choirboys and prepare them for Leipzig's Sunday church performances was also one of Bach's contractual assignments, another duty that he obviously considered a waste of time, since these were usually recalcitrant youngsters often devoid of musical talent. While he wrote motets (chants for unaccompanied voices—and what masterpieces they are), he would not deign to direct them. In Bach's mind, he was a capellmeister who prided himself in instrumental performances, not one inclined to take on the burden of conducting a bunch of schoolboys. This chore too was assigned to his more gifted students and other aides.

Through such astute delegation of unwelcome tasks, Bach was able to free himself to explore his own ideas and projects. "In redirecting his energies during these years," observes Christoph Wolff, the leading figure in Bach research and head of Harvard's Music Department, "he approached the status of a modern freelance writer." Bach had never been one to work well under the iron hand of patronage, be it church or court.

Posterity has affirmed that Bach's assessment of his musical priorities was far more astute than that of his Leipzig taskmasters. We are all the richer for his stubborn refusal to get involved with the drudgery they imposed upon him and for his insistence on "doing his own thing."

Detractors

Bach enjoyed high esteem in his own time as a virtuoso on the organ and harpsichord, but as a composer he had his severe critics—or worse still, he was ignored. We are accustomed to look at Bach's detractors with a superior smile, enlightened as we are by the knowledge acquired during the centuries that have since passed.

The cover of *Critischer Musikus*, a publication of Johann Adolf Scheibe, noted music critic and former Bach student. In it, Scheibe commented that Bach's work "would display more agreeable qualities...if they were less turgid."

Johann Adolph Scheibens,

Königl. Dänis. Capellmeisters,

Critischer

MUSIKUS.

Neue,

vermehrte und verbesserte

Auflage.

Leipzig,

bey Bernhard Christoph Breitkopf, 1745.

For example, we are apt to make good-natured fun of Leipzig's town fathers, who, when they selected Bach, thought they had picked a "second-rater." Indeed, they bemoaned the fact that the man they had wished to hire, Karl Heinrich Graun (1703–1759), had slipped through their fingers. Graun was a singer and composer who, in 1740, became capellmeister for Frederick the Great. An eminent figure then, he is little known today (except perhaps for his oratorio *The Death of Jesus*).

The bourgeois members of the town council clearly were not musical experts. These good burghers could not grasp the grandeur of Bach's music, which only began to be appreciated by the musical world many years after his death (see *Revival*). Has it not been truly said that "the glory of one's own time is hidden from the view of its contemporaries"?

An even more egregious example of this truth is the case of Johann Adolf Scheibe (1708–1776), a contemporary composer and music critic who, in his highly estimable journal *Der Critische Musikus* (May 1737), delivered himself of this judgment on the work of J. S. Bach: "The great man would be the object of admiration if he possessed more pleasantness and made his compositions less turgid and sophisticated, more simple and natural in character." Scheibe also paid Bach a left-handed compliment by declaring, "His music is exceedingly difficult to play because the efficiency of his own limbs sets his standards."

Such judgments sound somewhat ridiculous today, considering our own boundless admiration of the master. But the critical assault by Scheibe must be judged fairly in the context of his own aesthetic standards, for he was a musical "reformer" strongly committed to the gospel of Art Galant (see entry), which was becoming the fashionable style during Bach's own lifetime. This school favored compositions of a simplified melodic line, rather than Bach's erudite polyphonic style—music not *gelehrt* (scholarly) but *galant*. Art Galant composers, including Bach's own sons, deemed themselves superior to the master—more "with it"—deprecating what they construed as the "old hat" fugal constructions of the Leipzig cantor.

Although there was a kernel of truth in Scheibe's critique, Bach was nevertheless quite hurt and mounted a counteroffensive, which he entrusted to a friend, J. A. Birnbaum, professor of rhetoric at Leipzig University (see *Rhetorician*). Bach's cause was also taken up by Lorenz Mizler, who founded the famous music society that Bach would join in 1747 (see *Secretiveness*). The battle of wits involved many months of disputation in print, ultimately ending in a stalemate.

There was one gambit in Scheibe's attack that especially offended Bach. Scheibe had referred to the great Leipzig cantor as a *musikant*, which was a word that connoted the lowest grade of musicianship—a strolling player. Whatever Scheibe might have achieved as a musician and theorist (one who had once even studied with Bach in Leipzig), he was to be stigmatized by history as the man who not only misjudged one of his period's greatest figures, but who also had thus grossly insulted the master.

While Bach was obviously much annoyed by Scheibe, he did not permit himself to show any rancor against the critic's family. When called upon to judge a new organ that had been built by Scheibe's father, a famed organ builder with whom he had had previous dealings, Bach pronounced it admirable and faultless.

Bach-sniping continued long after the master's death, and by authorities that one would have expected to know better. No one made a more thorough study of the music of his time than the eminent English music historian Charles Burney. His judgments were the result

Dr. Charles Burney, a widely recognized music critic (and travel writer) in the latter half of the eighteenth century, did not rank Bach very highly. He accused the Leipzig master of heavy-handedness and a lack of sense for the graceful.

of intensive travel throughout Europe. In his great work *The Present State of Music in Germany, the Netherlands, and the United Provinces* (1773), Dr. Burney chastised Bach for his "heavy-handedness." Bach's genius, Burney said, "never stooped to the Easy and the Graceful." Apparently, Burney had never "stooped" to become acquainted with a work like the *Italian Concerto*, which Bach had published in 1735 as part of his *Clavier-Übung II*.

Perhaps one shouldn't be too harsh with Bach's contemporary critics. They were not as lucky as we, who can respond to the great body of Bach's music that still survives—the serious and the light—in printed editions and in recordings galore from which the miracle of Bach endlessly reemerges.

Education

Even in his earliest years, Bach was driven by what Henry James once called "the hungry futurity of youth." Today, we would call him a self-starter. Never in his life did he have to be coaxed to study. Rather, he was ever anxious, driven by his own initiative, and often under trying conditions, to penetrate the secret of his art.

He began his life under most adverse, not to say tragic conditions that would have broken the spirit of many a less rigorous young soul. But step by step and in unflagging application, he climbed the ladder of success, to dominate like no other composer the music of his own time, now rightly called the Age of Bach.

Sebastian's mother died when he was but nine years old. His father, Johann Ambrosius, remarried, but died a year later (see *Hometown*). No trace has ever been found of his stepmother. An orphan at ten, Sebastian was placed in the care of an older brother—Johann Christoph, fifteen years his senior—who was the organist of the Michaeliskirche in Ohrdruf, a small Thuringian town about thirty miles away from his birthplace, Eisenach. Johann Christoph was also accomplished at the harpsichord, having studied under Johann Pachelbel (whose *Canon* became something of a pop classic in America a decade ago). Family records report that the older brother instructed young Sebastian "in the first principles of the keyboard." In this, Johann Christoph followed a long-established tradition of the Bach clan, all of whose members were committed to the training of their young male offspring on the instruments they themselves had mastered and in the profession that had sustained the Bachs for more than two generations (see *Hometown*).

Already in this early stage, young Sebastian was possessed by a keen ambition to learn, to improve his knowledge and his budding musical prowess. This ambition, it seems, Johann Christoph was neither able nor willing to support. Grove's *Dictionary of Music and Musicians* describes him as one of the less brilliant members of the Bach clan. According to a well-known bit of Bach lore—akin to the once-popular Parson Weems yarns about the young George Washington—Johann Christoph looked at his upstart brother with a touch of jealousy. He denied Sebastian access to a group of rather advanced clavier pieces that the boy was anxious to study. Undaunted, young Sebastian eased the volume out of a cabinet and engaged in a nocturnal venture of copying the pieces secretly—by the light of the moon (see *Copying*).

Sebastian was to stay with his brother for five years, attending a rather progressive school of excellent repute, Ohrdruf's Lyceum. This school had a fine record of teaching Latin, Greek, rhetoric, and arithmetic in accordance with the principles of John Amos Comenius, an internationally famous Czech-born educational reformer, who in 1658 had published *Orbis Sensualum Pictus (The World in Pictures)*—the world's first illustrated textbook.

Young Bach's stay in Ohrdruf yielded significant benefits educationally, but his diurnal life must have been one of deprivation. The family of his brother Christoph—always a hesitant host—was growing, and the meager finances of the Bach clan required that Sebastian begin adding to the family income. This was to be accomplished in the traditional manner of so many Bach males: Sebastian was, at this early age (just turned fifteen), to become a professional musician, earning his keep.

Thus, in the spring of 1700 Sebastian made his way to the northern German town of Lüneburg—another of the important mercantile towns of the Hanseatic League—where he found employment as a choral singer and an instrumentalist for church services, weddings, funerals, and the like. As a singer in the church choir, he was eligible to attend classes at the Michaelisschule, which had a curriculum heavily weighted toward orthodox Lutheran theology, a training which seemed to suit Bach, since it would become the religious core of his sacred music. Aside from its fine educational facilities, Lüneburg offered an invaluable asset for an agile, self-motivated student—a large library of eleven hundred musical scores by composers, ancient and contemporary. No doubt Bach, showing himself already to be a tireless student of music old and new, delved into these treasures with abandon.

In Lüneburg, Bach was also exposed to other influences later to be reflected in his work. At the neighboring court of Celle, the reigning duke, Georg Wilhelm, had ambitions to make his dukedom a little Versailles. To achieve this end, he had assembled a fine orchestra, heavily committed to the French style of music. The teenaged Bach gained access to the court and at times may even have joined the orchestra in the violin section. This gave him his first taste of French music, which was imbued with a grace absent from the ponderous style of music to which he had till then been exposed.

It is clear that before long Sebastian was to become what today we would call a school dropout, devoting his energies primarily to the advancement of his musical career and giving up, through force of circumstance, any hope of furthering his academic career. Like many self-made men of the modern era, Bach would later see to it that some of his sons had the university education he himself was denied.

His transition to the status of professional musician became complete when, at Easter, 1703, at the age of seventeen, young Bach secured a position as violinist in the Weimar court orchestra of Duke Johann Ernst, then moved on a few months later to become the organist at the Neuekirche in Arnstadt, where he would stay for nearly four years.

It was during his Lüneburg stay that Bach had begun his habit of traveling afoot to distant towns to hear the outstanding artists of his region, themselves the repositories of musical trends from all over Europe. To these influences, Bach added the practice he had begun at Ohrdruf—copying in his own hand the works of other composers (see *Copying*). According to the obituary in Mizler's *Musikalische Bibliothek*, 1754, Bach taught himself the principles of composition through the intense study of the creations of his contemporaries and other famous composers that had preceded him. All that he learned from these quite respectable works of others was transformed through the miraculous alembic of his mind into something new and far greater. Sometimes bold, sometimes dramatic, sometimes lyrical—as yet still the work of a very young man, but already stamped with the individuality of genius.

As a composer, Bach was thus essentially self-taught, a truly amazing phenomenon when compared to the years-long training which today's composers are apt to undergo. In these lifelong pursuits, Bach didn't need to be coached or coaxed. He was born with a restless energy and an ambition to succeed. He was, in fact, a prime example of the kind of man who, in Freud's description, is possessed by an "inner tyrant" that compels him to bend his life to an obsessive "total work discipline."

Equanimity

The critical and material successes of his fellow musicians did not seem to disturb Bach's equanimity or move him to petty jealousy. Far from begrudging Telemann (see entry) the fame and the adulation he garnered, Bach established a warm friendship with this composer that lasted all his life (and beyond, judging from Telemann's touching memorial poem to JSB). Even Bach's unsuccessful efforts to establish a friendship with Handel (see entry), the greatest of his contemporaries, clearly show the Leipzig cantor's modesty and courtesy. Handel, the grand seigneur of music—vain, arrogant, and not lacking a streak of the dictatorial—may have found Bach beneath his notice, for he remained pointedly uninterested in Bach's attempts to meet him personally.

Bach's work—its preoccupation with sacred themes—conveys the picture of an artist spending endless hours in solitude, withdrawn, and perhaps even asocial. But contemporary reports make it clear that Bach was far from being a recluse. In his unofficial relationships, he was quite affable—obviously a man who cherished companionship. "Any lover of art, stranger or fellow countryman, could visit his household and be sure of meeting a friendly reception," his biographer, Forkel, writes. "These social virtues, together with his artistic fame, caused his house rarely to be without visitors." Indeed, this warmhearted hospitality, which kept Bach's Leipzig home full of comings and goings, led his son Carl Philipp Emanuel to liken the place to a "busy pigeon coop."

Bach was also bound by warm ties of loyalty to his extended family scattered throughout Thuringia, ties that were further strengthened by his first marriage to his second cousin, Maria Barbara. Although Johann Sebastian was to achieve the most exalted musical heights—as a performer and as a composer—and was to rise socially far above the rest of the Bach clan, he would always remain on friendly terms with his kinsmen, many of them humble musicians and teachers in positions of low prestige and meager income.

Bach took a special pride in taking young relatives into his Leipzig home for musical instruction, hoping that they might go on to a successful career in the family tradition. He never lost contact with the burgher and peasant classes in which the family was so deeply rooted.

The folksy, down-to-earth spirit of the Bach clan comes frequently to the fore in the music of its most renowned member. Exuding a *joie de vivre* and founded upon an inner contentment, the spirit-lifting beat of much of Bach's work is blatantly at odds with the dour, combative Bach seen in some of his official communications. Even a work of such ultimate solemnity as the *B Minor Mass* has movements of infectious and unrestrained jubilation. Dance rhythms of a decided upbeat quality are not infrequent in his sacred works, and they abound in his secular cantatas (see *Dance*). A work such as the *Peasant Cantata* amply proves that Bach understood the earthy pleasures of life.

Given the many quarrels, tensions, and frustrations of Bach's career, from what inner sources came the music that could either soar in spiritual splendor or gambol and frolic in ebullient pleasure? Surely the answer lies in the essential equanimity that animated his art. Isaiah Berlin has suggested that Bach was one of those artists "at peace with their medium—integral as men and artists...tranquil and solid and free from self-consciousness or obsession."

Eroticism

The sternness with which Bach seems to stare out at us from his portrait (only one truly authenticated one is known) hides an important and unexpected dimension of his character: a definite tinge of eroticism. It finds expression not only in his music but also in the texts which he selected for use. Even his religious cantatas—which we always envision as confined to orthodox thoughts—surprise us at times in their passionate text. Love between man and woman are here at times symbolically transposed into the Christian idiom, with the soul longing for Christ as the lover yearns for his beloved. Bach's love duet from Cantata 140 (*Sleepers Awake*) overtly expresses such ardent desire:

> *So come unto me, my fair and chosen bride,*
> *Thou whom I long to see forever by my side*
> *Within my heart of hearts thou art secured by ties*
> *That none can sever.*

In his jacket comments for an early Bach recording, the late biographer and musicologist Frederic V. Grunfeld observed that one does not have to be a psychoanalyst to note the "clear call of sexual urgency that often throbs in Bach's music. The passionate intertwining of melodies suggests the caresses of the bridal bed."

Bach also evoked in some of his cantatas and motets the close relationship of love and death, with death represented as a longed-for encounter with Jesus. Love and death often appear in Bach's work in a sort of "Freudian embrace," conjuring up the mystical swooning of Bernini's *St. Theresa* or the mordant sensualities of the *Liebestod* from *Tristan and Isolde*. As Diane Ackerman writes in *A Natural History of Love*, "Religious ecstasy and the ecstasy of lovers have much in common—the all-consuming fire in the heart and flesh."

More than any other composer, Bach reminds us that sensuality and spirituality, love and death, ecstasy and grief are not dichotomies but ever-merging voices in the unfathomable fugue of life.

Extraterrestrial

When the unmanned space explorer *Voyager* was launched in 1977, it carried, along with its heavy scientific gear, a recording of Bach's *Brandenburg Concerto No. 2* and some preludes from *The Well-Tempered Clavier*. This music was to be released into outer space as a resounding example of the earth's civilization.

The selection of Bach's music was the result of a discussion between Dr. Carl Sagan, a pioneer in interstellar communications, and Dr. Lewis Thomas, who was at the time chancellor of the Memorial Sloan-Kettering Cancer Center in New York.

Dr. Thomas, who died at the age of eighty in 1993, was not only a highly regarded scientist—a "cell-watcher," as he modestly called himself—but also expressed all through his life deep insights into the mysteries and magic of music. (See, for example, his remarkable and rewarding book *Late Night Thoughts on Listening to Mahler's Ninth Symphony* [1983].)

Among music's greats, Bach was without a doubt his favorite. Thus, it is no wonder that, in his discussion with Dr. Sagan about music as a means of interstellar communication, he came up with a ready answer, one which he later set forth in his book *The Medusa and the Snail* (1979).

"I would vote for Bach, all of Bach, streamed out into space over and over again. We would be bragging, of course, but it is surely excusable to put on the best possible face at the beginning of such an acquaintance. Any species capable of producing the music of Johann Sebastian Bach cannot be all bad."

In a 1979 talk before New York City's River Club, Dr. Thomas elaborated upon his gospel of Bach. Bach's music, he suggested, is much more than an aggregation of sound effects; it is an indication of "how the brain thinks"—or perhaps how it *should* think. "If you are looking around for signs of hope in humanity," he said, "pay close attention to Bach's *Art of the Fugue.*"

Musing on various government projects to promote research and education, Dr. Thomas once argued that our prime need was to promote sound thinking. Along these lines he whimsically suggested that a National Institute of Bach be annexed to Washington's sprawling bureaucracy. "I would rather pay my taxes for that than for anything else," Dr. Thomas concluded.

When this great scientist died, he left us with a consoling thought. From his lifelong biological research—summarized in his now-classic book *The Lives of a Cell* (1974)—he deduced that there is no physical pain present in the final moments of dying, an idea fathomed by his great patron saint, Johann Sebastian Bach, centuries ago.

Flattering the Mighty

B ach lived in an age when the feudal structures of society were beginning to crack. Individualism and self-esteem were, in his time, fostered by both the spiritual egalitarianism of the Protestant Reformation and the increasing power of capitalism. Nevertheless, one characteristic of feudal society still prevailed in the eighteenth century: commoners were expected to know their place and to exhibit fawning deference when addressing a member of the nobility.

In this respect, Bach was very much a man of his time. Though he was prepared to defend vigorously the integrity of his creative work and the prerogatives of his own position (see *Defending His Domain*), he knew what was expected of him when addressing an aristocrat in person or in writing—especially when seeking a favor of some sort. Though we may cringe a little when we read such puffy phrases in his letters, Bach did not hesitate to sign a petition to an aristocrat with these words: "Your most exalted magnanimous sublime Highness's ever obedient servant and slave."

After all, for nearly another century musicians, artists, and writers would often be dependent upon the aristocracy for positions, commissions, and other means of augmenting their incomes. Even so rebellious and egalitarian an artist as Beethoven would, in 1793, conclude his petition to his royal employer: "Your Electoral Excellency's most humble and most faithfully obedient Ludwig van Beethoven, Court Organist." What Beethoven really thought is better captured in the comment he is said to have made to Prince Lichnowsky two decades later: "There have been thousands of princes and will be thousands more; there is only one Beethoven!"

A further complication in the German states of Bach's time—

especially for a creative genius—was the fact that the wealthy bourgeoisie had risen to power. Still insecure in their status as the civic leaders of their communities, these rather pompous burghers insisted upon receiving the same sort of deference from all those persons that they considered to be of lower social status, including the musician hired to be Leipzig's cantor and choirmaster.

Even when Bach was furious at these bourgeois town fathers—and he seems to have existed in a state of permanent and bitter anger during his nearly three decades in Leipzig—he still remained conscious of his position and acquiesced in the servile forms of address that the social status of his adversaries demanded. Even an acid letter venting his complaints to the town council would be couched in such ripely flattering terms as "Your Magnificence, Most Noble, Most Distinguished, Steadfast Honorable and Most Learned, and Most Wise Highly Esteemed Gentlemen"—surely the exact opposite of what he thought of them.

In search of a new position, a court title, or perhaps even a gift of hard cash, Bach might augment his humble and submissive petitions with the gift of a musical manuscript. One of the most famous instances of this practice occurred in 1721 (when Bach was thirty-six), during his generally happy and productive tenure at the court of Prince Leopold of Anhalt-Cöthen (see *Anhalt-Cöthen*).

Recognizing that his patron, Prince Leopold, had after his second marriage begun to lose interest in his court orchestra, Bach began to cast about for a new place of employment. Leopold's realm, Anhalt-Cöthen, was but a tiny principality sandwiched between the large and powerful states of Brandenburg to the north, with Berlin as its principal city, and Saxony to the south, with Leipzig as its commercial center. Brandenburg itself had been absorbed into Prussia, a blossoming continental power, and within two decades Berlin would become the capital of Prussia's autocratic king, Frederick the Great. Nevertheless, Brandenburg was still a state of considerably more power than the tiny principality of Anhalt-Cöthen.

Apparently in the hope of acquiring the position of capellmeister at the court of Brandenburg's margrave, Christian Ludwig, Bach gathered together in manuscript form six concertos—some composed for this purpose, others perhaps a reworking of pieces composed for his Cöthen orchestra. These he dispatched to the margrave under the rather unassuming title *Six Concerts Pour Différents Instruments*. The manuscript was accompanied by a suitably fawning note in which Bach begged his Highness "most humbly not to judge the concertos' imperfections with the rigor of the fine and delicate taste which the whole world knows your Highness has, but rather to accept them as proof of my deep respect and servile obedience which I hope to show your Highness by submitting them to him."

Christian Ludwig of Brandenburg, to whom Bach dedicated a gift of *Six Concertos for Various Instruments* (1721). The compositions remained buried for almost a century until they were resurrected as the *Brandenburg Concertos*, which made the recipient and his domain immortal.

Since the margrave's orchestra was too small to tackle Bach's instrumentally demanding offering, the six concertos were promptly entombed in Brandenburg's court archive. There they were found at the margrave's death in 1734, wrapped and bunched together with some musical trivia to be sold for a total of two thalers. Luckily, the "lot" was picked up by Bach's faithful pupil Johann Philipp Kirnberger, who realized he had won a prize. Bach, however, received no reward for his flattering gift. Indeed, there is no indication that the margrave so much as sent Bach an acknowledgement, let alone an appointment, grant, or pension.

In one of those odd historical ironies, the six concertos ignored by the margrave would become a priceless treasure to future generations of music lovers, remembered by the name of the Prussian province ruled by a potentate who by now has disappeared into the proverbial mists of history. Thus, we know these once scorned works as the ever-inspiring *Brandenburg Concertos*. Bach's "humble gift" to the margrave was, in Martin Bookspan's words, "a veritable syllabus of the art of Baroque instrumentation and a matchless demonstration of the varied textures and sonorities possible to the Baroque orchestra."

Bach's signature, proudly displaying his title as "Royal Polish and Electoral Saxon Court Composer." An honorary title such as this was prized by Bach. He thought it more prestigious than the titles connected with his church positions.

When we think of this immortal master struggling for recognition—either exploited or ignored altogether by the kings, princes, and dukes of his times—we can only nod in agreement with Beethoven, who in 1812 wrote words that are a fitting epitaph for both himself and Bach, the musical giant who preceded him by nearly a century: "Kings and Princes can create professors and councilors, and confer orders and decorations; but they cannot create great men, spirits that rise above the earthly rabble; these they cannot create, and therefore they are to be respected." We not only have learned to respect these great spirits, but also to love them for the infinite enhancement they have given to our lives.

Frederick the Great

In 1747, the lives of two of the giants of the eighteenth century intersected. Johann Sebastian Bach was sixty-two years old when he set out to visit Frederick II, king of Prussia, a young monarch of thirty-five in the eighth year of a half-century reign that would earn him lasting fame as Frederick the Great. By this time, Bach had absented himself from his official functions as Leipzig's music director and had turned to composing music to meet his own creative needs.

We may wonder what led Bach, in the twilight of his life, to undertake an arduous trip to Berlin, some two hundred miles away. One reason for this venture (in which he was accompanied by his oldest son, Wilhelm Friedemann) was undoubtedly to visit his second son, Carl Philipp Emanuel, who had been principal harpsichordist at the court of the king of Prussia since 1738, two years before Frederick had ascended to the throne.

Carl Philipp Emanuel Bach, court harpsichordist to Frederick the Great. Pen and ink sketch for Adolph Menzel's famed painting: *Flute Concert at Sanssouci.*

The prospect of meeting the famed Prussian king surely provided another incentive for the trip. Bach always was keen to meet the mighty and gain their patronage. It must have been particularly tempting for the aging cantor to seek a connection with a court that could boast of a fine orchestra and was ruled by a highly cultured monarch who passionately loved music (as well as art, literature, and science). The

king's flute-playing had reached a professional level, and he wrote over one hundred concertos for this instrument—perhaps with some assistance from his renowned flute master, Johann Joachim Quantz. The current Schwann Catalogue still lists *"Concerto in C for Flute and Strings* by Frederick II (Frederick the Great) of Prussia."

Still, king and cantor lived in worlds far apart. The young monarch was well aware of his eminent position and inclined to be haughty. A convinced atheist, he pronounced that all religions "are founded on superstitious systems, more or less absurd." In contrast, Bach was a devoted Lutheran who never doubted the dogmas of the Christian faith—indeed celebrated them in majestic works of music.

Bach was to meet the king in his magnificent town palace, the Berlin Stadtschloss. (The famed Sanssouci Palace was at the time still under construction.) Unfortunately, this audience did not yield the formal recognition that Bach might secretly have hoped for. On the contrary, Bach seems to have feared that the encounter had been a minor calamity, that his performance had failed to come up to his host's expectations.

King Frederick II had of course heard through Carl Philipp Emanuel of Bach's fabled skill as an improviser. So shortly after the

Frederick the Great, king of Prussia, performing as flute soloist. At the harpsichord is Bach's son Carl Philipp Emanuel, who served the king from 1738 to 1767. *Courtesy of Deutsche Staatsbibliotek, Bildarchiv Preussischer Kulturbesitz, Berlin*

Bach performing for King Frederick II at the royal court in May 1747. The king asked Bach to improvise a six-part fugue based upon a theme the monarch had intoned. Dissatisfied with his performance and wishing to "atone" to the king, Bach composed his *Musical Offering*, based upon the "royal theme."

travelers had arrived at the palace (on May 7, 1747), Frederick went to one of his harpsichords and intoned a theme, asking his guest to use it as the basis for a six-part fugue. Bach began, but as he improvised, he found that this theme was not quite suitable to serve as the basis for a six-part fugue. Hence, he replaced the "royal theme" by one of his own invention, which he developed into a three-part fugue. The king and his entourage could hardly have noted the deviation and warmly applauded what they admired as the visitor's miraculous fugal wizardry (see entry). But Bach felt that he had not truly fulfilled the king's command. Interestingly, the noted Harvard music historian, Christoph Wolff, has recently disputed the notion that the "royal theme" was the king's invention, suggesting rather that it had been prepared by one of the many professionals in the court orchestra.

After returning home to Leipzig, Bach set about rescuing what he must have regarded as his impaired reputation. In the short time of three months, he composed one of the great masterworks of music, which we know now as the *Musical Offering*. Actually, Bach's own title

for it, *Musikalisches Opfer*, might be better translated as a *Musical Sacrifice*—that is, a sacrificial offering to the great king, making amends for what Bach construed as his "failure" at the court.

The royal theme King Friedrich intoned for Bach with the request to develop it into a six-part fugue.

Toward the fall of 1747, the work was delivered (printed and bound in a gold-embossed cover) to the Prussian court. It offered not only a six-part fugue on the "royal theme," but other ingenious variations of it. The centerpiece of the work was a trio sonata with the flute prominently featured, a special tribute to Frederick, who loved the flute above all instruments. (When later in life the king lost his front teeth and could no longer play, he remarked, "I have lost my best friend.")

The haste evident in producing this complex work was prompted not only by Bach's hope of regaining his standing with Frederick the Great (a standing which had been lost only in Bach's imagination); there was also a practical prospect urging him on. He wanted to have printed copies of the *Offering* ready for sale at the Leipzig Fall Fair in October of 1747. After his return to Leipzig from Potsdam in mid-May, Bach must have been gripped by "deadline fever" that urged him on to accomplish the feat in a manner akin to today's "instant publishing." Bach's great haste was evident in the printing itself, during which the parts emerged in a somewhat mixed-up sequence, a most unusual occurrence for Bach, the quintessential precisionist. (See *Music Publisher*.)

Bach obviously intended to have the *Musical Offering* ready because he envisioned a rare opportunity to achieve good sales for one of his works, especially one based on a theme by the king of Prussia. And news of the fact that Bach had been received by royalty was certain to add to his reputation among the musical cognoscenti.

To this day, music historians have conducted a vigorous debate about the order in which Bach intended to present the component sections of the *Musical Offering*. But there is no dispute about the greatness of the work that emerged from his Berlin adventure, a work conceived in some haste and yet containing insights of unfathomable depth.

Friendships

T he English Bach biographer C. Hubert H. Parry once observed: "I would be hard put to strike up a friendship with Beethoven. . . . But with Bach, I could sit down comfortably and quaff a stein of beer."

Admittedly, Bach's boiling point was a low one. He hated unjust infringements upon what he perceived to be his rights. He fought for years with Johann Gottlieb Görner, the organist of Leipzig's Paulinerkirche, who occupied a job (and thus garnered an income) that Bach believed was his, as the town's music director, by tradition if not by contract (see *Defending His Domain*). But after peace was made, Bach held no grudges. Görner later became a close associate of Bach's in the Thomaskirche—even though Görner's organ performances did not always come up to the master's high standards.

A feeling of collegial warmth bound Bach to his fellow musicians (see *Telemann*). Touchingly, Bach also accepted into this fraternity those musicians who were quite obviously several notches beneath his level of excellence.

A Bach contemporary, A. F. C. Kollmann, reported a pertinent incident that displayed the great man's modesty and tact. At one time, Bach was visited by a composer and organist named C. F. Hurlebusch—then quite famous, now long since forgotten. Bach prevailed upon him to play one of his published minuets. The visitor then presented Bach's young sons with copies of some of his other clavier works, encouraging them to study these pieces. Of course, as their father's pupils, they were technically already far beyond Hurlebusch. No hint of this fact was given to the visitor, who was greatly impressed with Bach's politeness and the friendly reception he had received. The irony, of course, is that this third-rate musician's work *had* been published, because his simplistic, melodious style was widely popular, while, with a few exceptions, the only way Bach could see one of his complex fugal works in print at the time was to finance the printing himself (see *Music Publisher*).

During his Leipzig stay—embattled years as they appear to us in retrospect—Bach was not without friends in the upper strata of society and academia. In 1730, he found a genuine admirer in Johann Matthias Gesner (1691–1761), who is recognized to this day as one of the pioneers of classical philology. As rector of the Thomasschule, Gesner exerted genuine efforts to make his friend's life a little easier. He saw to it that, in 1731–1732, the cantor's quarters in the Thomasschule were renovated to make them larger and more hygienic, a

Johann Matthias Gesner, rector of Leipzig's Thomasschule from 1731 to 1734—a classical scholar, and one of the few contemporaries who recognized Bach's greatness as a composer.

project that had startling results. Of the eight children born to the Bachs in the old quarters, six had died by 1732. In contrast, four of the six born after the renovation was completed survived to adulthood.

Equally important for Bach during these embattled years was Gesner's genuine admiration for the master's fabled abilities as a conductor. Gesner expressed this in a later panegyric: "Could you but see Bach presiding over thirty or forty musicians, controlling this one with a nod, another by a stamp of the foot.... Rhythm is in his every limb.... Great admirer that I am of antiquity, I yet deem this Bach of mine to comprise in himself many Orpheuses and twenty Orions."

Bach always provided a helping hand to his pupils. More than forty preserved commentaries attest to Bach's readiness to ease their way. No wonder they sensed in their preceptor—in spite of the strictness of his teachings—a warm core of goodness. Clearly, Bach's attitude toward friendship was fundamentally different from the stated cynicism of Beethoven, who once declared: "I considered certain friends mere instruments on which, when it pleases me, I play. I value them in accordance with their usefulness to me."

Fugal Wizardry

Music lovers are apt to open their hearts readily to a Schubert song or a Verdi aria. Their reaction to Bach tends to be less spontaneous. "Yes, we like him," they might say, "but isn't his music rather technical?" True, Bach created some highly complex musical structures. As a rule, however, his works speak to us with spontaneous simplicity and logic.

The basis of Bach's language is the fugue, whose structure has been endlessly explored. Of course, Bach did not invent the fugue. Long before his time it was music's accepted language. Its supremacy as the mode of musical expression had been rarely questioned since the beginning of the sixteenth century.

In both its most elemental and complex form, the fugue is a conversation between voices. Among them harmonic agreement prevails, though dispute is in no way discouraged. The fugue starts with the intonation of a basic theme. Once this is stated, another joins it at a prescribed interval. While the first voice is going on its merry way, the second voice makes its statement. There is a family resemblance between these two voices. Each states the thesis but states it with variants—extending it, shortening it, or surprising the listener with its rhythmic forays. In its elemental form, the fugue works with two interlinking voices. But the number of voices can rise to four—occasionally even to as many as five or six (see *Frederick the Great*).

In all fugues, one principle prevails: However self-contained the fugal voices and whatever rhythmic variants they pursue, they must relate harmonically to each other. (In pursuing relentlessly these variations, Bach at times creates what seems to us a dissonance, but he usually manages to resolve it quickly.) The voices of the fugue are independent but at the same time interdependent. Bach reminded his students that a fugue resembled a conversation, where one participant after another has his say.

We might think of a fugue more appropriately as a discussion group, in which each disputant in turn defends his thesis—civilly—and then sits down. Each one has a right to be heard, hence Mozart's wise hint: "If a fugue is not played slowly, one cannot hear the entrance of the subject distinctly and clearly, and consequently it is of no effect."

Still, Bach's voices rarely do "sit down"; they move forward in perpetual, yet harmonious dispute. At times, they pursue each other with unflagging abandon or even flee from one another. Yet however far the individual voices may stray, at the end they will always return to the point of departure, the cyclic form of the fugue reasserting itself. Bach always guides us back to the theme's simplicities. This is the basis of his fugal wizardry.

No one has ever matched Bach in his supreme command of this *ars perfecta*. Alfred Einstein, the eminent German-American musicologist, has suggested that in Bach's fugues streams of music which had been at work throughout the Middle Ages "celebrated their greatest victory" and showed themselves "at their most glorious." Bach absorbed, transformed, and ultimately transcended everything written in this form before his time. He became the fugal master incarnate.

Bach's fugues encompass the whole gamut of existence: "birth and death and everything in between," in the words of Albert Schweitzer. His was an inexhaustible power to build thematic elements into structures of breathtaking logic and beauty. Even while he remained bound to strict rules, Bach managed to convey in his fugues the deepest emotional messages.

It is the fugal pattern that distinguishes Bach's and most of the Baroque era's music from that of the Classical or the Romantic school. A Beethoven quartet can catapult us into emotional realms far beyond their starting point. In contrast, a Bach fugue ends, as a rule, where it began. This gives Bach's imaginings in sound—whatever mystic heights they may attain—a sense of consoling completeness. Bach always takes us safely home.

Gebrauchsmusik
Music on Demand

It has been estimated that it would take one of today's proficient music copyists—writing continuously—some forty years to replicate the hundreds of works and thousands of manuscript pages which represent the totality of the *oeuvre* Bach created in his lifetime. Compared with this cornucopia, the output of a more modern composer whom we consider highly productive—Mahler, Richard Strauss, or Prokoviev, for example—appears to be rather modest. What was it that drove Bach to produce such a massive body of work, including close to thirty cantatas and other immortal pieces of music in just the three years that marked the start of his Leipzig tenure (1723–1726)?

To put it simply, Bach was motivated—if not forced—to engage in this overproduction by the perpetual demand upon him to create *Gebrauchsmusik*. It was Paul Hindemith who labeled music that serves a practical, everyday purpose as *Gebrauchsmusik*—"music on demand," pieces written for a patron to enhance an outing, a wedding, a banquet. During the eighteenth century, Bach, Handel, Vivaldi, Telemann, Haydn, and Mozart all produced music to meet this sort of demand, usually under the pressure of very tight deadlines.

There simply was no time for a composer to wait for the muse to arrive. Assignments for the evening entertainments at a princely court, for example, had to be delivered with promptitude. Composers such as Bach and his contemporaries turned out the music for these soirées as routinely as the kitchen chef turned out food for the aristocratic table—and just as fast.

The need to produce *Gebrauchsmusik* on a tight schedule also applied to Bach's church work, especially in Leipzig. As the new cantor, he had taken on the burden of composing, rehearsing, and performing a new cantata every Sunday, filling a time slot of about twenty to thirty minutes during the weekly service. Bach probably set to work on Monday morning to have this *Hauptmusik* (as Bach called his cantatas—see entry) ready for rehearsal by Thursday. One can imagine him going through agonies in his race to meet the weekly deadlines, beset as he was by so many other duties, including such

Leipzig University students performing during a torchlight serenade. As the town's music director, Bach was required to compose such *Gebrauchsmusik*—"music on demand"—for festivities honoring visiting dignitaries.

unpleasant ones as training recalcitrant young choristers (see *Delegator*).

It is a miracle that the churchly *Gebrauchsmusik* he created in this high-pressure atmosphere was so often a composition remarkable for its serene beauty. Working as any craftsman might to produce the "goods" demanded by his "customers," Bach, in his genius, responded with creations that transcended their original function and limited audience. Detached from their parochial purposes, Bach's weekly "assignments" still speak to us, expressing things universal and nobly human.

In a similar vein, Bach's official position as music teacher at the Thomasschule (and privately as the teacher of his children) required the production of pedagogical works—pieces that taught the fundamentals of composition and furthered the competence of the technically advanced. The works in this category, essentially pedagogic *Gebrauchsmusik*, have gone on to have a life of their own, to become examples of Bach's high art that, here again, far surpass their original practical intent (the *Gebrauch*).

The epitome of Bach's masterworks in this category of pedagogical *Gebrauchsmusik* is unquestionably the *Well-Tempered Clavier*, which explores the harmonious and expressive use of all the tonalities accessible to this instrument. Packed with Bach's practical and educational hints, the *Well-Tempered Clavier* became in time the basic manual for piano training, what Schumann was to call "the young pianist's daily bread." Yet the work, far beyond its pedagogic intent, is replete with passages of profound depth and pathos.

Gesamt-Ausgabe
Bach's Complete Works

The fruits of Bach's lifelong striving have come down to us in his original manuscripts and the innumerable copies of his work created by his students. This enormous corpus is a grand monument to duty that would have done credit to a whole generation of composers. Even when one considers all the fine accomplishments of their contemporaries, it is Bach and Handel who have rightfully given the Baroque age its name (see *Baroque*).

The totality of Bach's creative output was made accessible by the first *Bach Gesamt-Ausgabe*, the complete edition of Bach's works. It was started after the formation of the *Bach-Gesellschaft* (Bach Society) in 1850, the centennial year of Bach's death, and completed in 1900. Altogether, forty-six volumes were issued, fulfilling the original promise of producing a complete edition of all the Bach works which were then known.

The *Bach Gesamt-Ausgabe* started with a modest sponsorship—some 240 subscribers, among them 23 members of royalty. With all its inadvertent editorial deficiencies, this first edition of the *Gesamt-Ausgabe* was to prove a major influence on the course of music. Nearly all of the nineteenth century's great composers fell under its spell. Brahms paid this venture a rare compliment when he ranked it with Bismarck's unification of the German Reich in 1871 as one of the pivotal events of the nineteenth century. The Bach venture was to prove decidedly more peaceable and enriching.

Each volume of the series seemed to fascinate Brahms, apparently more so than did the volumes of the complete edition of Handel's work that appeared at about the same time. As he made his way through the volumes, Brahms commented, "With old Bach there are always surprises and I always learn something new." In contrast, when a new volume of the Handel edition arrived, he is said to have put it on the shelf with the remark: "It ought to be very interesting. I will go through it as soon as I have time."

Richard Wagner had strong links to Bach. Wagner was born in 1813 in Leipzig and was baptized in the Thomaskirche, where Bach had for nearly three decades served as cantor (see *Leipzig Ordeal*). Wagner was first taught harmony and counterpoint at the Thomasschule by Christian Theodor Weinlig, its then current cantor—a student of Bach and one of Germany's most learned contrapuntalists.

Of course, Wagner rarely admired any composer except Richard Wagner. But in 1865, with the *Gesamt-Ausgabe* coming off the press, he became rhapsodic about "the musical miracle man that was Sebastian Bach." Wagner thought it was "impossible to characterize the riches" of Bach's music, the "loftiness and all-comprehending significance." And *The Meistersingers of Nuremberg* became a resounding tribute to Bachian counterpoint and the craftsmanship of the Baroque Age. That Wagner became a student of the *Gesamt-Ausgabe* is indicated in the diaries of his wife, Cosima Wagner, in which she tells of the stir each new volume created in their circle of friends. Cosima also recorded the fact that when discussions among Wagner's Bayreuth circle became too heated, the master would ask one of his associates to play a piece from the *Well-Tempered Clavier* "to clear the air."

In the late 1890s, Gustav Mahler also plunged into the volumes of the *Gesamt-Ausgabe* as they became available. As his wife reported: "He went into ecstasy over the miraculous freedom of Bach—to which probably no other musician has ever attained...." Thus aroused, Mahler pronounced: "In Bach, the vital cells of music are united as the world is in God."

To this day, the original *Bach Gesamt-Ausgabe*, reprinted and available at a reasonable price, has remained a useful research tool. Still, so much has happened in musicology since it first appeared that a critical updating was urgently called for. A *Neue Bach Ausgabe* (NBA) was started in 1950 under the imprint of *Bärenreiter Verlag* in Kassel, Germany. Still in the process of completion, it has grown to almost double the size of the original, and eventually will offer over one hundred volumes of Bach's works and supplementary commentaries. This project is said to be still five or six years from completion. It would seem that the more we learn about Bach, the more there is to learn.

Goethe and Bach

The beginning of the Romantic period in the early nineteenth century witnessed a renewed interest in the works of Bach, an interest that received powerful support from a figure who had little connection with music. Johann Wolfgang von Goethe (1749–1832), renowned as the author of *Faust*, was clearly the "universal man" of his age—dramatist, novelist, poet, and scholar. Yet he had no claim to musical gifts and never had learned to play an instrument. Nevertheless, as a man of classical culture, he considered it his duty to learn as much as possible about the musical art, and in the process he became an inveterate Bach-lover.

Goethe esteemed Mozart and bemoaned his early death, but to Beethoven he had a decided aversion. While agreeing with him that "the world is more pain than pleasure," Goethe found that Beethoven's music was "mad enough to drive one crazy." The best Goethe could say about Beethoven was that he "admired him with horror."

Goethe never showed any particular aptitude in selecting composers for the musical rendering of his poems. Schubert once sent him a sampling he had attempted. It was returned to Vienna without a

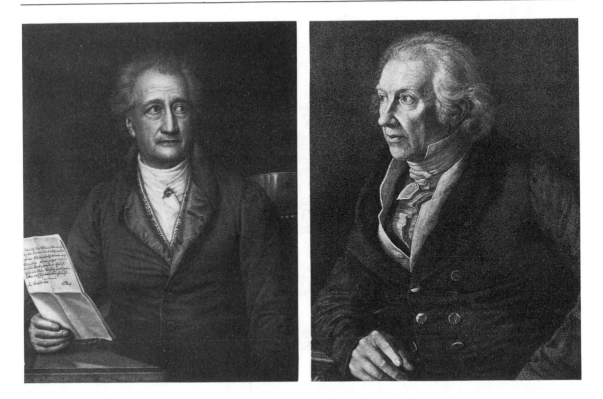

comment. Ironically, Schubert's gripping rendering of Goethe's poem, *Erlkönig*, was later to become one of the classics of German *lieder*.

Goethe's interest in Bach was awakened by his friendship with the Berlin composer Carl Friedrich Zelter. Having scorned Schubert, Goethe was rather partial to the *lieder* that Zelter had based upon his poems—though as a composer Zelter was in no way on a par with the masters of the Vienna school. Still, he had considerable merit as an organizer of Berlin's musical life and as director of the Berlin Singakademie, which he made the center of a Bach revival cult. Zelter was also the proud possessor of a manuscript of the *St. Matthew Passion*, not an original but a copy made in Bach's time that he had salvaged at an auction, where it was considered little more than "wastepaper."

Zelter conveyed his enthusiasm for Bach not only to his poet friend, but also to young Felix Mendelssohn, who was his star student. In time, Mendelssohn would gain fame as the period's outstanding performer of Bach's music on the organ and piano.

Mendelssohn and his guardian were often guests in Goethe's home, which by then was at its height as a gathering place for Europe's intellectuals. Piano works by Bach were prominent in Mendelssohn's

Johann Wolfgang Goethe *(left)*, the classic German poet, dramatist, and scholar. His interest in Bach arose through his friendship with the composer Carl Friedrich Zelter and the performances of Zelter's pupil, the young Felix Mendelssohn. *Courtesy of Stiftung Weimarer Klassik*

Carl Friedrich Zelter *(right)*, director of Berlin's Singakademie, which cultivated the music of Bach and provided, in 1829, the chorus for the revival performance of the *St. Matthew Passion*. *Courtesy of Deutsche Staatsbibliotek, Bildarchiv Preussischer Kulturbesitz*

Goethe watches as young Felix Mendelssohn performs during a visit to the poet's residence in Weimar—a gathering place for the cultural elite of Germany. Bach's music was always a part of the prodigy's program.

daily recitals, which Goethe encouraged and enjoyed with obvious relish. Aside from playing preludes and fugues from the *Well-Tempered Clavier*, Mendelssohn at times took a theme by Bach and developed it into one of his own fugues, keeping the old poet entranced for hours.

Very late in life, Goethe was prompted to make to Zelter an extremely profound observation about Bach, noting that it was "when my mind was in a state of perfect composure and free from external distractions, that I obtained the true impress of your grand master. I said to myself: it was as if the eternal harmony was conversing within itself, as it may have done in the bosom of God, just before the creation of the world."

Goldberg Variations

In the late 1730s, as Bach approached fifty, Leipzig officials expressed their dissatisfaction with his services, dubbing him "the incorrigible cantor" (see *Leipzig Ordeal*). But Bach was prudent enough not to permit the opinions, or the wishes, of his bureaucratic superiors to stifle his own creative impulses. His astute—perhaps somewhat cunning—withdrawal from officially assigned duties enabled him at this time to begin doing "his own thing": to pursue primarily those projects which met the needs of his art, rather than those enumerated by the tin-eared burghers of Leipzig (see *Delegator*).

Bach's efforts in this self-determined direction were crowned by a work of stupendous power, recognized today as the unquestioned high point of eighteenth-century clavier music. Such a peak of keyboard creativity would not be attained again until Beethoven's *Hammerklavier Sonata* (1818). The masterwork, undertaken in the last decade of his life, was of course the celebrated *Goldberg Variations*, whose publication is generally dated as 1742. The *New Yorker* critic Andrew Porter once observed that Bach "never again covered so wide a range of feeling in any other instrumental work he wrote," creating fugues "as naturally as a poet writes in verse."

The original manuscript actually bore a lengthy and rather unassuming title: *Clavier Übung bestehend in einer Aria mit verschiedenen Veraenderungen vors Clavicimbul mit 2 Manualen—Keyboard Exercises Consisting of an Aria with Sundry Variations for Harpsichords with 2 Manuals* (Keyboards). Music historians consider the work to be Bach's *Clavier-Übung IV*, last in the series of "keyboard-exercise" collections he assembled.

A majestic work like this could not long endure with such a utilitarian title. Oddly enough, however, the name under which it has become known to posterity—the *Goldberg Variations*—immortalizes not the music-loving patron for whom Bach was said to have created it, Count Hermann Carl von Keyserlingk, but rather the count's personal musician, the legendary keyboard artist and prodigy Johann Theophilus Goldberg (1727–1756).

A very wealthy and cultivated man, Keyserlingk was formerly the Russian ambassador, appointed by Catherine the Great, to the Dresden court of the elector of Saxony. The count had the rare privilege and adequate means to maintain as his own private harpsichordist the young Goldberg, who, though only fifteen when the *Variations* were written, had already become widely acclaimed as a virtuoso with brilliant keyboard technique. Goldberg was considered a romantic and eccentric figure by his contemporaries. One example was perhaps his use of the Greek-based middle name Theophilus in place of its prosaic German equivalent, his given name of Gottlieb. But then, another brilliant prodigy, Wolfgang Gottlieb Mozart, was to become famous with the use of the Latin-based Amadeus in place of that same prosaic German middle name. The romantic aura of both prodigies was surely enhanced by the fact that they both died while still young men.

According to the story recorded by Bach's first biographer, Forkel, and endlessly repeated since, Count Keyserlingk was frequently ill, suffering at such times from insomnia that forced him to spend the nights awake and in pain. He therefore requested that Bach (whom he knew well and admired greatly) write some music that Goldberg might play for him, to "cheer him up" during the many long nights in which he suffered so painfully—an early form of "music therapy."

However, the assumption that the *Goldberg Variations* were actually ordered by Count Keyserlingk does not seem to be borne out by the bland title Bach gave the work (*Clavier-Übung—Keyboard Exercises*) or the fact that the manuscript contains no reference at all to the count himself. In all probability, Bach wrote the thirty variations, a pianistic extravaganza, with young Theophilus Goldberg in mind—as a showpiece for this enormously gifted virtuoso. Goldberg had been a pupil in Dresden of Bach's oldest son, Wilhelm Friedemann. During the 1740–1742 period, the prodigy occasionally visited Leipzig for "graduate work" with Cantor Bach himself.

In any event, Bach surely sent the count a copy of the work once it had been engraved, and Keyserlingk quite obviously loved it. Reportedly, when attacked by painful insomnia, he would awaken Goldberg (who slept in an adjoining bedchamber) with the request "Dear Goldberg, do play me my variations."

That Count Keyserlingk thought of the *Variations* as his very own is also borne out by the fact that he apparently paid Bach quite well for them, though perhaps not as munificently as reported. Forkel stated that after receiving the manuscript, the Count sent Bach "a golden goblet filled with one hundred *Louis d'ors.*" This "goblet" is, undoubtedly, the "agate box mounted in gold" that is listed in the inventory of Bach's estate (see *Postmortem*). Indeed, this box was appraised as the most valuable art object in Bach's entire estate, valued at fifty thalers (perhaps $5,000 in current monetary terms). The cache of *Louis d'ors*—French gold coins the equivalent of approximately twenty thalers apiece—would thus represent an additional reward of perhaps $200,000 in today's money, almost three times the annual salary Bach was then receiving from the town of Leipzig, a most unlikely windfall.

The wondrous *Goldberg Variations* emerge from a deceptively simple and disarming theme. Bach based the mighty structure on a sarabande (a popular French dance) that, almost two decades earlier, had been included in the second *Noten Büchlein für Anna Magdalena* (a "little note book" of keyboard exercises that he had assembled for his second wife—see *Helpmate*). The quiet, gentle effect and slow pace of this sarabande theme in no way prepares us for the fugal fireworks to come in the ensuing variations. The sensitive listener must be enthralled by the theme's pensive pace—a love song of incomparable beauty and tenderness expressive of the affection that Bach felt for his young, musically gifted bride. The variations that follow depart drastically in mood from the loving gentleness of this theme, conjuring up feelings that cover the entire scale of human emotions, from unbounded exuberance to contemplation of the essential tragedy of life.

Some of the variations stray far away—and boldly so—from the theme initially intoned. But the work's unity is astutely assured by Bach through the work's basso line, always strongly stressed. Like a red thread, it leaves no doubt about the work's eminently sound and logical structure. Every third variation is a canon—a compositional form requiring enormous discipline and mathematical precision, in which the same melody is presented in different polyphonic lines, starting at different times. Hence, Bach wrote these "exercises" for a harpsichord with two keyboards, permitting two parts to be easily played at the same time. Only recently, Christoph Wolff, the famed Harvard Bach specialist, discovered—in Strasbourg, France—fourteen more canons by Bach based on the *Goldberg* theme.

For the performer, the *Goldberg Variations* pose enormous problems. In their complexity, they are accessible only to keyboard artists of the virtuoso class, beginning with the brilliant youngster Theophilus Goldberg himself. Considering the extravagant, though brutally short, career of this acknowledgedly fabulous performer, it is tempting to see some parallels between Goldberg and the virtuoso who in our time has brought back to us these *Variations* in all their glory.

Glenn Gould was virtually unknown when in 1955, aged twenty-three, he made his first recording of the *Goldberg Variations* at Columbia Records' famous Thirtieth Street Studio in New York. His extràpianistic modes of expression—singing, groaning, sighing—did not detract from his astounding interpretation of the work, which made the *Goldberg Variations* a best-selling album in 1956. A new recording of the work was made in 1981, shortly before Gould's untimely death at the age of fifty on October 4, 1982.

A Great Good Man

Many contemporary sources bear witness to the deeply human qualities of Bach—his kindness to friends and neighbors, for example. Yet those who knew him best have commented frankly on his contrasting behaviors when working with other musicians and with his pupils. Bach displayed infinite patience with students he felt would develop into fine musicians. But his patience vanished rapidly when confronted with professional incompetence. Once during a tense rehearsal in the Thomaskirche, Bach reportedly grabbed his wig in a rage and threw it at his old nemesis, the organist Johann Gottlieb Görner, shouting angrily, "You should have become a shoemaker."

But such outbursts of temper seem to have blown over quickly. Bach in his life practiced what he preached in his cantatas: affectionate interest in the well-being of one's fellowman. His basic goodness and willingness to help is particularly evident in his fond relationship with his young kinsman Johann Elias Bach, who lived with the cantor's family in their crowded Leipzig home (1737–1741). Although he was already thirty-three years old, Elias had enrolled as a student at Leipzig University. But he was also a skillful writer who acted as Cantor Bach's secretary, as well as a teacher for his younger children.

A telling anecdote has come down to us that reveals Bach's concern for his young cousin. Once when Elias was preparing to leave for a journey, Bach went to his wardrobe and insisted on loaning the young man his huge fur-lined boots and raincoat. Bach had found these items to be indispensable accessories during the many trips he himself had undertaken with seeming relish (see *Wanderlust*).

Elias never forgot the many kindnesses shown to him by the Herr Cantor during his Leipzig years, mentioning them again and again in his own writings. When he later became an organist in the town of Schweinfurt—a fine position that his famous cousin had helped him to secure—Elias, in gratitude, sent a cask of fine wine to Bach's home in Leipzig (see *Quaffing*).

Though Bach was to have his detractors in the world of music theory and was treated rather coolly by his own sons, he engendered great admiration, even adoration, on the part of colleagues, students, and friends. Georg Sorge, a well-known music theoretician of the time (though as a composer infinitely inferior to Bach), dedicated some clavier pieces to the master. In a prefatory note, Sorge noted that

Bach possessed a rare combination of personal qualities—he was an artist of unfathomable gifts and an individual of touching humanity. "The great musical virtues that your excellency possesses," Sorge observed, "are embellished by the excellent virtue of affability." (Sorge used the word *Leutseligkeit*—the urge to reach out with warmth to one's fellowmen, even the humble.) Sorge was particularly impressed by Bach's modesty, which he held to be an uncommon trait among artists, who, he suggested, were normally "full of conceit and self-love."

The fabled accomplishments of Bach as a composer are perhaps not the only cause of the warm affection in which he has been held by his admirers. History seems to judge the greatness of a composer by human as well as musical criteria. The qualities of the heart are as pronounced in Bach's music as those of the head, and it is their interplay that accounts for the never-ending wonder that fuels the Bachian phenomenon.

Handel

Johann Sebastian Bach and Georg Frideric Handel had some vital statistics in common. Both were born in 1685 (as was Domenico Scarlatti), within weeks of each other, in towns less than sixty miles apart. At the end of their lives, both men lost their eyesight and died after being treated by the same doctor (see *Blindness*). Both were enormously prolific composers, Handel's opus almost matching Bach's massive creative output. And both are now regarded as the great exemplars of the Baroque era.

Strangely enough, Bach and Handel never met in person, though it was no fault of Bach's that what promised to become a historic meeting never came to pass. In 1719, Handel, by then well established in England, paid a visit to his native town of Halle, some twenty miles from Cöthen, where Bach was capellmeister at the court of Prince Leopold. Bach apparently had received news of Handel's coming. Most anxious to meet his distinguished colleague, Bach traveled to Halle but failed to see his great contemporary. Deliberately or not, Handel had left town the morning Bach arrived.

Bach, stubborn in this as he was in almost all matters, didn't give up. Ten years later, when Handel again visited his hometown, Bach made another effort to arrange a meeting. Somewhat indisposed and unable to travel, Bach sent his oldest son, Wilhelm Friedemann, to invite Handel to come to Leipzig. Friedemann seems actually to have had an audience with the Baroque superstar, who haughtily refused to accept Bach's hospitality and make the reasonably short trip to Leipzig.

Perhaps Handel's reluctance stemmed from a sense that the two men really had little in common. Bach was a musician content with

Georg Frideric Handel was born the same year as Bach (1685), in Halle, a town less than fifty miles away from Bach's birthplace. As prolific as his Baroque contemporary, Handel led a far different life as a prosperous celebrity.

his small universe of the choir loft, the Collegium Musicum, and the concert room of small princely residences. In contrast, Handel was a citizen of the world who enjoyed life to the fullest, a man whose fame and influence were tremendous even in his lifetime. Handel was a world figure whose widely acclaimed career embraced Germany, Italy, France, and England. While his career had its ups and downs, Handel died a comparatively rich man, leaving an estate of £18,000 (today, perhaps half a million dollars or more)—a considerable fortune. Although Bach's income was quite respectable during his Leipzig years (see *Money Matters*), at his death his estate amounted to less than 1,000 thalers (about $100,000 in our day).

The audiences for which these two composers wrote could hardly have been more different. Handel's oratorios were created for a cosmopolitan audience in one of the world's great cities—the secular and pleasure-loving London public whose tastes had been formed by Italian opera. Bach wrote mainly for a provincial and devout congregation fixed upon salvation. Handel surely felt he had little to learn from the composer and performer whose patrons had consisted of minor aristocrats and small-town churches. Bach, on the other hand, had an insatiable desire to learn from all of his contemporaries. In fact, he was well acquainted with the work of his glamorous London-based colleague, having copied various works of Handel (see *Helpmate*).

Handel was, however, decidedly inferior to Bach when it came to the fugal development of his themes, which were beguiling when first intoned, but rarely developed to their full potential. Bach, with his superior force of creative intellect, was able to construct the most intricate and complex musical edifices upon what were sometimes unprepossessing opening themes. But his artistic elaborations of even rather simple themes—in his organ works especially—reached monumental proportions and the heights of spiritual grandeur. The difference between Bach's style of composing and that of Handel was perhaps best characterized by the observation that "whereas Handel plotted, Bach leaped."

In their death, also, the two composers had their significant differences. In 1759, Handel, blind and ill, conducted his greatest and best-remembered oratorio, *Messiah*, at Covent Garden. He died eight days later and was accorded a magnificent funeral—befitting royalty—at Westminster Abbey, where he was interred in the Poet's Corner. In 1750, also blind and ill, Bach spent his last days trying to complete his final masterwork, the *Art of the Fugue*. Upon his death, he was accorded the simple funeral of a small-town cantor and was buried near Leipzig's Johanneskirche—the exact place of his interment forgotten for nearly 150 years (see *Skull*).

Hauptmusik

Bach's cantatas—the close to two hundred church works thus designated that have survived—are, in number, richness, and depth, an essential part of his unfathomable *oeuvre*. Yet strange to say, Bach himself rarely used the word *cantata* to describe the vocal and orchestral works that he wrote for Leipzig's Sunday services. Instead, one generally finds the word *Hauptmusik* (principal music) hastily scribbled on the covers of his cantata scores. This is significant because the name that Bach gave these works reveals his intent in writing them. It was his desire to make instrumental music—which is

A cantata performance in Bach's era—notable for the presence of a variety of instruments, dominated by the mighty organ. Bach was a pioneer in providing significant instrumental support for the soloists and choir in cantata performances.

the innovative aspect of Bach's cantatas—a primary form of musical worship in Leipzig's churches (see *Instruments to the Fore*).

Giving instrumental support to the church's soloists and choir was still, in Bach's time, a fairly novel concept. Indeed, the designation "cantata" itself connoted a piece to be sung (*cantare*—"to sing"). Cantatas had been written in profusion before his time: his predecessor in Leipzig, Johann Kuhnau, had written hundreds, while Telemann purportedly produced more than a thousand of them. But even though instrumental accompaniment was often provided, these cantatas were—true to their name—essentially "singing pieces." They had been taken up with avidity by the Protestant church for its Sunday services because they elevated biblical text and ritual into a more inspiring musical offering.

Bach first applied himself to the cantata form when he was barely twenty-two years old, as organist in Mühlhausen (1707–1708). His early cantatas—when compared to the works of his predecessors— represent both a musical and a cultural landmark. His decision to make much greater use of instruments, so that they became a full partner with the human voice, was clearly influenced by the rising impact of Italian and French opera (see *Operatic Echoes*). In the operas of his time, the vocal and instrumental forms were integrated to re-create and to arouse the whole scale of human emotions. Bach's genius introduced this new musical genre into the weekly church service to provide, in fact, the *Hauptmusik*, the "principal music" of the service—vocal music and instrumental music combined to fulfill the believer's yearning for spiritual uplift.

Both the cultural climate and the state of religion were in a transition period just at the time Bach appeared on the scene. With the increasing impact of the prosperous bourgeoisie, the age of unquestioned faith was giving way to a more secularized lifestyle, as

"For the Glory of God," the invocation with which Bach ended many of his sacred works.

SOLI DEO GLORIA.

reflected in the decline in church attendance (see *Zeitgeist*). In this context, Bach's form of the cantata, or *Hauptmusik*, was an agent of both reform and revitalization.

Today, the overwrought texts of Bach's cantatas have become largely irrelevant to those who listen to these works—but not so the music itself. Bach's genius has bequeathed to our secular age universal music that is raised above the confines of dogma, music that can (in the words of the English music historian Wilfrid Mellers) "assuage and palliate some unassailable loneliness that lies within each human soul."

Heirs

When Bach died at age sixty-five on July 28, 1750, he had made no provisions to dispose of his belongings in an orderly way. This left Anna Magdalena, his wife of twenty-eight years, and his surviving daughters in a state of dire poverty. (See *Daughters.*) Strange indeed is the fact that a man who was so sensitive to the pitfalls of life should have shown this lack of foresight.

As soon as Bach closed his eyes, the Town Council sent its appraisers to his home in the Thomasschule to compile a highly informative but also saddening document: *Specification of the Estate Left by the Late Mr. Johann Sebastian Bach.* These officials did not find it worthwhile to list the voluminous collection of scores and papers that had been left behind by the deceased cantor. The cornucopia of Bach's musical works seemed to the appraisers hardly worth the paper it would take to list it. But this heritage—while unlisted in the estate *Specification*—passed on to (or was appropriated by) his two eldest sons, Wilhelm Friedemann and Carl Philipp Emanuel. In the end, they fared far better than Anna Magdalena, their stepmother.

The manuscripts that ended up in Carl Philipp Emanuel's column not only proved of profit to the recipient but also gave to posterity a priceless heritage that might otherwise have been lost. Carl Philipp Emanuel deserves much credit for preserving his father's treasure of manuscripts in impeccable order.

However, in keeping his father's cantatas in such good shape, Carl Philipp Emanuel obviously had a commercial prospect in mind. After he had taken possession of the manuscripts, he made some extra thalers by renting some of them out for performances or study

Carl Philipp Emanuel
Bach with friends in the
picture gallery of his
home in Hamburg, where
he was the capellmeister
and cantor from 1767 to
his death in 1788. Bach's
second son preserved
many of his father's
works, using them for
inspiration but rarely
performing them.
Courtesy of Elke Walford

purposes. He was known to be a sharp trader, rather pitiless in collecting fees. After his death in 1788, his widow continued the remunerative manuscript rental service he had started.

If Carl Philipp Emanuel treated his father's treasures with reverence, his brother, Wilhelm Friedemann, exploited them in a flagrantly irresponsible way. He was perhaps forced by circumstances to do so, for he had perpetual career problems. Bach's oldest son was exceedingly gifted—in the genius class himself. But after embarking upon a promising career as an organist, Friedemann ended up leading a dissolute, wandering life. Never able to hold a solid, responsible position in his later career, he often sustained himself by selling the manuscripts he had received from his father's estate, which numbered among them many of the master's priceless orchestral works.

Friedemann once offered Nikolaus Forkel—later renowned as Bach's first biographer—a cantata manuscript for twenty gold coins. More notorious is the report that Friedemann, while temporarily employed in the city of Braunschweig and harassed by his landlord for rent money, gave him in payment the invaluable manuscript of the *Well-Tempered Clavier*.

After all that he had done for them, Bach's most prominent sons seemed to have had little respect or affection for their father's memory. For example, nearly two decades after his father's death, the punctilious Carl Philipp Emanuel would achieve fame as a capellmeister in Hamburg—undertaking many functions similar to those his father had performed in Leipzig. But there is no record that he ever performed any of his father's works while in this post, though he was reported to have once performed parts of the *St. Matthew Passion* in a bowdlerized version, without giving any credit to its creator.

Bach's youngest son, Johann Christian, was born in 1735, when Bach was fifty years old. He must have been quite naturally the apple of his father's eye. Otherwise, how can it be explained that Christian received—even before Bach's death and before any acts of largesse to his other sons—a gift of "five harpsichords and one spinet." This was an endowment of considerable worth. Bach had been an ardent collector of instruments, which represented about one-third of his estate.

Did the five harpsichords that Bach gave to Johann Christian prove a meaningful gift to his youngest son? Perhaps in the beginning of Christian's career they did. But after moving to Italy in 1754, he completely abandoned the Bach musical and religious tradition, converting to Catholicism during his career as organist of the Duomo, Milan's historic Gothic cathedral. Christian achieved fame after he settled in London, where he was a favorite of Queen Charlotte at the Hanoverian court. In London, he married a prima donna and became a habitué of the town's aristocratic circles. Sir Joshua Reynolds painted two portraits of him.

Yet his death, like that of his father, was a tragic one. When he was only in his mid-forties, his health declined and he had to leave London, saddled, as it turned out, by a crushing debt of four thousand pounds. He died in 1782, prompting this touching obituary by a Mrs. Papendick: "This man of ability in his profession, of liberal kindness and worthy character, was forgotten almost before he was called to the doom that is the fate of all of us, to be buried forever in oblivion." This dour prediction was not to be totally fulfilled.

Some of Johann Christian's works, particularly his clavier concertos, are still performed to this day. So perhaps that gift of Bach's most valuable harpsichords to his youngest son was to find justification after all.

Helpmate

In the summer of 1720, when the thirty-five-year-old Bach returned to Cöthen from a trip to the spa of Carlsbad with his noble patron, Prince Leopold, he received a crushing piece of news. During Bach's absence, his first wife, Maria Barbara (aged thirty-six), had died and been buried. They had been married near the end of Bach's Mühlhausen stay (October 17, 1707), both of them members of the Bach clan, both orphans, and both in their early twenties. Their marriage of nearly thirteen years had been a particularly happy one.

But Bach's tragic experience seems to have fulfilled the folk saying "God closes one door and mercifully opens another." Little more than a year later Bach married Anna Magdalena Wülcken, sixteen years his junior. From the start, this second union was blessed with happiness—and an impressive number of children, thirteen in all. The prospects for success seem to have been bright from the start of Bach's second marital venture. Anna Magdalena was herself a gifted professional singer, descended from musicians on both her paternal and maternal sides; her father was a distinguished trumpeter at the neighboring court of Weissenfels. Apparently, Bach had met her during one of her guest appearances at Cöthen.

Upon her marriage to Bach in 1721, Anna Magdalena became the stepmother of the four surviving children from his first marriage: Catharina Dorothea (who at thirteen was only seven years younger than the bride) and the three boys—Wilhelm Friedemann, eleven; Carl Philipp Emanuel, seven; and Johann Gottfried Bernhard, six years old.

To the end of his life, Bach referred to his wife endearingly as *"meine Frau liebste"* (my most beloved wife). His second marriage proved to be such a happy one because the partners' deep mutual affection was closely intertwined with their love of music.

No doubt in an attempt to improve the keyboard-playing of his young wife, Bach assembled two charming instruction books: the first one, *Noten Büchlein für Anna Magdalena* (Little Notebook for Anna Magdalena), was dated 1722; the second, more progressive in content, was dated 1725. Some of the sketches that Bach assembled for the instruction of his young wife later became the basis for works that have become piano classics—such as *Clavier-Übung I–III*, the *Goldberg Variations* (see entry), and the *French Suites*.

More revealing, and truly touching, are the notations in the handwriting of both Bach and Anna Magdalena which are to be found in the two manuscript books. While some of Bach's entries convey his own thoughts, many of Anna Magdalena's are quotations from contemporary poets. (The authorship of some of the poems—especially those in the second *Noten Büchlein*—have not been established.)

There can be no doubt that the entries reflect the couple's glowing and growing mutual affection. In the second *Noten Büchlein*, we find a poem reminiscent, in its amatory ardor, of medieval love poetry:

> *If now my heart be thine*
> *as truly thine is mine,*
> *give thou the world no sign, love.*
> *No, not the slightest sign,*
> *for thus the love between us*
> *will ever stronger grow.*
> *Rejoicing in the secret*
> *which we alone will know.*

The intertwining of their love for each other with their love for music is touchingly expressed in one of Bach's own entries:

> *Oh how my heart with joy is filled*
> *To see your beauty blooming,*
> *Till all my soul with music's thrilled*
> *My heart with joy overflowing.*

In addition to their close emotional attachment, Bach and his wife developed, during their marriage of almost thirty years, a professional relationship that is unique in musical history. As a trained musician endowed with a fine handwriting, Anna Magdalena proved the master's invaluable helper. This was especially true during Bach's earlier years in Leipzig, when the task of copying his scores, and those of other composers, kept the household buzzing (see *Delegator*).

One of Bach's solo violin sonatas, "senza Cembalo," a manuscript copied by his second wife, Anna Magdalena, whose neat handwriting resembled that of the master himself. Königliche Bibliothek, Berlin

Anna Magdalena's clear, fine script so resembled that of the master's that it proved at times difficult to tell them apart. It was she who set out to copy sixty pages of Handel's *St. John Passion*. Bach finished the job by copying the remaining twenty-three pages. At one time, this entire manuscript was considered to be in Bach's own hand, but Spitta proved it to be the couple's collaborative effort. Quite a number of other manuscripts show Anna Magdalena's sure graphic touch and the resemblance of her "ductus" to Bach's own.

All through the ensuing years, Anna Magdalena remained the center of the household. Many testimonies—both from Bach's students and from the relatives who spent time in Leipzig's *Kantorei*—comment upon Frau Bach's infinite kindness and manifold household skills.

In view of the happiness and unstinting help this exemplary woman had given to her husband and her family, reports concerning her last ten years as a widow are shocking to note. Since Bach had left no will providing for her (see *Postmortem*), Anna Magdalena had to end her years in Leipzig's poorhouse meagerly sustained by alms. She died at the age of fifty-nine and was buried in an unnamed pauper's grave.

Hometown

The Bach clan of musicians was deeply rooted in Thuringia, to this day one of Germany's most attractive wooded vacationlands. In 1671, Bach's parents settled in Eisenach, a small medieval town

nestled in the shadow of its most important landmark, the Wartburg Castle. Martin Luther had been given refuge in this castle in 1521—thanks to the intercession of Frederick the Wise (elector of Saxony)—after having been banned from the Holy Roman Empire by the Diet of Worms, a tribunal led by the Catholic Emperor Charles V.

Imprisoned there for his own protection, Luther set about translating the New Testament from Latin into German, one of the epochal deeds of the Reformation. I can still remember a visit to the Wartburg with my parents—both Thuringians—when I was very young. I was awed by this romantic place, marveling at the big ink spot on the wall of Luther's cell, purportedly created when the rebellious monk had hurled an inkwell at the devil, who was trying to interfere with his sacred task.

Today, we tend to stress the effects of early impressions on the young, and thus must assume that Johann Sebastian Bach's childhood in a place so drenched with Lutheran images was a decisive influence upon his own lifelong commitment to the Protestant faith. Certainly, music was given prominence in the Lutheran church by its founder, who was himself a composer of hymns. The Protestant church music initiated by Luther would be brought to its ultimate flowering by the man who was born in the shadow of the Wartburg.

While Bach was endowed on his father's side with an impressive musical heritage, his mother came from a different background. She was a member of the Lämmerhirt family of Erfurt, its members mostly furriers by trade. The Lämmerhirts became one of the town's leading families, financially well-off. Twice Bach would be the recipient of

The Wartburg Castle, *(above left)* towering over Bach's hometown of Eisenach. It was here that Martin Luther translated the New Testament from Latin into vernacular German, contributing greatly to the spread of Protestantism among the populace.

A sixteenth-century woodcut *(above right)* depicting the legend of the devil entering Luther's cell at the Wartburg Castle, trying to prevent the translation of the Bible into German.

benefits from the Lämmerhirt estate. The first bequest, in 1708, probably enabled Bach, just turned twenty-three, to get married.

Members of the Bach clan tended to earn their livelihoods as church organists, cantors, and town musicians *(Stadtpfeifer)*. Highly respected and fertile, the Bachs were able to corner the musical employment market in this region. To be "a Bach" almost implicitly suggested that one was a musician. But it must be admitted that no true genius can be detected in this "orphean stream of Bachs," the seventy-nine ancestors of Johann Sebastian whom Karl Geiringer discusses in his book *The Bach Family*.

Bach's father (Johann Ambrosius Bach) was, from all appearances, a solid citizen with fine musical skills, primarily as a fiddler, but he did not have any outstanding creative gifts. His duties as a musician—both for the town and for the neighboring court of Saxe-Weimar—tended strongly to secular needs, civic and ceremonial. It was his duty to play at festive occasions, such as princely visits or the

Bach's father Johann Ambrosius (1645–1695), town musician of Eisenach and violinist at the court of Saxe-Weimar. He died when Johann Sebastian was but ten years old, a year after the death of his wife, leaving Sebastian an orphan. *Courtesy of Deutsche Staatsbibliotek, Bildarchiv Preussischer Kulturbesitz*

induction of a new town government. And he was obligated to sound an alarm bell when fire threatened the town's flammable roofs. Another bell under his command was not popular among the citizens. It would announce that tax time had arrived.

In 1684, Ambrosius petitioned the Duke of Weimar-Eisenach for relief from these duties. He wanted to return to his native Erfurt, where it might be easier to support his family of seven children (an eighth child was soon expected). The fact that this request was denied indicates the fairly low social standing of professional musicians of the time: Their masters seemed to have thought that they "owned" them. When Bach himself later embarked upon his own career at Weimar, he would suffer from this same sort of aristocratic arrogance on the part of *his* patron, Duke Wilhelm Ernst (see *Imprisonment*). And later in the eighteenth century, Mozart was to complain that he had to sit at the servant's table in the palace of the Salzburg archbishop (below the valets but above the cooks).

With Ambrosius forced to remain in Eisenach, his eighth child was born there on March 21, 1685, to be baptized in the town's Georgenkirche as Johann Sebastian Bach. Hardly ten years later, Sebastian would be orphaned by the death of his parents and compelled to leave Eisenach—a shattering tragedy for a young child. On the other hand, the devastating trick that fate played upon him may well have yielded unexpected but unprecedented riches. If young Sebastian had stayed in Eisenach, to be guided by his father, it is very possible that he would have become another Bach town musician, committed mainly to secular duties. In such a scenario, the world might never have known of Johann Sebastian Bach, the master of sacred music.

Imprisonment

Bach's tenure at the court of Weimar (1708–1717, age twenty-three to thirty-two) was a period of astounding productivity, especially in the field of organ music (see *Organist Supreme*). Though his master Duke Wilhelm Ernst, a highly cultured man, became very fond of this instrument, he was also a hard task-master. Bach *was* well-treated financially (Wilhelm Ernst even approved bills for the purchase of the composing paper which his court organist voraciously consumed), but Bach was also burdened with numerous, often arduous duties, including the creation of one cantata per month. In 1714, he assumed, additionally, the post of concertmaster in the duke's orchestra, in which he could demonstrate his prowess as a violinist.

Duke Wilhelm Ernst of Saxe-Weimar. He was a music-lover who greatly appreciated Bach's genius as a composer for the organ. Most of Bach's great works for this instrument were created during his Weimar period (1708–1717).

The following year, much to Bach's chagrin, he was snubbed by the duke when there was an opening for the post of Weimar's *Hofcapellmeister*, a superior position to which Bach felt he was entitled. Always a shaper of his own career, Bach was obviously not willing to chafe under such restrictive conditions. However, his efforts to break loose were stymied; worse still, they exposed him in the end to a month-long incarceration.

It was a petty dynastic squabble that delayed Bach's departure from Weimar: Duke Wilhelm Ernst had always been at odds with his young nephew and heir, Prince Ernst Augustus. To get the prince out of the way, Wilhelm Ernst made various attempts to marry him off, and in 1717 he succeeded in arranging a match. Prince Augustus was to marry a well-dowered widow, Eleonore Wilhelmina, the sister of Prince Leopold of Anhalt-Cöthen.

Concertmaster Bach undoubtedly met Prince Leopold during the preliminary discussions between the two royal houses. Keenly interested in music and anxious to build up his court orchestra, Leopold offered Bach the post as Cöthen's capellmeister. This was just the kind of job Bach was yearning for, and it seemed he promptly and cheerfully accepted (August 5, 1717). His prospective master sealed the deal with a *Geldgeschenk* (monetary gift).

But neither Bach nor Prince Leopold could have anticipated the possessive fury of Duke Wilhelm Ernst on hearing that Bach, who had gained some recognition as an organist during his Weimar years, would leave his employ. Worldly potentates prided themselves on adorning their courts with famed musicians, and Bach was well on the way to becoming one.

Thus, Bach's request for permission to take up his new post—made in a somewhat haughty tone—prompted an unexpected reaction. Weimar's court secretary records: "On November 6, 1717, the quondam concertmaster and organist Bach was confined to the

View of the city of Weimar, the ducal capital of Saxe-Weimar. Two of Bach's most gifted sons were born here: Wilhelm Friedemann (1710) and Carl Philipp Emanuel (1714). *Courtesy of Archiv für Kunst und Geschichte*

County Judge's place of detention for too stubbornly forcing the issue of his dismissal."

Bach's prison stay lasted for almost a month. He seems to have survived his confinement well, perhaps even welcomed it, since he was normally short of time to compose. But Bach's plot for his escape to Cöthen had been so well planned that Wilhelm Ernst must have concluded that resistance was futile. Still the duke did not grant Bach permission to leave without a parting shot. Bach's release notice of December 1, 1717, included a passage stressing the organist's "unfavorable discharge." This in hand, Bach made haste to pack up his family and leave for his new post in Cöthen—in what was almost literally a flight to freedom.

It was to prove a most portentous move for Bach personally and for the world of music, which gained the bonanza of chamber music works that Bach created at the court of his new sponsor, Prince Leopold of Anhalt-Cöthen.

Instruments to the Fore

When Bach, at thirty-eight, took up his new position in Leipzig in 1723, the town's church music was decidedly in need of a revitalization. The Sunday service consisted of no less than eighteen separate sections, starting at seven o'clock in the morning and lasting till vesper time at twelve—a formidable program for the congregation shivering during the winter in unheated churches (a heroic age). At mid-service, after the reading of the day's gospel, some communal singing, and other rituals, the preacher was scheduled to ascend the pulpit. Tradition prescribed that before the sermon, the cantata was to be offered, a musical reiteration and summation of the Bible text assigned to each Sunday's service.

This was Bach's chance to insert his *Hauptmusik* (see entry), or cantata, an orchestral and vocal interlude designed to arouse and refresh the believers' flagging spirits. To make his *Hauptmusik* the true agent of spiritual uplift, Bach had to overcome the rather subdued quality of the vocal cantata which up to this time had prevailed in Leipzig's Sunday services. He was able to create a far more dynamic and expressive form of sacred music by employing musical instruments in support of the soloists and choir. As Bach further expanded the cantata form into his novel concept of *Hauptmusik*, his need to acquire

Habit de Musicien

An allegorical print, entitled *Habit de Musicien*, demonstrates the increasing variety of musical instruments that became available during the eighteenth century. *Courtesy of Archiv für Kunst und Geschichte*

more musicians for "instrumental deployment" constantly provoked conflicts with his bourgeois superiors. Their refusal to provide him with the funds to further this innovation contributed to the bitterness of Bach's Leipzig years (see *Leipzig Ordeal*).

However, the modern hearer—even if not attuned to the religious message a cantata was intended to convey—receives a great musical bounty. A sacred cantata such as *Die Himmel erzählen die Ehre*

Gottes (The Heavens Recount the Glory of God) can be appreciated for its joyous music, even by those listeners who have little or no religious commitment.

The continuing popularity of these works, written for Sunday church services more than two centuries ago, is attested to by the large number of recordings that have been made of Bach's sacred cantatas. The current *Schwann Catalogue* lists some four hundred of them. The instrumental overtures with which Bach at times introduced his *Hauptmusik* have also been combined in recordings that give resounding proof of the master's genius for the symphonic.

Thus, Bach's Sunday cantatas, originally intended as sacred music for one particular religious community, have become universal music for all the world to enjoy.

Kaffee Kantate

It seems strange that in the hundreds of vocal works Bach committed to paper, events of his time are but rarely reflected. His church cantatas concern themselves almost exclusively with the metaphysical world, their subject man's fate rather than the facts of daily life.

However, among Bach's twenty-odd secular cantatas there is one that was clearly written in response to a particular social phenomenon of the time—the fuss caused by the growing indulgence in coffee drinking. What makes his *Kaffee Kantate* especially significant is that it was written in a lighthearted vein, making it a rarity within Bach's

In Bach's time coffeehouses had become all the rage—especially in England, where they were thought to foster rowdyism. In his *Kaffee Kantate*, Bach satirized the prevailing coffee craze.

111

monumental corpus of works. Albert Schweitzer thought the *Kaffee Kantate* had the earmarks of a modern operetta, "more Offenbach than Bach."

In Bach's time, coffee-drinking had become a rage, ubiquitous enough to be branded an abuse by the moralists of the day. The use of the coffee bean to make a soothing beverage had originated in Ethiopia by the fifteenth century. It spread first to Arabia where it was known as *qahwah*, which yielded the European words, *café, kaffee,* and coffee. By the mid 1500s, coffeehouses—where men drank coffee and socialized—were common in Persia and Turkey. A contemporary Turkish historian reported attempts to ban the beverage and the coffeehouses because they were thought to promote "loose living." By the 1600s, attempts at suppression in the Ottoman world ended and "on every street corner" coffeehouses appeared.

Coffee-drinking was imported into Italy from Turkey. By 1700, as Will Durant notes, "the three thousand coffeehouses in London were centers of reading as well as of talk," some of them later developing into exclusive clubs. In Paris, there were three hundred cafés by 1715, six hundred by 1750. "Such coffeehouses were the salons of the commoners," Durant adds, "where men might play chess or checkers or dominoes, and, above all, talk." In Germany, coffeehouses became places of relaxation for the bourgeoisie, and famed establishments, such as Zimmermann's Coffeehouse in Leipzig, offered concerts as well as social amenities for both local and visiting merchants.

Coffeehouses were of course male preserves. Women had to indulge the habit in their homes, which further alarmed the moralists. Housewives were accused of neglecting their domestic duties while passing time over "coffee socials" (*Kaffeeklatsche*). Rewards were even paid to volunteer "coffee-smellers," who devoted themselves to sniffing out offenders.

We do not know what moved Bach to take up the coffee issue, which seems so far removed from his typically transcendental concerns. Perhaps his job as conductor of Leipzig's Collegium Musicum (see entry)—a group that assembled in Zimmermann's Coffeehouse— prompted him to tackle the subject.

Some Bach specialists have even deduced that he revealed for once a piece of family history in this cantata. The father of its heroine, Liesgen, is distressed that his Lizzy will not give up her addiction to coffee at any price. The aggrieved father breaks out in a lighthearted aria:

Day by day I warn my Lizzy
Warn her till I am dizzy.

Since Bach's daughter Elizabeth was called Liesgen by her family, it seemed to these scholars that Bach had drawn upon his personal experience, moved perhaps by paternal concern. But this deduction does not hold up. Bach's daughter was only eight years old when he composed this musical plaint, so she could hardly be the inspiration for Liesgen, the cantata's coffee-mad heroine.

This rather droll cantata shows that Bach could compose works in sync with the musical trends of his time. The *Kaffee Kantate* was written in 1734, when Bach was almost fifty. This was but one year after the appearance of Pergolesi's *La Serva Padrona* (*The Strict Housewife*), one of the first comic operas, a genre that became highly popular in the course of the eighteenth century. However, no such success was accorded to Bach's *Kaffee Kantate*. It was revived briefly in 1925, when the British National Opera Company staged it as a theatrical presentation under the title *Coffee and Cupid*, and is occasionally featured in concerts devoted to the "Smiling Bach."

Did the Bach family itself indulge in the coffee-drinking habit? There are indeed indications that coffee was a favored drink in the cantor's household. The inventory of his estate reveals that the Bach kitchen was equipped with numerous coffeepots. An especially impressive one, in fact, was assessed for 18 thalers (about $2,000 today), six times more than "a little spinet" (3 thalers). These mundane entries suggest that the Bach family, like the heroine of his *Kaffee Kantate*, had indeed developed a strong "coffee habit."

Caricature of Giovanni Pergolesi (1710–1736), originator of *opéra comique*. In his *Kaffee Kantate*, Bach proved that he did not lack a sense of humor. The work antedates Pergolesi's *La Serva Padrona*, the prototype of *opéra comique*, a genre that was to take Europe by storm.

Keyboard Expert

One can hardly imagine a Rubinstein or a Horowitz donning overalls before a concert and rushing out to the stage to tune the grand piano on which he was to play that evening. In fact, wherever Horowitz went worldwide, he always took along his own grand piano and an expert technician to keep it in top-notch shape.

Johann Sebastian Bach—no mean virtuoso—always tended to his own instruments, and was very capable of doing so. In addition to his many other talents, Bach was a gifted instrumental mechanic, always prepared to make adjustments on the spot (see *Acoustician*). In a way, expertise in this area was a necessity for a performer in that age. Instruments as a rule were of a rickety construction and apt to go out of tune or to develop mechanical difficulties during a performance. Moreover, Bach's tuning skills proved to be a welcome source of income (see *Money Matters*).

Similarly, Bach's technical expertise in the construction of organs—recognized early—became almost legendary. That he, a

Woman playing the clavichord, a rather fragile instrument, popular for domestic use. Because of its wispy tone, it was rarely used in professional performances. Bach favored the clavichord and had several in his own instrument collection.

beginner, was entrusted with the testing and inauguration of the new organ in Arnstadt's Neuekirche (1703) points to his impressive insight into the instrument's mechanics—even at the start of his career. When quitting his next job in Mühlhausen, after but a brief stay, the consistory of St. Blasius asked him to continue to supervise the construction of its new organ. Some twenty documents in his own hand attest to his acoustical and mechanical insights, which he was always anxious to apply to the invention of new musical forms. A man who certainly knew pianos, Artur Schnabel, described Bach's constant zeal to enhance the effect of his compositions by using the best instrument available. "As soon as a new instrument appeared, he wanted even those works which were written for the previous instruments to be played on the improved instrument."

His alert interest in technological progress makes Bach seem like a Janus-like figure—a composer whose works were rooted in the past but who was possessed by visions of an instrumentally progressive future. This paradoxical aspect of his music is particularly evident in his attitude toward two of the keyboard instruments predominant throughout his career—the clavichord and the harpsichord (cembalo).

The older and domestically widely used clavichord had qualities that the mechanically more advanced and sturdier harpsichord lacked. The clavichord had a modest but superior dynamic range—a greater capacity to play notes from a *piano* (soft) to a stronger *forte* sound. The clavichord was also as a rule lower-priced than the harpsichord. This made it the favored instrument for home use.

Though virtuosi found it beneath their dignity to use the clavichord, many remained sentimentally attached to this older instrument, upon which they may have had their first lesson in keyboard music-making. In fact, Bach's son, Carl Philipp Emanuel, who was to become a prominent composer of cembalo (harpsichord) music, seems to have kept a clavichord in his Hamburg music room, obviously just for sentimental reasons. He celebrated its virtue in a 1784 pamphlet entitled *Farewell to My Silbermann Clavichord.*

When Johann Sebastian first came on the scene, the harpsichord was already the preferred instrument among professionals, even if it was incapable of producing the subtle dynamic shadings of the more fragile clavichord. The harpsichord was an indispensable instrument in ensemble playing, its ability to mark strong rhythmic accents supplying the "backbone" for orchestral performances. But the harpsichord could not match the "singing qualities" and tonal shadings that clavichords were capable of producing. It was clearly Bach's lifelong hope that the harpsichord could be improved in its dynamic range.

In 1710, success seemed to have been achieved in this direction when the Italian instrument maker, Bartolomeo Cristofori, unveiled in Florence his *gravi-cembalo con piano e forte*. This "pianoforte" was designed so that the hammer hit the strings and rebounded, allowing the strings to vibrate in varying intensity and tonal strength. It was a promising start, but Cristofori's pianoforte saw no further development.

Much more promising was the work of Bach's good friend, the organ builder Gottfried Silbermann. If Bach was the musical genius of this age, Silbermann was the prodigy of keyboard instrument builders, having at his death forty-seven masterful organ projects to his credit. He was apparently a rather eccentric character, forced to leave his Alsatian homeland in 1709 after entering into a liaison with a nun. Although he was to become the revered head of an instrument-building family, he never married. Besides constructing magnificent organs, the Silbermann family also created clavichords and harpsichords of great repute, including the clavichord that Carl Philipp Emanuel had so loved that he wrote a eulogy for it.

The harpsichord (cembalo) was stronger in tone than the clavichord, providing robust rhythmic accents that held orchestral performances together. But it lacked dynamic range.

Silbermann surely shared Bach's desire to expand the dynamic range of the harpsichord. Following the lead of Cristofori, he experimented with the production of a pianoforte. Bach does not seem to have been overly impressed with the results. Johann Friedrich Agricola—one of Bach's students and the court composer for Frederick the Great—reported that one of Herr Silbermann's pianofortes was tried out by Capellmeister Bach. He greatly admired the instrument's tone, but complained that it was weak in its high registers and was too hard to play. This criticism deeply offended Silbermann, causing a decided estrangement between the two friends.

Bach's negative feelings were not shared by other performers. Indeed, among the professional and amateur purchasers of Silbermann's new instrument was Frederick the Great (see entry). When Bach first demonstrated his virtuosity to the king during his Berlin

In Bach's time and under Bach's influence, the harpsichord grew from its limited role in support of other instruments into a solo instrument.

Bartolomeo Cristofori's "forte piano," unveiled in Florence in 1710. It was designed to combine the dynamic range of the clavichord with the tonal strength of the harpsichord. *Courtesy of the Metropolitan Museum of Art, the Crosby Brown Collection of Musical Instruments*

visit in 1747, it was proba-bly on a Silbermann pianoforte, one of the many the King had assembled.

Though there was tension for a time between Bach and Silbermann, they later reconciled. Nevertheless, no Silber-mann pianos appear in the inventory of Bach's estate. In fact, the inventory list does not mention a clavichord either, although this was a type of instru-ment that surely would have pleased Bach in its

tonal range. The poor construction and the wispiness of its resonance must have been below his professional standards.

In the field of acoustics (see entry), Bach deserves to be given pioneering status. Equally impressive were his progressive ideas in the field of instrument technology. He was at one time even credited with the design of a new string instrument, the viola pomposa—its name indicative of both Bach's tendency toward the grandiose and his desire to extend the sound barriers prevailing in his time. Recent research has disproved this claim. Nevertheless, while Bach may never have built or designed a musical instrument himself, he certainly inspired others to do so.

The Last Bach

Johann Sebastian Bach founded a family of dynastic proportions. Four of his sons remained prominent figures in musical life after their father's death (see *Paternal Devotion*). Two of them—Carl Philipp Emanuel and Johann Christian—would diverge markedly from the musical style that their father had brought to perfection, becoming practitioners of the Art Galant style. But they also kept the Bach name alive during an era that had almost forgotten the Leipzig cantor.

By the mid-1800s, the Bach male line was extinct. When the sons of Wilhelm Friedemann and Carl Philipp Emanuel passed away, the son of Johann Christoph (the "Bückeburg Bach") became the last of the amazing Bach progeny. Wilhelm Friedrich Ernst was thus the only grandson of the Leipzig cantor to live past the end of the eighteenth century, and he did so in a state of relative anonymity. It was Mendelssohn's dedication to the revival of Bach's music that brought once more into the limelight—and with a sad note of finality—this aged last member of the once-

Self-portrait of Felix Mendelssohn at the organ. The great Romantic composer was dismayed that Leipzig had never erected a memorial in honor of Bach. To raise funds for such a monument, the twenty-four-year-old virtuoso gave a number of Bach organ recitals.

119

proud and miraculously productive family.

In 1835, when Mendelssohn was only twenty-four, he became conductor of the world-famous Leipzig Gewandhaus Orchestra, an organization descended from Bach's modest group of instrumentalists, the Collegium Musicum (see entry). Imbued with a deep love of Bach (see *Revival*), Mendelssohn pronounced it a scandal that Leipzig had never honored the memory of its great cantor with a monument. Robert Schumann had been thinking along the same lines, complaining that "as yet no outward symbol testifies to the living memory of the greatest artist who ever dwelled in this town."

In order to raise funds for the creation of a Bach momument, Mendelssohn gave a memorable organ recital of Bach works in the Thomaskirche on August 10, 1840. He afterward remained active in negotiations with the town authorities, seeking to bring the project to fruition. Three years later, the plans of Mendelssohn and Schumann finally found realization: a monument of modest proportion—featuring only a bust of Bach—had been placed in front of the Thomasschule, under the window of Bach's erstwhile study. A few days later, in his music magazine, *Die Neue Zeitschrift für Musik*,

A Bach monument, in front of the cantor's office of the Thomasschule, was dedicated in 1837. During the ceremonies, the "last Bach" was also honored" Wilhelm Friedrich Ernst, Bach's grandson, was then the only direct descendant of the once-mighty Bach family. *Courtesy of Archiv für Kunst und Geschichte*

Schumann described the touching surprise that was a highlight of the dedication ceremonies: "Honour was paid not only to Bach but also to his only surviving grandson, a man of eighty-four, still full of energy, with snow-white hair and fine features.... No one knew of his existence, not even Mendelssohn, who had lived many years in Berlin and who had prided himself in following every trace of Bach he could discover."

In contrast to his grandfather's youthful wanderlust, Wilhelm Friedrich Ernst for the most part lived an uneventful life, though he was a fine pianist and made a few concert tours that brought him acclaim. Eventually, this last Bach found a quiet niche in Berlin as harpsichordist and capellmeister to Prussia's beloved Queen Maria Louise, who, Schumann reported, granted him a life pension of two hundred thalers annually—probably in excess of fifteen thousand dollars in our currency. Wilhelm Friedrich Ernst died two years after the monument's dedication, and with him ended the saga of the Bach dynasty.

But a new saga was in the offing. Only a few years hence, in 1850, the publication of Bach's enormous opus was to begin, with the forty-six volume *Gesamt-Ausgabe* (see entry). Even if the Bach family itself had disappeared, the music of the Leipzig cantor in its infinite variety was to begin a new reign.

Leipzig Ordeal

It is one of the supreme ironies of Bach's life that after an almost idyllic period of employment as capellmeister at the court of Prince Leopold of Anhalt-Cöthen (see *Anhalt-Cöthen*), he should have been fated to spend the remainder of his years not very happily as Leipzig's cantor. In his late thirties and with a large and still-expanding family, Bach himself had hesitated before accepting the Leipzig appointment in 1723. And indeed, after he took that post, nothing was to quite work out as he might have hoped.

To be sure, the cantorial position at Leipzig happened to be a very prestigious one, due both to the caliber of men who had filled the post, and to Leipzig's long-standing reputation as a commercial center and a bastion of learning and religion. Yet, paradoxically, it was these very factors that contributed to Bach's long travail in Leipzig.

It has been said that a man cannot serve two masters. In Cöthen, Bach was the highly respected conductor of a court orchestra, and

Leipzig *Bürgermeister* Abraham Christoph Platz, who observed that since the town in 1723 had been unsuccessful in hiring the best cantorial candidate, "we had to settle for a mediocre one"—namely, Bach!

Prince Leopold was his *only* master, a man who (in Bach's words) "both loved and understood music" and who truly appreciated the genius of his capellmeister. In Leipzig, Bach would be called upon to serve many masters, very few of whom could appreciate his artistic gifts and creative achievements.

As the cantor of Leipzig's principal churches, Bach was under the thumb of the Consistory, composed mostly of lay people who supervised the church services. His attempt to direct music for the town's university would bring him into conflict with the chancellor of that institution. As principal music teacher of the Thomasschule, he had to kowtow to its rector, an eminently practical young man who thought a musical education was totally superfluous in the dawning age of enlightenment. It was a situation that has its echoes in our country's public schools today, when computer skills are increasingly stressed while courses in music and art slowly disappear from the curriculum.

As director of music for the town of Leipzig, Bach was subject to the dictates of the Town Council, whose members, three *Bürgermeister* (mayors), two deputies, and ten assessors—proved especially difficult to please. Elected for their financial skills, these prosperous burghers apparently lacked any musical knowledge whatsoever.

In this environment, with an overabundance of masters, Bach, an independent soul, would fight vigorously to preserve his independence and to uphold his traditional prerogatives (see *Defending His Domain*). He would fight equally hard to provide the town and its churches with music of the highest performance standards, a goal for which his tin-eared superiors had little understanding or sympathy.

Sadly, Bach himself was never to hear his music played in Leipzig as he conceived it. Performances in the town's Thomaskirche and elsewhere during Bach's time were definitely inferior to what a modern choral or orchestral ensemble has to offer. Even by the standards of his time, the instrumental and vocal resources on hand in Leipzig were not of the quality necessary to provide the fine performances he envisioned.

It is not just third-person reports alone that chronicle Bach's

The churchyard of Leipzig's Thomaskirche. At left is the Thomasschule, where Cantor Bach was responsible for the training of young students as church singers. The Bach family had quarters in this building from 1723 until the master's death in 1750.

difficulties in obtaining decent performances of his work. We are fortunate to have the evidence in his own inimitable prose, spiced at times with a touch of sarcasm. Bach let loose a cannonade of complaints in his *"Short but Most Necessary Draft for a Well-Appointed Church Music,"* submitted to the Town Council in August 1730. His continuous warfare with the council members reached its highest pitch with this verbally aggressive petition. The fact that the memorandum dispenses with the usual submissive forms of address (see *Flattering the Mighty*) seems to indicate a willful and deliberate circumvention of etiquette, thus revealing the depths of anger Bach had reached in his first seven years at Leipzig.

Bach noted that when he came to Leipzig he had expected the support of a group of well-trained town musicians, but what he had found was largely a group of incompetents. He added that every request for better-trained, better-paid musicians—such as those at the electoral court of Dresden—had been rejected by his penny-pinching superiors.

Enraged, Bach argued that to provide the town with a proper and inspiring church service would require an orchestra of eighteen to twenty instrumentalists and a chorus of twelve to sixteen singers, some of whom would serve as soloists. In reality, he normally had far fewer of each at his command. He was dependent upon students from the Thomasschule, who sang for room and board as well as a free musical and general education. These boys of varying talent had hardly time enough, let alone skill enough, to prepare for a new cantata or motet performance each Sunday. Even when supplemented by the more talented music students from Leipzig University, Bach's vocal resources were spotty at best.

As for instrumentalists, all the Town Council had approved was "four town pipers, three professional fiddlers, and one apprentice," most of them lacking in the necessary artistry. As Bach ironically observed, "Modesty forbids me to speak at all truthfully of their quality and musical knowledge."

The town's leaders ignored his complaints and his request for additional financial support. Instead, as the council minutes reveal, the members unleashed a torrent of complaints about their music director: Bach was stubborn; he refused to perform the tasks assigned to him (see *Delegator*); he would ignore directives, and leave town without asking permission. In sum, he had proven himself time and again, to their disappointment, to be an "incorrigible cantor."

The most astonishing and unwarranted complaint of all was the one voiced by the chancellor and *Bürgermeister*, Dr. Jacob Baron, who stated that Bach "had done nothing" during his seven-year tenure, and even when apprised of this fact, had shown "little inclination to work." Actually, during these seven years Bach had worked with superhuman zeal to lift Leipzig's church music to new heights of excellence. Shortly after his arrival, he had completed and performed the three-hour-long *St. John Passion*. During the first three years of his Leipzig tenure, he had written close to thirty cantatas. The continuing flood of church music produced by Bach had been crowned by the *St. Matthew Passion*, first performed in 1729—a majestic and complex four-hour work (see *Radiant Masterwork*). Seemingly, Dr. Baron and the Town Council overlooked—or were unable to comprehend—that in seven years Bach had composed, and arranged for the performance of what is arguably the greatest body of church music ever created.

After the town's burghers had rebuffed his plea of 1730, Bach must have been thoroughly disgruntled. Later that same year, he unburdened himself to an old friend, Georg Erdmann, who was once his classmate in Ohrdruf and Lüneburg (see *Education*) and now was an influential diplomat in Gdansk, Poland. Bach compared his present miseries with the fulfilling post he had enjoyed at Cöthen in the employ of "a gracious prince." Not only was the Leipzig position not as remunerative as he expected, Bach wrote, but the cost of living turned out to be very high. Bach added that the authorities who employed him "are odd, and little interested in music," with the result that he had encountered "almost constant vexation, envy and harassment." He told Erdmann that he felt compelled to seek his fortune elsewhere, asking the diplomat's help in finding a suitable post in or around Gdansk.

Of course, Bach was fated to stay on in Leipzig until his death two decades later. Paradoxically, this man with so many masters was (in Leipzig) ultimately his *own* master, carried to freedom by the wings of his genius. His output of sacred music declined after 1730, and he began to recycle his older compositions, devoting himself more and more to the composition of secular music. The Collegium Musicum (see entry) occupied much of his time in the near term, as did special commissions from towns and members of the nobility outside Leipzig. In his final years, Bach turned ever more inward with the creation of some of his most glorious compositions—his monumental "summation works" (see entry), including the *Musical Offering* and the *Art of the Fugue*.

Fuss and fume as they might, the town officials could do little about their stubborn cantor and the manner in which he chose to spend his time. By 1749, it seemed as if they could hardly wait for Bach (now almost sixty-five) to pass away to make room for a cantor less recalcitrant. Rather tactlessly, they interviewed a prospective candidate, one Gottlob Harrer, to replace the Herr Cantor—"in case he should die." Today, if these good burghers are remembered at all, it is only as footnotes to the biography of their "incorrigible cantor."

Librettists

It was Puccini who expressed the opera composer's perennial quest for librettos and pleaded, "Give me texts that will make the world weep." Richard Wagner, it seems, despaired of ever finding a librettist who could match the magnificence of his music, and decided therefore to write all his opera texts himself. Bach wrote no operas, though he came close to doing so in his secular cantatas. But he was in a perennial need of librettos for his sacred cantatas, masses, and wedding and funeral music.

This textual problem hardly existed for the composers that had preceded him. For them, the Bible proved to be a bottomless resource, providing a vast storehouse of sacred texts and psalms for use in their librettos. But a whole new school of meditative and more emotionally oriented librettists was to arise in Bach's time. Influenced by German Pietism, they placed great emphasis upon the believer's yearning for a personal dialogue with God. In their poetry, the writers of this new generation gave expression to the believers' thoughts, fears, and hopes, offering consoling meditations upon the Bible's message.

Boldly leading this group was Erdmann Neumeister (1671–1756), preacher at the Jacobikirche in Hamburg. Bach probably had met this pastor during his own tenure as an organist in Weimar. Sensing a new religious *Zeitgeist*, Neumeister, himself a poet and librettist of talent, was forward-thinking enough to take note of the growing popularity of opera in Germany. He understood that operatic arias—in which the hero or heroine so dramatically give voice to their innermost feelings—could be readily adapted to sacred and inspirational purposes. The Hamburg pastor forthrightly declared that "a cantata is nothing but a piece of opera performed in a church."

When starting as a writer of cantatas in Mühlhausen (1707–1708), Bach still relied essentially on biblical texts. He was

Erdmann Neumeister, pastor of the Jacobikirche in Hamburg from 1715 to 1755. He wrote numerous cantata texts, meditative in character and often operatic in form. Several of these texts were adapted by Bach for his own cantatas.

unequaled in his knowledge of the Bible and continued to draw heavily on this resource during the ensuing years. By mid-career, however, he felt keenly the need for a new type of text. During his first years in Leipzig, Bach had turned to the creation of *Hauptmusik* (see entry)—highly expressive, spiritual cantatas. Thus committed to the avant-garde Neumeister mode, Bach began his search for capable librettists.

Among the writers who would first supply Bach with this new kind of libretto text was the Leipzig poetess Marianne von Ziegler, a member of the town's social elite. Later to be the author of a book on poetics, *Essays in Rhyme* (1728), von Ziegler supplied the text for nine of Bach's early Leipzig cantatas. But in the end, it seemed that her writing wasn't quite to his taste.

Continuing his outpouring of sacred music, Bach turned next to a local poet, Christian Friedrich Henrici (1700–1764). Writing under the pen name of Picander, he was not a serious writer, but one who garnered applause for his comic and satirical poems, which he collected and published in 1729. The texts that he created for Bach tend, as a whole, to be overly sentimental, at times even embarrassing, making use of such strange metaphors as, "Christ, you are my waterbath."

Yet here again we have one of the paradoxes of the Bach phenomenon. He was able to take a mundane text, with its verbally overloaded Baroque style, and translate it into music that could lift the hearts and inspire the minds of his listeners—perhaps even more so in our time than his, given the widespread search for spiritual meaning so prevalent in our day despite our material progress and prosperity. Picander himself once expressed the hope that his own "lack of poetic charm" would be overcome by the beautiful music "of the incomparable Herr Capellmeister Bach."

The handy and facile Picander became what today we would call Bach's "house poet," ready to help whenever an emergency arose. One occurred on November 19, 1728, when Bach's adored former master—Prince Leopold of Anhalt-Cöthen (see entry)—died suddenly at the age of thirty-eight. At that time, the fifty-three year old Bach was hard at work composing the *St. Matthew Passion*, with Picander as his librettist. This masterwork was to be ready for performance on Good Friday, 1729 (see *Radiant Masterwork*).

The composition of the *Passion* was probably close to completion when Leopold's untimely death intervened and Bach was compelled to think of a musical memorial for his former master. Rather than start from scratch, he apparently decided to make use of the initial movements of the *St. Matthew Passion*. With Picander's textual assistance, Bach speedily transformed the passages thus far written into a *Trauer Kantata* (funeral music) for the deceased.

An ever-ready versifier, Picander could turn his pen from the spiritually profound *St. Matthew Passion* to a work as ephemeral and rambunctious as Bach's *Peasant Cantata*. Picander stood by faithfully supplying Bach with texts for both routine works and those demanding speedy delivery, among them some festive cantatas Bach was compelled to produce on short notice. In the 1740s, with Bach's interest in cantata-writing markedly waning, Picander ceased to write librettos and became the head of Leipzig's liquor-taxing authority. But he remains a prime example of the show-business axiom: You may achieve lasting fame when you "hitch your wagon to a star." Picander did it—and it worked.

The Man and His Music

A biography in dictionary form, even one as informal as this, is pledged to provide hard facts and entertaining or illuminating anecdotes. Yet the phenomenon of J. S. Bach is not easily captured within alphabetic categories alone. There is something in the Bach story that transcends the ordinary data of life, something that seems to be intimately connected to his music in a most fundamental way. We have the sense, when we listen to a work by Bach, that we are encountering the essence of the man himself—that we gain insight into what he thought and how he felt, his philosophy of life and his beliefs about the mission of music.

If we listen to a work of Stravinsky, for example, we are at a loss to know what manner of a man set the notes on paper. No such puzzlement prevails if we listen to Bach. The man—with all the intangible elements of his character and creative genius—seems to be represented by his music with a fidelity that may well be uniquely Bachian.

Be it an aria, a chorale, a cantata, or even one of the vast numbers of instrumental solo pieces, there is something embedded in each work that informs us that its creator was a man of deep beliefs and human goodness. Every line of music that Bach composed conveys his insistence upon order and his profound faith in God's benevolence.

Bach's music, by his own confession, is the language through which he hoped to attain a closer rapport with the Almighty—to plead with Him for mercy and forgiveness, to search for succor or to find relief from mortal anguish. Even his secular pieces were composed, according to Bach himself, in order to praise the Lord for the

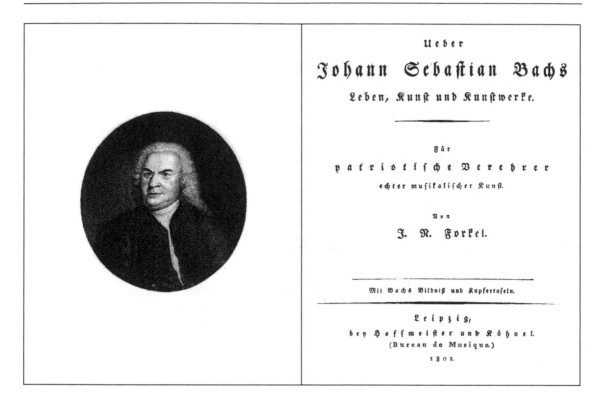

Title page of the first biography of Bach (1802), written by the music director of the University of Göttingen, Johann Nikolaus Forkel, who was born in 1749, the year before Bach died. Patriotic in tone, it was largely based upon information supplied by Bach's son Carl Philipp Emanuel, stressing the master's human qualities.

creation of a world of beauty and delight. An assured *bonhomie* and an existential contentment are immediately conveyed to us when the first measures of a piece by Bach are intoned.

In this regard, Bach fulfilled the mission of his art as did few other musicians. Freud (not known for a close attachment to music) described this mission most aptly: "What the artist tries to accomplish with his art is to awaken in us the same emotional attitude, the same mental constellation as the one that produced in him the impetus to create." Thus, a work of art in its ideal incarnation is "an effective expression of the intentions and emotional states of the artist." It is the intimate self-revelation that Bach is able to present to his listeners that gives his music an exceedingly personal touch. The marvel of his music lies in the fidelity with which it evokes the man who created it.

Money Matters

From the abundance of sacred music that Bach has left to us, one might easily deduce that its composer was a man deeply, perhaps exclusively, concerned with matters transcendental. The salvation of the human soul, the prospect of eternal life—these are the subjects of many of his cantatas, chorales, masses, and Passions. One might easily assume that the composer himself was little concerned with the mundane problems that beset ordinary men.

An early-seventeenth-century thaler. Its purchasing power has been estimated as roughly equal to a thousand dollars in our current monetary value. *Courtesy of the American Numismatic Society*

This, however, is decidedly not the case. Notwithstanding Bach's unquestionable piety, he was at the same time very much a dweller of this earth. Many documents reveal that the Holy Cantor was also an astute businessman. He knew his worth and insisted on his proper recompense. As the Bach biographer Charles Sanford Terry once observed: "Bach had an agile interest in money. He fought for his rights—especially the right to be paid. . . . He was not wrapped in metaphysical asbestos."

Bach's life story abounds with examples that reveal a man well aware of life's economic realities. His zeal to earn money is evident in the career moves that he made during the first twenty years of his working life. They began, astonishingly, when he was but fifteen years old and was paid 12 thalers a year as a choir boy in the Michaeliskirche of Lüneburg (see *Education*). When his voice changed, he apparently was asked to remain as accompanist and choral assistant, which continued to afford him a meager sustenance.

From this time forward, we can observe a constant rise in Bach's pay scale. As the Arnstadt organist (1703–1707), his yearly salary was 84 thalers. As the Weimar court organist (1708–1717), he was initially paid 200 thalers a year, increased to 250 thalers in 1713. His salary doubled again in 1717, when he became capellmeister for Prince Leopold of Cöthen. Finally, there was the Leipzig appointment, which he accepted in 1723. As indicated in the famed Erdmann letter (see *Leipzig Ordeal*), Bach, now forty-five, estimated his annual income to be about 700 thalers (more than $70,000 in today's money), after some seven years on the job—although his income, derived from several sources, was variable.

Thus, Bach's career resumé indicates that he continually strove for material betterment and greater financial reward—a rather atypical attitude for a churchman. Actually, Bach's 700-thaler income was quite respectable, considering that Leipzig's mayor (*Bürgermeister*) received a salary of 1,600 thalers (more than $160,000), while a city judge earned somewhat less than the Thomasschule cantor, about 650 thalers. Bach complained, in the Erdmann letter, that his apparently ample income was offset by the high cost of living in Leipzig. In Thuringia, he noted, he would have been able to live better on a 400-thaler income.

Still, these salaries seem to be rather meager incomes when measured against the phenomenal rewards garnered by the opera divas of the day. Faustina Bordoni, a Dresden prima donna, and her husband, the composer and capellmeister Johann Adolph Hasse are reputed to have had a joint yearly income of 6,000 thalers (today, a very substantial income of more than $600,000). This renowned couple was quite friendly with Bach, providing hospitality to him during his occasional visits to Dresden. (See *Operatic Echoes*.) The situation is hardly different today, when a movie star, or even a teenaged rock star, commands an annual income at least ten times that of the president of the United States.

Bach's estimated Leipzig income may appear satisfactory for his station, especially for a man who twenty-three years earlier had started out with no money, no connections, and an altogether limited education. But there was something quite uncertain about the sum that Bach, with a fair degree of pride, had quoted. The base salary that Bach received from the town treasury was a mere 100 thalers. The rest of his income was earned by means of *Akzidentien*—what today we would call fees from freelance work—some of it guaranteed by the town to be the cantor's personal monopoly.

To write funeral music and conduct musical services at a deceased's grave was one of the more remunerative sources of Bach's income. No wonder Bach looked forward to these sad occasions, seemingly without too much sentimentality. His pragmatic attitude is demonstrated in the Erdmann letter: "If the death-rate is higher than *ordinairement* then the fees increase in proportion; but if the air is healthy they fall accordingly, as last year, when there was a reduction of over one hundred thalers in the fees I would normally receive from funerals."

Wedding ceremonies also offered additional income opportunities. As always, what could have been mere *Gebrauchsmusik* (see entry), or music on demand, became for Bach an opportunity to produce true gems, as in his *Wedding Cantata—O Longed-for Day, O Blessed Time* (BWV 210). But it was the lost income, and not the lost opportunity to create a masterwork, that made Bach angry when he heard that one of Leipzig's bridegrooms had sneaked out of town with his bride in order to circumvent the cantor's fee for wedding music. In a furious letter, Bach admonished the *Bürgermeister* and the church authorities that they must see to it that his freelance income was protected in the future. This missive is a reprimand by the cantor, full of anger and umlauts: *"Ich bitte Sie in der Zukunft meine Einkünfte kräftig zu schützen"* (I request that in the future you give powerful protection to my income). Harsh notes of this sort have led to the conclusion that Bach sometimes acted more like a shrewd accountant than a Holy Cantor.

With his family responsibilities always growing, Bach had to hustle for money. And one must observe that he was capable at times of being a rather inventive hustler, searching out opportunities to make a thaler here and there. Receipts have come down to us in Bach's own hand that show how he made a little money on the side as a "sales agent," renting and selling clavichords, mostly those of his friend Gottfried Silbermann. The year before his death, Bach sold for 115 thalers (perhaps $12,000 today) a fine Silbermann instrument to a Count Branitzky, a visitor to Leipzig from Bialystok, Poland.

Records also reveal Bach's activity in the field of bookselling. Based on announcements in contemporary newspapers, we know that he kept for sale in his house the basic musical manuals of the time, among them Johann David Heinichen's *Der General Bass* (1728), and the *Musik Lexikon* of his distant relative and Weimar friend, Johann Gottfried Walther (1732). The works of his sons, Wilhelm Friedemann and Carl Philipp Emanuel, were also at times advertised in Leipzig's newspapers as "available for sale in the Herr Cantor Bach's home at the Thomasschule."

Did Bach's continual struggle to support his considerable household pay off in the end? Was he able to build up a reasonable reserve to sustain him in his later years, or to provide for his family in the event of his death? Sadly, the answer to both questions must be a resounding no. When Bach died without having made a will, the estate he left behind—including his considerable collection of instruments, his library, and household furniture—might seem to us rather substantial, almost 1,000 thalers (in excess of $100,000), after debts were paid. (See *Postmortem.*) But the actual cash reserve that he had accumulated was a mere 270 thalers—about the same amount of money he had earned each year as a court organist in Weimar, when he was still in his twenties.

Music Publisher

The tired old adage "publish or perish" applies not only to academic circles. Be it poet or musician, every creative person strives to see his or her work in print. Bach was no exception, though in this area he proved unfortunate. Of more than a thousand works listed in Bach's work inventory, the Bach-Werke-Verzeichnis (BWV), less than a dozen were printed during his lifetime. In large part, this was because his complex fugal works did not appeal to a mass audience as did the simpler, more melodic works of such composers as the then-famous, now-forgotten organist C. F. Hurlebusch, who was widely published (see *Friendships*).

After Bach's death in 1750, music-publishing took a decided upswing, but the demand for his work was extremely limited. During the ensuing decades, as the Art Galant style held sway in Europe (see *Art Galant*), Bach's fugal style was largely forgotten, many of his manuscripts gathering dust on the shelves of Leipzig's Thomasschule. Bach's first posthumously printed composition, *The Well-Tempered Clavier*, was commercially published in 1800, half a century after his death. Between 1800 and 1802, just three publishers issued editions of this work. Only after Mendelssohn's presentation of the *St. Matthew Passion* in 1829 sparked a revival of interest in Bach's music (see *Revival*) did the manuscripts of his great works begin to be printed. The *Brandenburg Concertos*, for example, had to wait until 1850 to become available in a published version.

Bach's cantatas fared even worse. Of course, after Bach's death in 1750, the demand for cantatas in general must have been slack. They required a large apparatus of soloists, chorus, and orchestral musicians, inaccessible to most congregations, especially in the light of an increased secularism during the Age of Enlightenment (see *Zeitgeist*). In any event, Bach's cantatas were the last category of his works to reach the printing press—essentially with the publication of the *Gesamt-Ausgabe* (see entry) between 1850 and 1900. The sole exception was the cantata *God Is My King*, which Bach had composed in Mühlhausen when he was twenty-two years old. This work was printed then at the expense of the Town Council.

Since it didn't pay to print Bach's cantatas, the Leipzig publisher Johann Gottlob Immanuel Breitkopf had some of them hand-copied and carried them in this form in his music catalogue, to serve the small community of Bach enthusiasts (see *Vienna Bach Circle*). One wonders how the master would have felt seeing the recent Schwann

> Clavier Übung
> *bestehend in*
>
> Præludien, Allemanden, Couranten, Sarabanden, Giquen,
> Menuetten, und andern·Galanterien;
> Denen Liebhabern zur Gemuths Ergoezung verfertiget
> *von*
> Johann Sebastian Bach,
> Hochfürstl Anhalt-Cöthnischen würcklichen Capellmeister und
> Directore Chori Musici Lipsiensis
>
> Partita I
>
> In Verlegung des Autoris
> 1726.

Bach's first venture in self-publishing (1726): *Partita I* for harpsichord, "offered for the delight of dilettantes." Five more partitas followed in succeeding years, to be combined as the *Clavier Übung I* (1731). It has been conjectured that this title page was engraved by Bach himself.

Catalogue, which lists seventy-three recordings of the *Brandenburg Concertos* alone.

When it came to having their works published, many of Bach's contemporaries were luckier, more astute or more capable of pandering to the popular tastes than he. Telemann's works were widely distributed in print. His *Six Quartets* first appeared in Hamburg in 1730. There seems to have been some problem with this release, prompting Telemann to go to Paris and have the pieces republished. To protect his property, he applied for a "royal privilege." This marks him as a pioneer in the field of music copyright. In the meantime, Cantor Bach seems to have scanned the market for publications by his famous colleague. "Herr Bach of Leipzig" appears in the list of subscribers to an edition of Telemann's *Flute Concertos* published in Paris in 1738.

Handel, too, had no trouble finding publishers for his scores. His *Concerti Grossi* were first released by John Walsh in London, and they proved so popular that they had to be reprinted within weeks, with additions and emendations. Walsh also published some of Handel's oratorios, paying the composer a less-than-royal royalty of £10 each (still, it was better than Milton's emolument of £5 for *Paradise Lost*).

Since Bach was unsuccessful in finding a publisher for the overwhelming stream of works he produced, he set out with typical self-reliance to publish under his own imprint, starting inconspicuously in 1726. Seemingly as a trial balloon, Bach first published his *Partita I for Clavier*. This publication was followed periodically by others (*Partita II to Partita VI*), until he combined the six individual offerings in one volume, finely printed and ready for sale at the Leipzig Fair of 1731. The title page read, *Clavier-Übung I: Six Partitas Offered to Music Lovers to Lift Their Spirits (Gemüts-Ergötzung)*. The title page of this work bore the identification "*Opus I.*" Perhaps Bach added it as a tongue-in-cheek comment, well aware that he had been a prolific composer for more than twenty years. Before *Opus I*, he had already written compositions such as *The Well-Tempered Clavier, Part I*, the *St. Matthew Passion*, and the *Brandenburg Concertos*—all works which would by themselves have made him immortal.

Forkel described *Clavier-Übung I* as causing "a sensation." But this is hardly borne out by the fact that it was never reprinted in Bach's time. Since then, however, the work has appeared in hundreds of editions.

Over the years, Bach's publishing program seems to have undergone a change, shifting from pieces primarily targeted to beginners and less sophisticated music lovers to more serious works. *Clavier-Übung III* offered chorale works, while *Clavier-Übung IV* unveiled the *Goldberg Variations* (see entry), the zenith of clavier music in the eighteenth century, marking a peak in the genre not achieved again until Beethoven's *Hammerklavier Sonata* (1818).

Bach's career as a publisher ended with one qualified success. The publication of the *Musical Offering* in 1747 under his own imprint was at best a *succès d'estime*. Bach was proud of the "celebrity endorsement" that Frederick the Great (see entry) had provided him, though it is doubtful that the king ever heard the *Offering* as a completed work. Bach distributed copies of it to his friends as his *Prussian Fugues*. He arranged for a second printing of a hundred copies. We are informed about this publication in a letter Bach wrote to his second cousin, Johann Elias Bach, who asked for a copy. Publisher Bach replied, "If Herr Cousin desires a copy, you only have to give notice by mail and add a thaler. The rest shall then be complied with."

The mention of the thaler should not be overlooked. Even if Bach wrote music that reached empyrean heights, he was not apt to neglect the practicalities involved in earning a living (see *Money Matters*). Nevertheless, the master's ventures into the publishing of his own music were few indeed when compared to the enormous number of his works fated to remain unpublished for a century after his death.

Newness

One feature of the music scene in Bach's time may be hard for us to understand today: the constant clamor by the public for new works. Bach felt compelled to provide new cantatas for Leipzig each Sunday; Handel wrote one or two operas every year for his London audience; Telemann ground out new compositions in enormous numbers (fifteen hundred cantatas, twenty-odd Passions—a compository fertility which earned him at one time a place in the *Guinness Book of World Records*).

This unceasing demand for new musical works explains both the prodigious output of many eighteenth-century composers and the phenomenal speed with which they worked. Handel once noted that Telemann could write a cantata in the same time that it took most people to write a letter. But Vivaldi perhaps holds the record. Supposedly, he completed his opera *Tito Manlio*, in five days. He also boasted that he could compose a concerto faster than a copyist could copy the parts.

It seems somewhat paradoxical that our era, which prides itself on newness and "nowness," has a totally different attitude toward music (except for rock, rap, and other music directed toward the youth market). Works written by serious contemporary composers are performed rather sparingly. To offer a program of modern music does not as a rule create a run on the box office, whereas classical music remains in constant demand.

The idea of a repertory of standard works worthy of repeat performances was unknown to the era of Bach. Craving ever-fresh sensations, the public was lukewarm toward music previously performed. The first thing a newly appointed cantor did was to throw

Johann Kuhnau, Bach's distinguished predecessor as Leipzig's cantor. He was noted for his "Biblical Sonatas." Bach clearly viewed Kuhnau's work as outdated and undertook to provide his own music for all occasions, religious and secular.

away all the music produced by his predecessor and go on a binge, composing his own new body of work. (See *Gebrauchsmusik*.)

Following the pattern of his time, Bach ignored the considerable *oeuvre* of Johann Kuhnau, who had preceded him as cantor of Leipzig's Thomaskirche. Kuhnau, a distinguished musician and scholar, had created a respectable backlog of cantatas, motets, and chorales for Leipzig's Sunday services. Bach must have considered them old hat. Even more important, perhaps, they were not *his*. Almost from the moment Bach was installed as the town's new cantor in mid-1723, he started afresh with an outpouring of liturgical works. Within a year, the musical underpinning for Leipzig's principal church services was entirely Bachian, and Kuhnau's work was quickly forgotten.

In the field of secular music too, Kuhnau had cut a considerable figure. He is rightfully considered one of the period's leading composers of piano music—notably his *Clavier-Übung* (Keyboard Exercises) of 1689 and 1692, which codified his teachings. These works fell by the wayside and were forgotten when Bach's keyboard technique set new standards.

The works collected in the various editions of Bach's own *Clavier-Übung* truly embody newness, especially when one compares them to Kuhnau's rather simple exercises. The complex, sophisticated, and absorbing music that Bach had composed as "keyboard exercises" have remained ever new and ever "now"—a basic component of the classic repertory of our own time.

Numerology

B ach said his goodbye to the world in 1750 by dictating to his star pupil and son-in-law, Johann Christoph Altnikol, a version of the chorale *Before Thy Throne I Stand*. Its theme is first conveyed in fourteen notes which are the numeric equivalent of his name: B-A-C-H. To arrive at this conclusion, one translates each letter into the number of its place in the alphabet: B = 2; A = 1; C = 3; H = 8 (total 14). Bach was fond of "smuggling" into his works this cryptic musical signature (see *B-A-C-H*). Furthermore, if we reverse the digits 1 and 4, we end up with the sum of notes (41) used in Bach's "death-bed chorale." A mystifying coincidence? Hardly.

Bach was a convinced and adept practitioner of numerology. The application of its principles in his final musical offering to God seems like an attempt to send his maker a message in a very personal code. Numerology itself is based on the belief that God's creation of the cosmos and everything that happens within it is ruled by numerological relationships established by the Creator himself. Numerologists hold that those who penetrate this code might even be empowered to predict the future. Moreover, if they could make use of these codes in their own activities, then perhaps they might be able to influence future events.

The Bible is replete with incidents inviting numerological interpretation. Using the numbers scale, God would of course be symbolized by the number 1; Jesus Christ, the number 2; the Trinity, 3. The number 5 was assigned to the Crucifixion, connoting the five wounds inflicted on Christ during this ordeal. Those who were taken with this form of mysticism hoped that their appeals to God would be more effective if based on such numerological principles. Bach believed in them firmly.

Hourglass and numerological table from Albrecht Dürer's engraving *Melancholia*. Bach, like Dürer, believed that numerological symbols influenced man's fate.

In many of his cantatas and passions, he apparently allowed the accepted magic numbers to be his guide in the shaping of his music. A typical example is the treatment of the central chorale of the *St. Matthew Passion: O Haupt voll Blut und Wunden (Oh Sacred Head Now Wounded)*. Guided by the numerological symbol for the Crucifixion—5—Bach was at pains to intone the melody in this work five times. In the chorale prelude *These Are the Ten Commandments*, the basic theme appears ten times. There are many other examples that bear out his practice of translating numerological text references into their musical correlates.

Similarly, Bach's numerological beliefs seem to have guided his association with Lorenz Mizler's famed Society of the Musical Sciences. Mizler probably had invited Bach in the early 1740s to join his ranks. But Bach apparently hesitated for what might have then seemed a rather mysterious reason. He would have become the group's thirteenth member, but seemingly he wanted to become its fourteenth. Hence, he had to wait until another eminence had joined the roster. The one who took his place as number thirteen was a worthy candidate—none other than Georg Frideric Handel. Only after Bach could join as number fourteen in 1747 did this dedicated numerologist accept Mizler's invitation. Why all this fuss about being the fourteenth member? Once again, 14 is the numerological equivalent of the letters in his name, B-A-C-H (see entry).

He even carried this numbers game a little further. In the portrait by E. G. Haussmann that he was required to submit to the

The portrait of Bach by
Elias Gottlieb Haussmann
submitted in 1747 to
L. C. Mizler's Society of
the Musical Sciences.
Bach's six-buttoned coat is
a reference to the six-part
fugal riddle he submitted
as an "approval piece" for
acceptance as a member
of this society. *Courtesy
of Archiv für Kunst und
Geschichte*

Mizler society, Bach is shown displaying the *Probestück* (approval
piece), a work he had to compose to officially gain entry into this
select circle. This piece presents a variation in six voices of the
chorale *Vom Himmel Hoch*, a structure which is subtly referred to in
the six buttons that show on his coat in the portrait submitted when
entering Mizler's ranks. (What naive games this giant was prone at
times to play.)

Many Bach scholars have made astounding claims as a result of
joining in this numbers game. Indeed, the musicologist George J.
Buelow came up with a startling discovery when he found that the sum
total of measures comprising Bach's *B Minor Mass* equals 2,345 in all.
If one adds up the four digits in this figure, one arrives at the number
14, the familiar musical signature of the composer of this masterwork.

Oldest Son

Triumph and tragedy were strangely intermixed in the life of Bach's oldest son, Wilhelm Friedemann. He was expected by right of primogeniture to become the head of the succeeding generation of the Bach family. But it was not birth order alone that suggested that Friedemann might play this role, for he was also endowed with considerable gifts. While attending Leipzig University, Friedemann proved himself a brilliant student. In later years, he would at times be favorably compared with his father, both for his virtuosity and for his improvisational skills as an organist.

Bach himself certainly spared no effort to help his beloved "Friede" attain the stature in the music world that his heritage suggested. To ensure that his oldest son would acquire sound musicianship from the start, Bach had by 1724 compiled the *Clavier-Büchlein für Wilhelm Friedemann Bach*—a basic text and guide book explaining the musical elements (such as rhythm and ornamentation) that he wished his fourteen-year-old son to master.

As Friedemann matured, he was called upon to play the role of an assistant in his father's far-flung musical enterprise, such as the presentation of cantatas. (It has been suggested that Bach's early organ cantatas were composed with his first-born son in mind.) Friedemann probably joined his father at times in performances at Leipzig's Collegium Musicum (see entry), which was surely an excellent proving ground for a promising career.

Yet, for all his native genius, Friedemann was temperamentally flawed. He lacked the often painful self-discipline to write down and give structure to the free-floating improvisations on the organ in which he and his father both excelled (although he did create some

Wilhelm Friedemann, Bach's oldest son. He was the most gifted of Bach's progeny and served a long apprenticeship as his father's student and assistant. Yet he lacked his father's self-discipline, wasting his gifts in dissipation. *Courtesy of Archiv für Kunst und Geschichte*

fine organ and harpsichord music). Friedemann's failure in this area exemplifies an essential truth: The gift of a creative imagination has to be paired with the more mundane qualities of diligence and discipline in order to give birth to a masterwork. Johann Sebastian Bach possessed these qualities in rich measure. His first-born son, Wilhelm Friedemann, reputedly a genius, tended to be undisciplined, not inclined to transpose his imaginings into printable form.

Obviously, Friedemann also suffered from the fact that he was raised within the long shadow of his father. He must have been frustrated by the feeling that he could not measure up to the standard set by his father's genius and industry. And it is quite obvious that the father did not help his oldest son to overcome his self-indulgent bent, but rather fostered it, with the result that Friedemann became helpless without his paternal guidance.

Title page of the *Clavier Büchlein* (1720), the instructional manual Bach compiled for his oldest son, Wilhelm Friedemann, when Wilhelm was ten years old. It explains basic elements of music—such as rhythm, ornamentation, and harmony—that Bach considered vital to the boy's training.

This is exemplified by Friedemann's first official assignment in 1733, as organist of the Sophienkirche in Dresden, a town alive with artistic and musical activities. To secure this job, Friedemann did not have to lift a finger. His father smoothed the way. Both his application for the post and an accompanying sample of his composing skill (signed "Wilhelm Friedemann Bach") are said to have been written not by Friedemann, but by his father.

After Bach's death, Friedemann's career underwent a decided decline (see *Heirs*). He neglected his duties, abandoned his family, and became a wanderer, tending to drunkenness and living for many years a vagabond's existence. Friedemann spent his last years in Berlin, grinding out a living by giving occasional organ recitals. The son who was designated by primogeniture to be the crown prince of the Bach dynasty—and backed from the first by his father's love—died in 1784 at the age of seventy-three, penniless and virtually unknown.

Operatic Echoes

To link Bach with opera seems at first somewhat paradoxical. Revered as the "Holy Cantor," what in the world could he have had to do with what in today's parlance would be called an entertainment medium? Yet it is true that Bach, the ultimate church musician,

was markedly influenced by the opera of his time. With unrestrained enthusiasm, he tried to adapt some of its most popular elements to his own *Hauptmusik* (see entry), in an effort to bring church music more in tune with the public's rapidly growing secular taste.

Almost from the beginning of Bach's career, opera was moving to the fore as the medium incorporating these new tendencies. Its composers beguiled their audiences with florid, storytelling recitatives; melodically entrancing arias; choruses that commented dramatically upon the ongoing action. Italian opera carried these captivating elements to their heights. Indeed, Venice and Naples could be seen, like Hollywood and New York today, as the centers of an international entertainment industry. France was to take up the torch in the person of Jean-Baptiste Lully, the great French court composer and conductor who came to a tragic end (see *The Dance*).

Even though opera did not enjoy in Germany the popularity it evoked elsewhere in Europe, Bach, with the insatiable hunger to learn from his contemporaries that he displayed throughout his life, had

Opera performance in Dresden (1719). Bach is said to have visited this opera house a number of times. He was friendly with its music director Johann Adolf Hasse, and leading diva, Faustina Bordoni, a husband-and-wife team renowned throughout Europe. *Courtesy of Deutsche Fotothek, Dresden* ample opportunity to experience the world of operatic glamour. When he was only a teenager, struggling to establish himself at the Michaelisschule in Lüneburg (see *Education*), the peripatetic lad was within a few hours' walk of one of the oldest operatic establishments—the Hamburg Opera House. In Bach's time, a renowned composer and conductor, Reinhard Keiser, was its guiding spirit. It is not unreasonable to suppose that the musically inquisitive young Bach sampled at least a few of the more than one hundred operatic works created by Keiser, who was said to have combined "light and pleasing melodies together with dramatic expressiveness." (It is worth noting that Handel was for a time first violinist in Keiser's orchestra, and that his first opera, *Almira*, had its premier in Hamburg in 1705.)

There had even been an opera house in Leipzig for a few decades until 1720. Telemann claimed to have composed for it more than twenty operas. Though it had closed it doors three years before Bach took up his post as Leipzig's cantor in 1723, its music surely was still well remembered.

Clearly, the most important source of operatic influence for Bach during his Leipzig years was Dresden, the Saxon capital. Known as the "Florence on the Elbe River," Dresden presented, architecturally and culturally, the acme of Baroque splendor and power in Germany. It boasted an outstanding orchestra with "musicians well-paid by His Royal Majesty, relieved of all concern for their living... excellent to hear," as Bach himself, stuck in Leipzig, observed pointedly and with perhaps a touch of envy. Dresden also boasted a widely acclaimed opera house, which was dominated by productions in the Italian style. Forkel reports that Bach had on a number of occasions taken Friedemann to Dresden "to hear the pretty tunes." (Richard Wagner was to become capellmeister of the Dresden Opera in 1843, where in earlier years his own operas *Rienzi* and *Der Fliegende Holländer* had their debuts.)

Bach became friendly with the two luminaries of the Dresden Opera—its music director Johann Adolf Hasse and his wife, the famous diva Faustina Bordoni, both in their thirties when Bach first made their acquaintance (see *Money Matters*). Hasse himself composed operas for the Dresden company which featured his wife in the leading role.

Bach clearly appreciated the instrumental innovations of the opera world. Notwithstanding his stern Lutheranism, he had come to see the need to revitalize church music in order to provide greater spiritual uplift for the congregants. This led him to enliven his church cantatas with stronger instrumental support, operatically inspired arias, and orchestral interludes (see *Instruments to the Fore*).

When the thirty-eight-year-old Bach accepted the post of Thomasschule cantor in 1723, he apparently had a reputation for such progressive tendencies that was well-known to his prospective Leipzig employers. His contract with the ultra-conservative town masters stipulated that the music he was to compose for church services "shall be of such nature as not to make an operatic impression." Bürgermeister Graupner, who was favorably inclined toward Bach, warned him to avoid "theatricality." The antagonistic attitude toward opera prevailing among the town's leadership was well expressed by Johann Christoph Gottsched, a big wheel at Leipzig University, who called opera "the most preposterous absurdity ever invented by the human mind."

Of course, Bach, being Bach, did not accept this judgment. He clearly recognized that church music had to adopt a less turgid, more secular style, a conviction he also expressed in his famed memorandum, *"Short but Most Necessary Draft for a Well-Appointed Church Music"* (1730) in which he noted, "The state of music is quite different from what it was, since our artistry has increased considerably and the former style of music no longer seems to please our ears."

Bach was not alone in perceiving that the sacred music of the Lutheran service could benefit from adopting operatic elements. A well-known contemporary preacher and librettist, Erdmann Neumeister declared blandly, "A cantata is a piece of opera performed in a church" (see *Librettists*), while Johann Mattheson, in his *Der Musikalische Patriot* (1728), confessed, "a note which gives me pleasure in an opera can do the same in church."

Bach shared this conviction and acted upon it. "There is more musical drama in many of his church compositions," Bach specialist Arthur Mendel once observed, "than in any opera of his time."

Organist Supreme

That Bach was the greatest organist of his time has never been doubted. He was born to the organ. For three generations, many members of his family had found an honest sustenance as organists. Although solid craftsmen all, none of the clan's members was to bear comparison with Johann Sebastian as a composer, performer, or technological authority on the "royal instrument."

The essence of Bach's creative genius comes most powerfully to the fore in his organ works. As Christoph Wolff, a leading Bach authority and an organist himself, observes, "The organ was the starting point of his development, the germ from which in great measure his characteristic creations grew and spread."

Favoring the full flowering of Bach's genius in this area was what seemed to his contemporaries to be a virtual revolution in organ technology taking place as he came upon the scene. As in so many European industries of the time, craftsmen were advancing rapidly in their technical knowledge and skills, vastly improving the tonality and range of these majestic instruments. The great advance during this period in the design and construction of organs was perhaps culturally and socially similar to the electronics advances of our own time. Just as few public institutions today would be without the most up-to-date computers or sophisticated sound equipment, so too did the congregations of Bach's time vie with each other to build the most impressive organs they could afford. Many churches raised funds just to contract for building the latest organ models (sometimes at the expense of thousands of thalers) or to bring their old instruments up to date.

The vastly improved sound technology of the new organs found its counterpart in structures that were visually imposing, with organ pipes reaching as high as thirty feet. The instruments' highly complex array of pipes were often fitted into a decorative setting that turned them into veritable works of art.

This burgeoning art of organ design and construction was, in some ways, Protestantism's response to the splendor of Baroque architecture, with which Catholicism had impressed its believers and absolutist monarchs their subjects. As a composer, performer, and expert in the instrument's construction, Bach came to embody this organ renaissance more than any musician of his time. The noted classical scholar Gilbert Highet once pungently observed, "The counterpoint of Bach built an invisible Versailles to the glory of God."

During Bach's lifetime, organ building took great strides. Congregations vied with each other to improve their instruments or to acquire new ones at the cost of thousands of thalers.

Bach reached the heights of his accomplishments as a composer for the organ early in his career, when he was still in his twenties and held the position of court organist to Duke Wilhelm Ernst of Saxe-Weimar (1708–1717). It was during this Weimar tenure that he composed no less than thirty-nine monumental organ works—preludes, fugues, toccatas—more than he would compose in the three decades that were to follow. He was said to have been inspired in this feat by the pleasure that the duke took in his playing, "which fired him to try every possible artistry in the treatment of the organ."

The Weimar years essentially saw the emergence of Bach's organ style, both in its touching intimate utterances and its grandiose fugal structures. These works eclipsed with one stroke the respectable creations of his predecessors such as Frescobaldi, Froberger, Böhm, Pachelbel, Buxtehude, and countless other fine practitioners. Bach must have been well aware of the wonders that the new organ technology held in store for the instrument's sonic range. Yet like Moses, who was permitted to see the Promised Land but not to enter it, Bach was confined to career assignments in which he never was lucky

ORGANIST.

enough—except when sneaking away for guest appearances—to display his full artistry on a truly up-to-date instrument.

Still, his vast technical knowledge of organ construction and registration seems to have enabled him to coax great sounds from technically inferior instruments, mixing subtle but seemingly unrelated timbres or blasting forth with heaven-storming force. Philipp

Emanuel reports: "No one understood the choice of registers as well as he.... Organists were terrified when he sat down to play on their organs and drew the stops according to his taste... but then they heard an effect that astounded them."

The organ was always to remain the indispensable core of his creative life. It has been truly said: Imagine the organ removed from Bach's works, and the soul would be gone.

Pageantry

The Leipzig marketplace, April 21, 1733, as the townspeople celebrated the accession of Friedrich August II as elector of Saxony. Bach composed a secular cantata that prominently featured tympanies and trumpets. *Courtesy of Stadtgeschichtliches Museum, Leipzig*

In addition to his numerous duties as a church musician and teacher, Bach, as municipal music director *(Director Musice Lipsiensis)*, was also required to produce concerts and provide secular cantatas for civic occasions, celebratory and "upbeat" in spirit. The most popular of these were written for public pageants, much-longed-for interruptions in the often dull routine of town life, in an age far removed from the never-ending media and entertainment circus of our own time.

In that long-ago era, the Leipzig town fathers eagerly grasped every opportunity to amuse and impress their citizenry with public

152

displays. Whatever the excuse—honoring a visiting potentate, observing the birthday of a famous professor, or celebrating the marriage of a princess—it was turned into a festive occasion, with spirits lifted and excitement raised by torchlight parades, ringing church bells, and exploding cannons. The university authorities also readily sponsored such public events, especially if they were likely to win the support of a mighty monarch or some other dignitary who happened to visit the town and had some money in the bank. It fell to Cantor Bach to provide the appropriate musical underscoring for such festivities.

A typical opportunity arose in October 1734, when Leipzig had the chance to stage such a public ceremony. A year earlier, the elector of Saxony, Friedrich August II, had been chosen as the king of Poland (where, confusingly, he was titled Augustus III). Actually, the elector spent little time in Poland but held court mostly in Dresden, where

Johann Gottfried Reiche, Leipzig's outstanding trumpet player, who had the principal role in Bach's cantata for a 1734 pageant in honor of the elector of Saxony. He fainted from smoke inhalation during the torch-lit event and died the next day. *Courtesy of Archiv für Kunst und Geschichte*

Bach had visited him in 1733 in order to present him with music for a mass (see *Catholicism*). Now, a year later, the elector had suddenly decided to come to Leipzig in order to celebrate (or to have his subjects celebrate) the first anniversary of his accession to the throne of Poland. The town made haste to welcome the monarch in style.

On October 8, as night fell on this solemn occasion, some six hundred university students equipped with torches were assembled to provide a dramatic setting in Leipzig's marketplace, where the town's Collegium Musicum would perform a secular cantata composed and directed by Herr Bach. The latter apparently had received only three days' notice to compose this imposing tribute, using tympani and trumpets to provide an appropriately monarchical air. This festive cantata was based upon the text *Preise dein Glück, Gesegnetes Sachsen* (Praise Your Good Luck, You Blessed Saxony). Under the pressure of his tight deadline, Bach reputedly wrote much of the text himself.

That Bach had succeeded in this emergency assignment is attested by this item which appeared in the local paper the next day: "His Royal Highness together with his Royal wife, did not leave the window as long as the music lasted—but most graciously listened to it—and his majesty found pleasure in it."

However, there was a tragic consequence to this otherwise joyous occasion. Bach had enlisted for the event the services of the sixty-seven-year-old Johann Gottfried Reiche, a prominent local trumpet player who was also a well-known composer for this instrument. (He ranks an entry in the recent Grove *Dictionary of Music and Musicians*.) Strained by his forceful blowing and no doubt adversely affected by the smoke of the students' torches, Reiche was felled by a stroke during the pageant and died the next day.

Paternal Devotion

Johann Sebastian Bach sired twenty children, ten of whom (six sons and four daughters) survived to adulthood. The mere statement of this fact generally prompts a reaction of disbelief...or perhaps a mixture of irony and sympathy. Neither is warranted. Bach was in remarkable control of the vast family he founded. Indeed, the Bach clan bears a striking resemblance to certain commercial ventures of modern times, with Johann Sebastian serving as the CEO for the sprawling branches, closely managing the affairs of his highly diverse progeny.

The founding of a large family was of course quite in keeping with the parental philosophy of the time. The Bach dynasty, however, was *both* a family *and* a musical enterprise. Whether guided by instinct or conscious planning, he managed to bring the two spheres—Bach the father and Bach the musician—into an exemplary and creative harmony.

What is amazing is the zeal and endless dedication with which he devoted himself to the upbringing of his children, musically and otherwise. Of course, it must be noted that the four daughters who survived him (see *Daughters*) seemed to have played a minor role in this well-managed enterprise.

Bach himself clearly thought of his first-born son, Wilhelm Friedemann, as the preeminent heir to his own domain and lavished a great deal of attention on the boy's education. Yet Friedemann, who clearly possessed some of his father's genius, was never to achieve the stature and accomplishments that Bach must have hoped for. (See *Oldest Son.*)

In contrast to Friedemann's often slovenly life, the career of Carl Philipp Emanuel—Bach's second son and four years younger than the first—was far more successful. He spent the first thirty years of his career—not very happily—as harpsichordist at the court of Frederick the Great (see entry). Then, in his fifties, he made a startling change, becoming the cantor and music director for the great Hanseatic port city of Hamburg, where he remained until his death in 1788.

Paul Henry Lang, in his *Music in Western Civilization*, credits Philipp Emanuel with the development of the sonata form, in which he "established the musical dialect of the Classical style: symphonic themes, development of somber intensity, harmonic intricacies, and a disarming humor." Hence, it was Philipp Emanuel, not the first-born son, Wilhelm Friedemann, who inherited a leading position in the world of music after Bach's death. He was much admired by Haydn, Mozart, and Beethoven—and tends to be the only one of Bach's five musician-sons who produced works that are still performed today with some frequency.

We can deduce a certain degree of respect, but something less than filial love, in Carl Philipp Emanuel's attitude toward his titanic father. Perhaps there was a sense of oedipal rivalry in this; perhaps resentment in response to a perceived favoritism that the father had shown to Wilhelm Friedemann, the older son.

Johann Christian was the youngest of Bach's sons. By a twist of fate, Christian was just fifteen years old in 1750 when his father died.

Johann Christian Bach, The master's youngest son, who totally abandoned his father's heritage. Converted to Catholicism, he gained distinction at the English court as composer of operas and concertos in the Art Galant style.

Bach himself had been orphaned at ten in 1695 (see *Hometown*). Like his father, Christian was taken into the household of a musically accomplished older brother, in this case the Berlin home of Carl Philipp Emanuel. Two decades younger, Christian would be second to Philipp Emanuel in the esteem he gained in the world of music, mainly through his accomplishments in the highly popular medium of opera (see *Heirs*).

A fourth son, only three years older than Christian, had a far less glamorous career. Johann Christoph was educated at both the Thomasschule and Leipzig University and, in the year of his father's death, became capellmeister in Bückeburg, two hundred miles northwest of Leipzig, from which he seems never to have strayed. He was the last surviving Bach son, dying in 1795.

Ironically, Bach's paternal devotion was perhaps most evident in relation to the least successful of his musician sons—the troubled Johann Gottfried Bernhard, who was born in 1715, just a year after Philipp Emanuel. Unlike his two older brothers, this third Bach son was not university-educated, receiving only tutoring in music and staying in Leipzig to help his father in his many cantorial tasks. In 1735, Bach must have seen a chance to provide a post for this son who had not yet left the parental fold. Always a solicitous guide to his children, Father Bach must have thought that the time was ripe for Gottfried (now twenty years old) to be on his own. Hence, he secured a position for him as organist in Mühlhausen, a town where he himself had spent a short time twenty-seven years earlier.

Gottfried Bernhard was a competent organist, but once on the job he seems to have been afflicted by youthful impatience and recalcitrance, a state not unfamiliar to his father, who had exhibited just such rebellious tendencies when still a youth. In addition, Gottfried Bernhard got involved with some young men of dubious character, incurring debts that his father had to pay off, while the son returned home in disgrace.

In 1735, Bernhard was established in another town once served by his father—Arnstadt (see *Abendmusik*). He was organist for a time at the Marienkirche, where he continued to show some of his father's youthful stubbornness and boldness, prompting a congregant to comment: "If Gottfried Bernhard Bach continues to play his way, the organ will be ruined in two years and half of the congregation will be deaf."

The following year, in October 1736, Father Bach once again secured a position for Bernhard in a town where he himself had long-established connections. The position of organist at the Jacobikirche in Sangerhausen had been promised to Bach some thirty years earlier, but was then given to another candidate. In his letter to the town authorities, Bach suggested that "divine providence" had made it possible at long last for the town to redress the balance by appointing his son Bernhard to the same post. But it was not long before Bernhard pursued his dissolute ways. Within two years, he was so badly in debt that he had to leave town hurriedly and find a safe haven in parts unknown.

Informed of this misbehavior of his son and mortified to discover a black sheep in his family, Bach wrote a letter to an old friend of his in Sangerhausen who had first sponsored Bernhard's appointment. One of the most touching documents in the Bach archives, this letter reveals Bach's pride of family and the infinite care he lavished on his children. But what obviously caused Bach almost hysterical anguish was the fear that Bernhard's misdeed would cast a shadow on his own record as a man of unassailable honesty. Bach offered to settle his son's account promptly and ended his letter with the plea: "Since I have opened my heart to Your Honour, I am very confident that you will not associate me with my son's misconduct, but will understand that a father, whose children are close to his heart, will do all that he can to advance their welfare. . . . "

For a while, nothing was heard of Bernhard, a fugitive from justice. At last, news arrived in Leipzig that he had found refuge at the home of a member of the clan, a Nicolaus Bach in the town of Jena. Bernhard seemingly wanted to redeem himself and had registered at the University of Jena in the hope, perhaps, of receiving the academic training he had missed as a youth. But his belated efforts were in vain. In 1739, only four months after his matriculation, Bernhard suddenly died of a "fever." He was twenty-four years old.

Whatever their individual fates, or the judgments of posterity as to their individual achievements, the progeny of Johann Sebastian Bach certainly comprise the most outstanding musical dynasty in Western history. But it would be unfair to ascribe all the credit for these gifted children to the master himself. His two wives surely provided additional genetic and environmental support for the musical gifts of the sons. Bach's first wife, Maria Barbara, was his cousin, a member of the Bach clan of musicians and daughter of an organist, while his second wife, Anna Magdalena, was the daughter of a court trumpeter and was reputed to be a gifted singer. Maria Barbara was the mother of Wilhelm Friedemann, Carl Philipp Emanuel, and Gottfried Bernhard, while Anna Magdalena gave birth to Johann Christophe and Johann Christian. Surely the Bach children had been destined for musical distinction.

Pictorialism

Steeped in the musical principles and practices of his time—even if he did not theorize about them (see *Theory and Practice*)—Bach was a staunch adherent of *Affekten-Lehre* (the doctrine of the affects). This theory inspired the composers of the time to translate words and sentiments into easily comprehended musical metaphors. Bach displayed an amazing inventiveness applying this theory in his works, sacred and secular.

He was only nineteen years old when he produced his first known clavier work—one that relied heavily upon pictorial effects—the *Capriccio on the Departure of His Beloved Brother* (1704). The brother in this case was the twenty-two-year-old Johann Jacob Bach, who had secured a position as oboist at the court of the king of Sweden. In the *Capriccio*, the assembled Bach family is conjured up musically. Slow, almost mournful tones convey their sadness at the thought of their young kinsman's departure, perhaps never to return. To suggest the arrival of the coach that will carry Jacob away, Bach's music becomes more lively, deftly weaving into a rather jaunty fugue the sound of the posthorn. Even the cracking of the coachman's whip is musically depicted by Bach in this vivid scene.

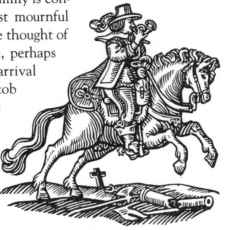

A rider sounding a posthorn. Bach's earliest known piece of program music, *Capriccio on the Departure of His Beloved Brother* (1704), features the sound of the posthorn, developed into a lively fugue interspersed with the crack of the coachman's whip.

Johann Sebastian was only at the beginning of his career when he composed this work—a searcher still. His *Capriccio* was undoubtedly influenced by the work of Johann Kuhnau, who had developed program music into a fine art in his "Biblical Sonatas," among them his still-famous harpsichord composition, *The Fight Between David and Goliath*. Twenty years later, Bach would become Kuhnau's successor as cantor of the Thomaskirche in Leipzig. But in his immense output both before and after assuming that post, the *Capriccio* would remain Bach's only experiment in pure programme music.

Even if he did not further pursue this musical genre, Bach would always lean toward pictoralism—composing music that illustrates the text. Albert Schweitzer described this technique, noting: "If the text speaks of drifting mists, of boisterous winds, of roaring rivers, of waves and ebb and flow... of Satan rising in rebellion, of angels poised on the clouds of heaven, then one sees and hears all this in his music."

Many such examples occur in the *St. Matthew Passion*: trembling strings reflect the tremors of the heart grieving for Jesus; when the cock crows thrice at Peter's denial, the music echoes it realistically. In an aria from the *St. John Passion*, "I follow thee with joyous steps," a flute enters just behind the singer and, in Schweitzer's words, "almost treads on his heel as it follows the vocal line."

His secular cantatas especially offered Bach many opportunities to exercise his gifts of pictorialism. A prime example is in the cantata *Aeolus Appeased*, where, in the aria "How lustily I will laugh," the singer bursts into a twenty-five-note paroxysm of laughter.

These examples of Bach's adherence to *Affekten-Lehre*—the translation of words into sounds—give us just a glimpse into his working methods. His *ouevre* as a whole—gigantic in proportion—defies explanation and will forever remain a mysterious gift of fate.

Postmortem

Like so many aspects of Bach's life, the events surrounding his death are replete with painful paradoxes. His musical confessionals, chorales, cantatas, and Passions suggest that Bach looked forward to his own demise with an expectant yearning. Never has a man's "death wish" been more touchingly expressed than in Bach's chorale *Come Sweet Death, Come Sweet Repose*. Bach often reminded his fellow believers that in the fullness of life they should never forget the warning *"Memento mori"* (Remember that you must die).

Bach himself certainly did not flinch from facing death. And yet he had made no provisions for his own demise. Neglecting to make a will, he left his affairs—when he died at the age of sixty-five on August 18, 1750—in an unmanageable mess. This neglect was quite atypical of him, the exemplary and orderly architect of vast musical structures. But it doomed to a life of misery Anna Magdalena, his beloved wife of twenty-eight years, as well as three of the four daughters who survived him (see *Daughters*).

The material and financial remains that Bach left behind were, altogether, not impressive. When no will was found, the town sent to the cantor's house its official appraisers, who speedily prepared a *Specification of the Estate Left by the Late Johann Sebastian Bach*. One of the most revealing Bachian documents that has come down to us, it states that the deceased left a cash reserve—Bach's entire life savings—of almost 270 thalers (less than $30,000 today), with an outstanding debt of more than 150 thalers. Silverware, candlesticks, cutlery, and the like added up to 251 thalers. The most valuable item in this latter category was a tobacco box of agate set in gold. With all probability, this was the reward that Bach was said to have received from Count von Keyserlingk for the writing of the *Goldberg Variations* (see entry).

The *Specification* also listed the wearing apparel Bach had left behind. One would hope that the inventory was not complete and that

Bach's wardrobe contained more items than the listed three coats, eleven shirts, and one pair of shoe buckles. The mention of "a writing desk with drawers" among the household belongings conjures up thoughts of the endless number of masterworks that Bach must have written upon this sturdy piece of furniture, valued at more than three hundred dollars in today's money.

When Bach's valuable musical instruments and his extensive library are included, the net value of his estate was less than 1,000 thalers (about $100,000 in our currency)—little more than a year's income during Bach's Leipzig years. According to the prevailing law, one-third of the dead man's estate, modest as it was, would go to his widow Anna Magdalena, who at Bach's death was forty-nine years old. The remaining two-thirds of his possessions had to be divided equally among the ten surviving Bach children, two of them still under age (see *Daughters*). Each of them could have received only a pittance. And what would eight-year-old Regina Susanna have profited from her bequest of Martin Luther's complete works in eight volumes? Bach's musician sons—Wilhelm Friedemann, Carl Philipp Emanuel, and Johann Christian—fared best (see *Heirs*).

Another benefit that somehow could have accrued to Bach's widow was squandered. In the library of the Thomasschule, Bach had assembled the vocal scores of many of his cantatas, filed in impeccable order, each neatly marked with its title and its place in the liturgical year. Bach's successor must have decided that this "old stuff" was taking up shelf space he needed for his new cantatas and disposed of numerous Bach manuscripts as bulk *Makulatur*—useless waste material. Some of these manuscripts were even reported to have found their way into butcher shops, where they were used as wrapping paper. Today, of course, they would be worth millions of dollars.

In the face of Bach's neglect and this official bungling, Anna Magdalena's declining years were to be sad ones, and how little she deserved this (see *Helpmate*). This talented and devoted wife and mother died in 1759—the widow of the once mighty Leipzig cantor and princely capellmeister was buried in an unmarked pauper's grave.

Prades Festival

The bicentennial of Bach's death was marked worldwide in 1950. In July of that year, an enthusiastic crowd of Bach-lovers made a pilgrimage to Prades in the French Pyrenees, facing the Spanish border. Prades was at the time a sleepy little town with only a single,

Violinist Joseph Szigeti
(*left*) and cellist Pablo
Casals, rehearsing for the
Prades Festival of 1952.
The festival was first
staged in 1950, to
commemorate the two-
hundredth anniversary of
Bach's death.

twenty-two-room hotel. However, St. Pierre's Cathedral in Prades became the center of a Bach festival that turned out to be one of the most important and influential musical events of the time. Among the outstanding musicians in attendance at the festival were Alfred Cortot, Joseph Szigeti, Rudolf Serkin, and Isaac Stern. The festival's energetic organizer was the violinist Alexander Schneider.

The festival also marked the public reemergence of Pablo Casals, who had established himself, in previous decades, as a cello virtuoso of world renown. Seventy-three years of age at the time—still a refugee from Franco's dictatorship—Casals was to become the festival's guiding spirit and its most memorable soloist. Under his leadership, the festival was later to be moved to Puerto Rico, where in 1956 the great cellist would establish his home.

Casals, himself a member of a family of musicians, had started to play the piano at the age of five. At fifteen, he was already acknowledged as a cello virtuoso. Early on, he became an ardent student of Bach's solo *Cello Suites*. "For twelve years," he confessed, "I worked on them and I was nearly twenty-five before I had the courage to play one in public." After a career as a touring virtuoso, Casals, a man of immutable integrity, retired in 1936 to Prades, an exile from his native Spain, in protest against Franco's destruction of the Spanish Republic. Curtailing his musical activities for a time, Casals devoted himself to providing charitable help for displaced fellow musicians.

During his triumphal reappearance on the world stage at the 1950 Prades Festival, Casals performed four of Bach's suites for solo cello. This was the unforgettable high point of the occasion, a performance that was made into one of the great classic discs available to music lovers.

From early youth, Casals had been inspired not only by Bach the musician, but also by Bach the man. The Leipzig cantor remained the

Pablo Casals as young cello virtuoso. He had begun studying the Bach *Cello Sonatas* when he was fifteen. It was twelve years before he had the courage to play them in public, Casals later noted. He had come to Prades in 1936, at age fifty-four, an exile from the Franco dictatorship in Spain. He died in 1973.

cellist's patron saint throughout a long life (Casals died in 1973 at the age of ninety-six). In his memoirs, Casals paid touching tribute to Bach, who had provided him with a sense of order and consoling serenity.

"For the past eighty years," Casals reported, "I have started each day in the same manner. It is not a mechanical routine but something essential to my life: I go to the piano and play two *Preludes and Fugues* by Bach. . . . it is a rediscovery of the world of which I have the joy of being a part. The music is never the same to me—never. Each day it is something new, fantastic and unbelievable. That is Bach, like nature. . . . a miracle."

Precisionist

B ach's lifelong allegiance to fugal technique left him open to some good-natured sniping and left-handed compliments from both contemporaries and modern commentators (see *Detractors*). It prompted Colette to call him "the celestial sewing machine." Others looked at him as a cold-hearted constructionist, more interested in the form than the content of his music.

While Bach surely followed orthodox fugal precepts in most of his works, he also has endeared himself to music lovers by creating beautiful, even haunting melodies. What greater ones have ever been written than the *Air on the G String*, or the *Shepherd's Music* from the *Christmas Oratorio?* Yet even in these celestial melodies, Bach applies a strong, repetitive beat. It is this strict rhythm that at times keeps listeners from recognizing the melodic enchantment of such pieces.

Of course, Bach lovers appreciate the beauty of works like these, but they recognize also that the unfailing rhythm in almost all his creations provides an element of reassurance and order, so much needed in our age of befuddlement. It simply adds to the miracle of Bach that within this strict rhythmic discipline—"life-ordering"—he *was* able to create singing and soaring melodies. The great English Bach expert Charles Sanford Terry has well described this symbiosis: "Bach's opus disproves the illusion that he was a cold mathematical precisionist. Rather it reveals him as one of the tenderest and most emotional of men—with a poet's unshakable soul and a technical skill that was miraculous."

Quaffing

B ach-lovers may be inclined to believe that the Holy Cantor now surely dwells up above in the empyrean heights, talking to God. It was perhaps such a poetic fancy that prompted William Buckley to announce, "If Bach is *not* in heaven... I am not going." Still, it's a fact that when he was alive, Bach had a decidedly worldly streak—he frequently engaged in a little innocent quaffing. Indeed, various documents clearly reveal that Bach, even in his younger years, enjoyed his stein of beer and a few glasses of wine.

Perhaps this was a predilection that ran in his family, quite evident in the clan's yearly get-togethers (see *Quodlibet*). Bach himself, eighteen years old, was censored during his stay as organist in Arnstadt (1703–1707) for a flagrant misdeed: His superiors were outraged to note that their young organist "had gone to the wine cellar during the Sunday service." It has also been recorded that shortly after his marriage to Maria Barbara (October 17, 1707), Bach twice bought a considerable amount of Rhine wine, albeit achieving by this wholesale purchase a reduced rate (reflecting his characteristic parsimony).

Even during Bach's tenure as cantor of the Thomaskirche in Leipzig (1723–1750), beer seems to have been a staple of his household. In a letter to a young cousin, Bach holds out special praise for *Gose*, a Leipzig specialty—beer brewed by quick fermentation. Quantities of this potion must have always been kept ready in the Bach household, which was well known for its warm hospitality.

Beer-drinking was especially attractive to Bach because as a church official he was exempt from the beer tax. In 1732, he received a refund for the tax he had previously paid on three barrels purchased

This advertisement for a German wine is both a spoof and a welcome reminder of a more worldly side of the "Holy Cantor." Bach was indeed a wine-lover, and he seldom passed up the chance to add to his supply.

from a local brewery. Requests of reimbursement for wine delivered whenever he journeyed to another town for an organ inspection also appear regularly as items on "expense accounts" that he submitted after each trip. Typical is the 1724 statement he presented after he spent time in Gera, where he had been hired to appraise and play a newly installed organ. As a fee, he received 3 thalers (more than $300 in our money), plus 10 thalers for transportation and 7 thalers for wine. The latter amount seems rather generous and must have pleased the bibulous traveler.

No doubt Bach's love for wine was well known among his students and friends. They were ever anxious to show their affection by sending the master a new supply. This noble impulse had its problems in Germany, divided as it was into many small states and principalities, each one claiming taxing power for merchandise crossing its borders.

This troublesome fiscal problem is illustrated in a letter preserved in New York's Morgan Library, and at one time reprinted under the title *"Bach and Taxes."* This letter is addressed to his "Most Noble and Esteemed Cousin" (Johann Elias Bach). It also gives amusing evidence that Bach the wine-lover had to play second fiddle to Bach the parsimonious householder. Noting that the "noble gift" of a barrel of wine had arrived somewhat damaged, Bach's letter presents a detailed account of the costs involved in having the gift delivered: "carriage charges, 16 groschen; tip to the delivery man, 1 groschen; fee of the customs inspector, 1 groschen; inland duty, 5 groschen; general duty, 3 groschen." Since there were 24 groschen to a thaler, it had cost Bach more than $100 in today's money to claim the wine. Bach ended his acknowledgment rather blandly by asking the sender, his "honoured cousin," to "desist from further gifts" on account of the excessive local expenses.

The heaven-storming aspects of Bach's nature, especially in his mighty organ works, were offset contrapuntally by the realist in him, who never lost touch with the demands of his diurnal existence. To make and save a few extra thalers ranked high in his scheme of living—higher even than his evident enjoyment of beer and fine wine.

Quodlibet

The *quodlibet* ("whatever you want") was a well-established form of vocal improvisation in Bach's time. It arbitrarily juxtaposed various popular melodies for ensemble singing. This generally produced a somewhat disharmonious but hilarious "musical mish-mash."

Members of the Bach clan rejoiced in this form of musical fun-making. Once a year they gathered together in one of Thuringia's principal towns—Eisenach, Mühlhausen, or Erfurt—for a "cousins club" reunion. Most of these Bachs were cantors, organists, or town musicians. The celebration started, as Forkel tells us, with the singing of a chorale. But soon the beer began flowing liberally, and the merrymakers would start singing songs and *quodlibets* of a very worldly, even mildly sexual nature. Forkel notes that the musicians "not only laughed heartily at themselves but made those around them roar with laughter."

Although we have no report that Johann Sebastian attended one of these gatherings, he was deeply steeped in his tribe's traditions. Hence, the *quodlibet* remained a musical form that he occasionally utilized. The *Bach-Werke-Verzeichnis* (BWV) lists under BWV 524 a *quodlibet* written for the 1707 wedding of Johann Friedrich Fuchs and Salome Roemer.

He even made use of two *quodlibet* themes in his towering clavier work, the *Goldberg Variations* (see entry). These two melodies occur after the last variation of this masterwork, fugally intermixing musical quotations from the following German folk songs.

> *I have been away from you so long,*
> *come closer, closer, closer.*

and

> *Cabbage and turnips early and late.*
> *If my mother had cooked more meat,*
> *I would have stayed.*

A popular German *quodlibet,* an amusing improvisation based upon a folk tune. Bach ended his *Goldberg Variations*—a masterwork of the fugal art—with this popular ditty.

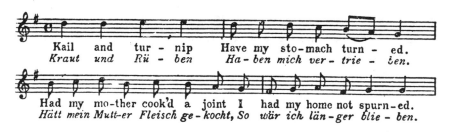

Kail and tur - nip Have my sto - mach turn - ed.
Kraut und Rü - ben Ha - ben mich ver - trie - ben.

Had my mo-ther cook'd a joint I had my home not spurn-ed.
Hätt mein Mutt-er Fleisch ge - kocht, So wär ich län - ger blie - ben.

Bach's use of the *quodlibet* in this manner shows perhaps his intent to relieve profound fugal composition—of which the *Goldberg Variations* are one of the supreme examples—with a light note of jest. As Wanda Landowska observed, "It seems that Bach, by ending his imposing work with a joyful *quodlibet,* meant to symbolize the patriarchal tradition which ran in his family from generation to generation," and, one may add, to which he remained bound throughout his life.

Radiant Masterwork

The *Thematic-Systematic Index of Bach's Works* (*Bach-Werke-Verzeichnis*, or BWV, 1950) is a book of some seven hundred pages, listing more than a thousand of the master's works. It stands to reason that not every entry is a winner. Nevertheless, the grandeur of Bach's *oeuvre* never ceases to amaze us. Is it presumptuous or even futile, therefore, to select but one of Bach's works and mark it as his "ultimate achievement"? I hope this is not the case, for I have long settled upon my own personal favorite among Bach's works, and hereby nominate the *St. Matthew Passion* for this distinction.

Admittedly, my nominee may be put forth with a tinge of prejudice. I have listened to Bach's *St. Matthew Passion* innumerable times, beginning very far back—in 1913. My acquaintance with this radiant masterwork began in the Bach town of Leipzig, when I was ten years old and a member of the boy's chorus of the Thomaskirche. Since then, each hearing of the *St. Matthew Passion*—be it in live performance or via recording—has reinforced my judgment.

Of course, in holding this opinion, I find myself in the best of company. Bach himself seems to have looked upon the *St. Matthew Passion* as his ultimate achievement—even considering his great summation works: the *Musical Offering* and *Art of the Fugue* (see *Summation Works*). During each of the creative periods of his life, Bach would focus on one specific field of music-making: e.g., the organ in Weimar; the orchestra and the harpsichord in Cöthen; cantatas during his first few years in Leipzig. (See *Universality*.) But he seems to have worked on the *St. Matthew Passion* at various times, if not indeed all the time, from his Weimar days (1708–1717) until very late in his life.

The Crucifixion by Albrecht Dürer. Bach's *St. Matthew Passion* is a powerful drama whose music recounts the death and burial of Christ.

The text of the *St. Matthew Passion* recounts the fateful events of Jesus' earthly mission between the Last Supper and His Crucifixion and burial. Bach translated this, "the greatest story ever told," into a music drama of truly Aeschylean proportion. To do so, he employed a musical force of unprecedented size and penetrating power: two choruses (supplemented by a boys' chorus in the opening movement), two organs, two orchestras, a harpsichord, and five vocal soloists. The awesome and noble structure of this work has been rightly compared to the structure of a great medieval cathedral—both of them triumphs of human faith.

The *Passion's* opening itself is a mighty display of vocal and instrumental forces. From this powerful opening onward, the work's eighty-two pieces project the full dimensions of the tragedy of Christ's death. In its last piece—Christ's burial—all of the tumultuous and tormenting passages that have preceded it are resolved in a mood of solace and deep peace.

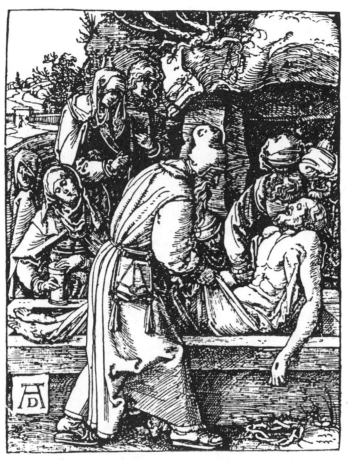

Laying Christ to rest—
the subject of the *St.
Matthew Passion's* final
movement, which
expresses a spirit of deep
peace and solace.

When the *St. Matthew Passion* was first performed in the Leipzig
Thomaskirche on Good Friday, 1729, its impact was extraordinarily
powerful, but profoundly disturbing. Many members of the congregation—which was said to have included numerous clergymen and
noblewomen—seem to have reacted with a sense of shock, if not
dismay. A report about this premier, which appeared three years after
the event, stated: "When this theatrical music began...people were
thrown into the greatest bewilderment...and said: 'What will come of
this?' An old widow of the nobility said: 'God save us, my children! It's
just as one were at an opera-comedy.'"

The greatness and nobility of the *St. Matthew Passion* clearly
escaped Bach's contemporary audience, but it is these qualities that
have lifted it into the realm of Bach's ultimate masterwork. As the
English music critic Jamie James observed: "If such a thing exists as
divine inspiration—this must be an instance of it."

Bach himself was not encouraged by the reception of his

masterwork, in whose creation he had expended all the psychic and physical energy of his genius. The Leipzig city clerk, Andreas Bienengräber, visited Cantor Bach on March 17, 1731, and must have queried him: "What about a *Passion* performance this coming Good Friday?" The Clerk reported Bach's sour reaction to the Town Council: "He [Bach] did not care, for he got nothing out of it anyway... and it was only a burden."

For all practical purposes, the *St. Matthew Passion* was forgotten after Bach's death—until 1829. A century after its first performance, the Berlin Singakademie, under the direction of the twenty-year-old Felix Mendelssohn, presented it in a glorious revival (see entry). This work has today become—through innumerable performances—the symbol of all that Bach sought to achieve through his genius and his faith.

Recycling

Burdened throughout most of his life with obligations and deadlines, Bach became an adept borrower of melodic material—from his predecessors, from his contemporaries, and from himself. This practice was known at the time as "parodying" and was a widely practiced compositional technique.

Composers were unhampered by copyright laws, so most of them helped themselves freely to musical ideas found in the work of their confrères. The music historian Donald J. Grout has noted that in Handel's *Israel in Egypt* "sixteen out of thirty-nine numbers employ themes—often entire movements—snatched from other composers." This practice of musical piracy was so commonplace that it was scarcely even commented upon. Since almost everyone did it, a well-known composer was as likely to *be* copied as he was to copy someone else.

Bach used this method of "parodying" the work of others far more subtly than many of his contemporaries. He merged borrowed material with his own ideas, generally ending up with a piece of a higher order—more sophisticated, more animated, and rhythmically more daring.

Typical of the many works he absorbed, transmuted, recast, and vivified are the Vivaldi *Violin Concertos Op. 12*, which he converted into keyboard works for two, three, and four harpsichords. In the process, he added so much vitality and rhythmic thrust to the original scores that we rightly consider these works to be Bach's very own (see *Vivaldi*).

More startling still is the technique of borrowing from his own works in order to meet the needs of a current assignment, especially if Bach was faced with a tight deadline (see *Gebrauchsmusik*). In his mind, good music was adaptable to any purpose, secular or sacred—a philosophy that served him well. In his crowded schedule, Bach often found himself hard put for time to develop ideas that were totally original. His solution, often, was to borrow from his own works, usually secular pieces composed earlier, upon which he could draw for inspiration and adaptation.

In 1733, for example, he had composed a cantata celebrating the birthday of the Queen of Saxony (see *Ye Trumpets Resound*). The exultation Bach expressed in this musical tribute was easily retextured the next year into a passage asserting humankind's joy at the birth of Christ—an aria included in his five-part, three-hour *Christmas Oratorio*.

Another prime example of such "self-parody" can be traced in Bach's *Hunting Cantata* (The Hunt Is My Delight), composed for the birthday of the duke of Weissenfels in 1713 (see *Wanderlust*). Bach—in his late twenties at the time—is said to have used the cantata again in its entirety the following year for the birthday of another duke, with just a change in name. He was to further reuse its opening aria in a later pentecostal cantata—a strictly religious piece—where it appears as the endearing melody *Mein Gläubiges Herze* (My Heart Believing).

Bach's secular *Hunting Cantata* was also to furnish themes both for the melody of *Air on the G-String* and for the chorale prelude, *Jesu, Joy of Man's Desiring* (which became a much-beloved perennial in a piano version recorded by Dame Myra Hess). Reusage of secular pieces in Bach's church compositions gave the latter works at times an unexpected worldly air, an upbeat character that helped to revitalize the weekly or holiday service (see *Instruments to the Fore*).

One reason Bach was able to recast themes previously developed in earlier works was his disciplined sense of order, an unfailing characteristic throughout his life. In modern terms, we would say that he kept a well-organized scrap file. From time to time, some of his students or colleagues tried to borrow a score from Bach's own archive, be it for study or performance. He apparently granted these requests for a while. But he must have changed his mind, since his trusted helper, Johann Elias Bach, had to tell one inquirer, "The capellmeister will not allow the score to go out of his hands, because he already lost many things in this way."

Bach became as parsimonious in musical matters as he had always been in money matters (see entry)—clearly, he did not believe in wasting good material. He kept his "scrap file" in impeccable order, for ready reference. When he had written something that especially pleased him, he returned to it and recycled it in the form of a "parody," with rarely a seam showing. To apply a modern metaphor: The master never threw away his good oranges without giving them an extra squeeze.

Revival

On March 11, 1829, an event took place in the halls of Berlin's Singakademie that seemed "like the opening of the gate of a long-closed temple." Bach's *St. Matthew Passion*, first performed in 1729 and forgotten for almost a century, was heard again. This was a truly daring venture, spearheaded by the twenty-year-old Felix Mendelssohn. Close to a hundred years had passed since Bach's death, a period that had not dealt kindly with the master's memory. Not only the *St. Matthew Passion*, but most of Bach's stupendous output had faded from public consciousness, as the art of the fugue gave way to Art Galant (see entry).

With the beginning of the nineteenth century and the dawn of the Romantic era, conditions seemed favorable for a Bach revival. The long reign of the Age of Enlightenment (see *Zeitgeist*) had ended in the horrors of the French Revolution and the Napoleonic Wars. In the aftermath of these epic events, the cultural impulse, which previously had tended toward cold rationalism, now showed renewed interest in man's deeper feelings, including religious contemplation and romantic love. The times called forth an emotionalism that was akin to the spirituality and introspection that Bach had embraced a century earlier. Hence, this change in the *Zeitgeist* brought Bach's music into a prominence considerably greater than it had enjoyed in his own age.

Even in the years of his neglect, Bach had always had his admirers, especially among his former students, many of them now settled in Berlin. These dedicated musical missionaries eventually kindled a wave of enthusiasm for Bach that helped to restore the master to his rightful place in the world of music. Besides young Mendelssohn, Karl Friedrich Zelter, founder of Berlin's Singakademie, was a leader of this movement (see *Goethe and Bach*).

It was perhaps fated that Zelter and Mendelssohn (his star pupil) would one day collaborate on the revival of one of Bach's acknowledged masterworks. When Felix was only ten years old, his grandmother had presented him with the *St. Matthew Passion*, copied from a manuscript that Zelter had acquired earlier at an auction.

To perform this great work one day gradually became, during the succeeding years, an exciting vision in the young genius's mind. But Zelter, much as he might have liked to undertake such a bold venture, felt it was too overwhelming a task to tackle and urged Mendelssohn to give up the idea. At eighteen years of age, Felix was already a world-renowned virtuoso and composer, and his passionate enthusiasm succeeded in winning Zelter over. The task was indeed a formidable one, as Zelter had feared. Simply to train the chorus of the Singakademie to perform the *Passion* took almost two years.

Young Felix Mendelssohn, who in 1829 realized his long-held dream of presenting Bach's *St. Matthew Passion*. The performance at the Berlin Singakademie—a hundred years after the *Passion's* first performance, led by Bach—helped to spark a revival of interest in his works.

Mendelssohn felt it was necessary to bring the work more in line with current tastes. To this very young musician, Bach's work seemed far too long, and overloaded with Baroque ornamentation. The tempo and dynamic markings that Mendelssohn neatly penciled into his conducting score were designed to infuse the *Passion* with the highly-charged emotionalism of the Romantic era.

In his preparations for the great day, Mendelssohn had the energetic backing of one of his close friends, Philipp Eduard Devrient (1801–1877), a prominent actor who had offered to sing the role of Christ in the planned performance. At one time, as Devrient reported in his memoirs, the two spoke of "the strange chance that just a hundred years had to pass...before this *St. Matthew Passion* would again see the light." "And to think," Felix added with a smile, "that it would take an actor [Devrient] and a Jew to revive this greatest of Christian musical creations."

The announcement of the great event caused a stir within Berlin society, thanks to the work of many volunteers and newfound friends of the Bachian cause. The nearly one thousand seats of the Sing-akademie quickly sold out, while over a thousand more music-lovers pleaded in vain for tickets. Mendelssohn's sister, Fanny, later remarked that when the great day arrived, the hall had "all the air of a church... the most solemn devotion pervaded the whole.... Never have I felt a holier solemnity vested in a congregation than on that evening." In the audience were members of the Prussian royal family and the town's intellectual leaders, including the philosopher Georg Friedrich Hegel, who would later discuss Bach's music in his university lectures.

The performance, with Mendelssohn conducting from the piano, left an unforgettable impression on the audience. Those who had witnessed the event quickly spread the news of Bach's rediscovery. This surely was in sharp contrast to Bach's first performance of the *St. Matthew Passion* in 1729, which received such a shocked and disapproving response that it probably was never staged again during the composer's lifetime (see *Radiant Masterwork*).

The Berlin performance of 1829 had to be repeated ten days later,

Choral singers in rehearsal. The Romantic era, marked by a heightened emotionalism, saw a renewed interest in vocal music, including Bach's choral works.

when it was sold out again, with other cities quickly following suit. The number of performances and the study of this work—as well as the publication of other Bachian works—steadily increased throughout the nineteenth century. Mendelssohn's revival of Bach and his *St. Matthew Passion* in Berlin had truly opened the gate to the wondrous Bachian temple that had till then been shut tight.

Rhetorician

There is a certain satisfaction in being able to identify almost immediately the composer of a musical work we chance to hear. Somehow, Bach's music always permits instant recognition. Its beat, structure, and decisive melody shows the inimitable hand of the master, and we can smilingly declare, "Bach! Who else?"

Bach himself would probably have been hard put to explain his music's attraction—its characteristic beat and style. By all accounts, he was emphatically a practicing musician not given to theorizing, a fact often bemoaned by his contemporaries (see *Theory and Practice*). Still, it was the age-old theory of *rhetoric* that guided Bach to compose as he did, marking his style from early on in his career.

A composer guided by this ancient doctrine believed that for music to reach its hearers, and properly affect them, it should follow the three-part rule proposed by the rhetoricians of antiquity. First, state your thesis clearly and attractively (*declarare*). Second, vary what you have said, exploring your thesis from different angles (*explorare*), making your audience understand the argument you have advanced. Third, return again to what you have stated at the beginning, so as to drive home your main argument with the force of repetition (*repetitio*). These rules, it was held, also applied to music, which could be seen in essence as "singing rhetoric" (*klingende Rede*).

Bach was a firm believer in these classic rules. Thus, he begins most of his creations—and he wrote thousands of them—with a clear and simple statement, a musical thesis which, upon hearing, we can readily perceive. He then elaborates on this thesis, lets it resound in different variations, always related to the initial thesis, to which he returns by way of a musical round-trip. This may take twelve measures as in one of the little marches written for his children's instruction, or two-hundred-plus measures as in a choral or orchestral composition.

Greek orator addressing the citizenry. Bach became acquainted with the principles of rhetoric during his early education, sparse as it was.

Even in so majestic a work as the *St. Matthew Passion*, Bach intones at the outset a simple, concise melody—a *dispositio* ("this is what we are going to talk about"). No matter how elaborate the variations which follow—the musical trip he has prepared for us, be it pilgrimage or joyride—Bach always returns to this basic starting point. It is the rhetorical structure upon which Bach built his music that makes it instantly recognizable.

How can we account for the fact that Bach, when composing, followed these rhetorical principles? Did Bach, always busy, ever have the time to study the classic Latin rhetoricians, such as Cicero and Seneca? Although he did not have a university education, the lack of which he always regretted, the schooling he had received in his youth at the gymnasium in his home town, Eisenach, and the Lyceum in Ohrdruf were impressive in their strict adherence to the ancient tradition (see *Education*). Records preserved from both schools indicate that young Bach had received instruction in the classical *trivium*: grammar, rhetoric, and logic. He had even earned credit for studying Cicero's *De Oratore*, a classic of rhetorical literature.

While composing, Bach the practicing musician may rarely have had time to think of Cicero. Nevertheless, his pen was guided unconsciously by the rhetorical principles he had imbibed as a youth. These principles provided that unique logic and conclusiveness which are the hallmarks of Bach's music—and the means by which it can be instantly recognized, even by the casual listener.

Rhythm

Bach's contemporary and colleague at Leipzig's Thomasschule, Rector J. M. Gesner, once saw the Herr Cantor conducting and was stunned by the speed and briskness of his tempos, which seemed to be reflected in Bach's agitated movements. "The rhythm seems to take hold of his limbs," Gesner observed.

The rhythms Bach applied in both his sacred and secular works are as a rule inventive and at times daring, in contrast to the restrained rhythm prevalent in the works of his predecessors. A restless stir is often to be noticed in Bach's works. The music both of his contemporaries and of his predecessors sounds simplistic when compared to Bach's, so full of rhythmic wizardry. The Bach biographer Charles S. Terry observed that the master unhesitatingly introduced rhythm into staid church music, thereby injecting it "with the dynamism of his own personality." Terry also noted that the "genuine" church composer of that age had "an uneasy suspicion of rhythm" and thus did not "dare to open his soul to it." That Bach at times did so is a measure of his genius.

We only have to hear one or two measures of a piece of music to recognize the Bach touch. The assertive beat gives us a sense of security—the certainty that even after many convolutions we will be led back to a logical finale (see *Rhetorician*).

Bach's music, secular and sacred, is often music to march by, whether in tempos slow or fast. In 1840, Mendelssohn confirmed this effect while preparing for a concert to raise funds for a new Bach monument in Leipzig (see *The Last Bach*). He had been practicing for a week on the organ of the Thomaskirche. Afterward, he confessed that he couldn't walk along the street without falling into the rhythm of Bach's pedal passages.

Secretiveness

Bach did not like to comment on his own music or recount the events of his life. At various times, Johann Mattheson, a respected music journalist of this time, invited him to provide biographical data for publication in the *Musical Honor Arch* (*Ehren-Pforte*), the musical *Who's Who* of the day. Bach ignored the requests. He also beseeched his son, Carl Philipp Emanuel, to be at pains not to provide the world with anecdotes of his early adventures. As the son observed, his father had voiced "unreasonable objections to giving an accurate and systematic account of his life."

When asked to explain his art, Bach used subterfuge to deflect attention from himself. Typical in this regard was his purported reaction to the praise he received after one of his majestic organ performances. "There is nothing to it," the master is said to have declared disarmingly. "It is just a matter of touching the right key at the right time. The organ does the rest." His refusal to get involved in a discussion of his work is shared by many artists, who are determined to preserve the mystical aura of their creativity.

Not only did Bach refuse to reveal biographical data, he seemed very reluctant to have his portrait painted (camera-shy, we would call him today). The only fully authenticated portrait we have of him is the one that Elias Gottlieb Haussmann produced in 1747, three years before the master's death at the age of sixty-five. It was probably commissioned by Lorenz C. Mizler, a highly active commentator who headed the Society of the Musical Sciences. This was an exclusive and highly prestigious club that admitted to its ranks only a small number of musicians and composers. Once chosen, a new member had to submit a sampling of his compositional skills and also a portrait (see *Numerology*).

It is this Haussmann painting that was used in the mid-1800s to identify Bach's skeletal remains—which in turn served a decade later as the basis of Leipzig's world-famous Bach monument (see *Skull*).

Skull

The end of Bach's life is not lacking in macabre elements. The man who had given endlessly to Leipzig and the world was treated badly by the town fathers even after his death (see *Leipzig Ordeal*). Bach's demise was hardly noted or commented upon in the local press. A mere two sentences pronounced from the pulpit of the Thomaskirche, a church he had served with zeal—was all that marked his passing.

Even Bach's interment on Friday, July 31, 1750, seems to have attracted few mourners beyond the members of his immediate family. In contrast, when Beethoven passed away in 1827, the citizenry of Vienna followed his coffin by the thousands, the largest funeral procession the city had ever seen.

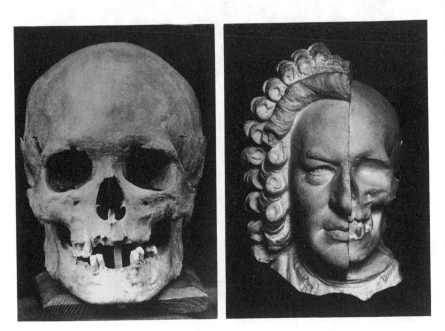

Bach's skull was recovered more than a century after his burial in an unmarked grave in Leipzig's Johanneskirche cemetery. The 1885 centennial of his birth led to a search for his remains, which were found in an oak coffin and transferred to the Thomaskirche that he had once served so faithfully.

A bust of Bach's head—reconstructed in 1898 from his skull—by the noted Leipzig sculptor Carl Seffner. It matched with great fidelity the authentic portrait by E. G. Haussmann, then in the C. F. Peters Music Library.

A Bach monument by
Carl Seffner, erected in
1908, dominates the
churchyard of the
Thomaskirche. Close by
are the headquarters and
museum of the Neue
Bach-Gesellschaft, a
mecca for Bach lovers.

In truth, Bach had been fading from the scene during his final years. He was snubbed by the town's officialdom, which had already interviewed a potential replacement. And he was considered to be outdated as a composer by the new generation of music-lovers, already attached to the Art Galant style of music (see *Art Galant*). Increasingly blind, Bach had turned inward, devoting himself to the last of his great summation works, the *Art of the Fugue* (see *Summation Works*).

Still, one would have expected that a musician of Bach's stature would have been given, at the least, an honored resting place in the Thomaskirche's burial ground. Instead, his remains were interred in one of three anonymous coffins grouped together in the cemetery of the humble suburban Johanneskirche, out on the eastern limits of town. Not even a modest memorial plaque marked Bach's last resting place. For more than a century, no one knew of the exact location of his grave—and no one, it seems, much cared.

The bicentennial of Bach's birth in 1885 revived an interest in the question of his grave's location. If its precise site was unknown, tradition placed it six paces from the church's south door. Also, it was known that, in contrast with others who died in his time, Bach had been buried in an oaken coffin. After three days of fruitless digging, such a coffin was found, containing the skeleton of an elderly man— well proportioned, of medium height, with massive skull and heavy jaws.

At this point, Professor William His, head of the anatomy section of Leipzig University, was called in for consultation. He and his associates conducted extensive research in an attempt to relate the skeletal finds to a copy of the Bach portrait by E. G. Haussmann, which was in the possession of Leipzig's C. F. Peters Music Library. In these efforts, Dr. His was greatly helped by the town's leading sculptor, Carl Seffner, who was asked to create a bust of Bach, based upon the rediscovered skull. The result was startling. The bust Seffner produced matched with unmistakable fidelity the Haussmann portrait.

A decade later, Seffner was assigned by the city to create a Bach monument to replace the rather humble memorial erected in 1847 at the suggestion of Mendelssohn. Seffner's monument to Bach today dominates the Thomaskirche's courtyard, with the headquarters and museum of the Neue Bachgesellschaft close by. It has become the site of pilgrimages by an ever-growing circle of Bach-lovers from the world over.

Songs of Faith

Chorales

Music was a strong element in the Protestant religion from its inception. Martin Luther himself was a fine lutist, who loved to gather his family together to join him for an "evening sing." Luther once declared: "Music is a gift of God. It removes from the heart the weight of sorrow and the fascination of evil thoughts." Given this predilection, it is no wonder that music was to play such a prominent role in the liturgy of the religion he founded.

Luther's use of music to accompany prayer established a new means of addressing the Almighty. In the Catholic ritual, it was the priest who was called upon to intercede with God. But Luther believed that every mortal soul could appeal directly to the Almighty. And the Creator would be more inclined to mercy, so the Lutheran theory held, if He was addressed through the medium of music—"the language of God to which angels dance."

In Luther's day, the chorale, a communal song of faith, became a special source of courage for Protestantism, a young and struggling religious movement. The faith's early adherents were to find strength in joining together to sing their hymns of belief, at times defiantly. Foremost and best loved among Luther's vocal confessionals was *Eine Feste Burg ist Unser Gott* (A Mighty Fortress Is Our God). Heinrich Heine was to call it "the *Marseillaise* of Lutheranism."

Luther adapted some of his chorales from popular, even folksy, songs whose themes and moods varied widely. At times, they shouted forth a common plea for help; at other moments, they expressed a more submissive mood, giving voice to the sinners' hope for mercy. The healing power of music was greatly enhanced by the fact that these chorales were "we songs." The individual—pleader or sinner—gained strength in being a part of the congregation, united in lyrical appeal to the Almighty. Joining voices and sharing faith provided great solace to these believers and assuaged their sense of isolation.

There can be no doubt that Johann Sebastian Bach became the quintessential musical representative of Lutheranism: his chorales preached—in music. It was a position Bach attained through both personal conviction and family heritage. Three generations of Bach

church organists had faithfully performed chorales for each Sunday service. At fifteen years of age, young Sebastian, a fine singer, was already earning a living at the Michaeliskirche in Lüneburg (see *Education*). There he probably acquired an excellent knowledge of chorales and a lifelong loyalty to the teachings they conveyed. Such chorales were to become the bedrock of his mighty corpus—371 of them, according to the collection that his son, Carl Philipp Emanuel, published between 1784 and 1787, more than three decades after his father's death. (A series of heretofore unknown Bach chorale preludes was discovered in 1982 by Harvard Professor Christoph Wolff in the Yale Library.)

The very first works credited to Bach were chorale preludes. And it is perhaps not incidental that his final creation was a chorale that Bach—blind and on his deathbed—dictated to his son-in-law and star pupil, J. C. Altnikol (*Before Thy Throne I Stand*). This chorale was added by Carl Philipp Emanuel to the unfinished manuscript of the *Art of the Fugue* to help overcome the fragmentary character of this final Bach masterwork (see *Summation Works*). A great many of Bach's

Martin Luther, a fine lutist, provides the music for a hymn sung by his children. Luther made music a basic element of the religion he founded. And Bach would become the foremost representative of Protestant church music.

Chorus and instrumentalists performing a chorale under the leadership of the church's pastor. Bach was a pioneer in providing strong instrumental support to the chorale, a highly expressive "song of faith." Bach's chorale preludes for the organ are among his most inventive works.

approximately two hundred surviving sacred cantatas resound with a chorale—consoling, admonishing, and stirring the believer. Similarly, chorales form the high point of Bach's Passions, oratorios, and motets. In the *St. Matthew Passion*, the most touching elements generally are the chorales, which comment on the tragic events, point to a moral, and give voice to heartrending pity (see *Radiant Masterwork*).

Once, when Robert Schumann played a Bach chorale prelude for Mendelssohn, the latter confessed, "The melody seemed interlaced with garlands of gold, evoking in me the thought: were life deprived of all trust, all faith, this chorale would restore it in me." Among the most popular of the Bach works available to us today are the recorded

Leipzig trumpeters intone Bach's *New Year's Chorale* from the tower of the Thomaskirche. (ca. 1910). These midnight performances seemed truly magical to the author when he was a young boy. They made him a Bach-lover for life. *Courtesy of Underwood & Underwood, New York City*

piano versions of various chorale preludes performed by artists such as Ferruccio Busoni and Dame Myra Hess.

Perhaps it is admissible for the writer, by now revealed as an ardent advocate of Bach's music, to recall an event that brings to mind the immense power that Bach chorales can have even on a child, especially one fortunate enough to be born right in the center of Leipzig's "Bach country." As I related it recently in my autobiography (*Picture Man*): "On New Year's Eve, my parents had made it a habit of inviting their friends. As the midnight hour approached, the guests grabbed their hats and coats and rushed to our expansive balcony facing the Thomaskirche. The city lay in almost total darkness, but as the church bells chimed twelve, as if by magic, the church's top lighted up and seemed suspended in mid air. Without delay the town's trumpeters began to intone Bach's *New Year's Chorale*:

> *The old year now has passed away*
> *For this we thank you Lord today*
> *That thou has kept us through the year*
> *When danger and distress were near.*

It was a scene that became imbedded deeply in my youthful mind and made me a Bach lover for life."

Summation Works

In the last decade before his death in 1750, Bach took on the task of editing and finalizing much that he had produced during his years of intense creative labor. In the process, he became the builder of musical superstructures which he could pass on to posterity as a legacy—the essence of his mighty achievement.

All through his career, Bach had applied himself to the tasks of the day and had done so with an unwavering sense of duty. But there

Portrait of Bach in his last years, when he was withdrawing more and more from his official duties, turning instead to the inner needs of his genius. The great works of these last years represent a final summing up of Bach's art.

also had always existed another force in his psyche—the yearning to transcend the daily routine and to produce works that were summations of his art, self-contained anthologies. Moreover, Bach had a mania for completeness and for organization. "He would not suffer anything that was half-finished, unfocussed, impure," one of his contemporaries, C. F. Crämer, observed. In Bach's enormous *oeuvre*, few unfinished, fragmentary compositions can be found.

This urge to build complete musical structures is discernable even in some of Bach's earlier works, such as the *Well-Tempered Clavier*. In this work, Bach utilized eleven fugues and preludes he had previously included in the *Clavier-Büchlein* assembled for the instruction of his oldest son, Wilhelm Friedemann, in 1720. Bach expanded these germinal pieces, adding to them until he had produced twenty-four preludes and fugues, written in every major and minor key. The first volume was completed in 1722, before Bach left Cöthen, and he repeated the feat with a second volume in 1744. Even in this latter volume, he developed preludes and fugues from pieces he had written more than two decades earlier. The "Forty-eight" have remained an unsurpassed fugal masterwork and have been rightly called "a total library of human emotions," or, as Schumann said, "the daily bread of the piano student."

Urged on by a similar striving for unification and summation within each musical form that he explored, Bach had retrieved (from the archive of his manuscripts) a *Kyrie* and *Gloria*, which he had combined and sent to Dresden in 1733 in quest of a post at the court of Elector Friedrich August II (see *Catholicism*). To these compositions he added, in the ensuing years, other sections of the Mass, some previously written and some newly composed, to complete the supreme and sublime structure of the *B Minor Mass*.

The *St. Matthew Passion*, first performed in Leipzig in 1729, was also reworked and burnished anew in later years (see *Radiant Masterwork*). And he seems to have even improved upon the earlier *St. John Passion*, first performed in 1724. Gerhard Herz, a leading Bach authority and the author of *Bach Sources in America* (1984), has observed: "It is touching to see the aging master attach meticulously newly written half pages to the worn marginal borders of the opening movement of the *St. Matthew Passion*, or to see his fingers stiff with cramps and arthritis revising a passage in the *St. John Passion*."

Bach's increasing tendency to revise, finalize, and consolidate works previously written hardly indicates that his creative powers were at the time in decline, forcing him to focus upon his earlier works. On the contrary, it was his fully matured creative genius that Bach now brought to bear—still impelled by the resilient spring of his ambition—as he turned from works written for performance to works that summarized his art in abstract terms. This is analogous to the aging painter who abandons his involvement with swirls of color and turns to a stark black-and-white medium in order to focus attention upon his most fundamental artistic statement, stripped of all the crowd-pleasing chromatic distractions.

Thus, in the last three years of his life, Bach was to produce two of his great "summation works"—the *Musical Offering* (1747), written as a tribute to Frederick the Great (see entry); and the *Art of the Fugue*, left incomplete upon his death in 1750. The latter was clearly meant to be a recapitulation of Bach's fundamental creative themes and techniques.

Glenn Gould—arguably the greatest interpretor and executor of Bach's keyboard works in recent times—has well characterized Bach's

The last notes of the thousands Bach wrote in his lifetime: the abrupt ending of the *Art of the Fugue*. As he died, Bach—now blind—was dictating his final chorale to his son-in-law and star student, Johann Christoph Altnikol.

later years of harvest: "Despite monumental proportions, an aura of withdrawal pervades their works. Bach was withdrawing from the pragmatic concerns of music-making into an idealized world of uncompromised invention." These final works of grandeur emerge as building blocks of a transcendent structure—nothing less than the summing up of Bach's life and art.

Telemann

One of the remarkable qualities noted by many of his contemporaries was Bach's total lack of professional jealousy. To "improve his art" was a primary impulse throughout his career. Wherever he found guidance or inspiration serving this end, he accepted it and absorbed it without hesitation and false pride. This impulse prevailed even in his unselfish relationships with other composers, though lesser men might have viewed the accomplishments or public acceptance of their fellow artists with a tinge of jealousy.

Among Bach's immediate colleagues, Georg Philipp Telemann (1681–1767), certainly ranked the highest—higher than the Leipzig cantor—on the scale of musical acclaim. Yet Bach's relationship with this quicksilver musician always remained friendly and cordial. Though Telemann was only four years older than Bach, as a young man he had held important positions in Leipzig and in the court of the prince of Sorau. Close relations were established between the two musicians during a three-year period when Bach was organist to Duke Wilhelm Ernst of Weimar (1708–1717) and Telemann worked nearby in Bach's hometown of Eisenach, as capellmeister of the ducal court to which Bach's father had been loosely connected.

During this period, Telemann became the godfather of Bach's second son, Carl Philipp Emanuel. This act of friendship took on a somewhat symbolic significance when Carl Philip Emanuel became a major proponent of Art Galant as it reached its height in the mid-eighteenth century, a musical style of which Telemann had been the German pioneer during the prior decades. Indeed, when Telemann died—seventeen years after Bach and after a laudable reign as music

Georg Philipp Telemann was highly popular with the music-loving public of the day. Bach maintained friendly relations with this talented, facile composer, who became the godfather of Bach's son, Carl Philipp Emanuel. *Courtesy of Deutsche Staatsbibliotek, Bildarchiv Preussischer Kulturbesitz*

director of the churches of Hamburg—Carl Philipp Emanuel became his successor.

The friendship between Telemann and the elder Bach seems even more remarkable when one considers that their compositional and personal styles were very different. Bach's serious, erudite manner prevailed even in his worldly music, with nobility in every line. In sharp contrast were Telemann's often carelessly composed, at times trivial, creations, characterized by an easy melodic line. So effortless did Telemann's art seem, that later generations denigrated him as lacking in depth and originality. But in the first half of the eighteenth century, Telemann's lively and upbeat music was infinitely more popular than Bach's. Telemann was published widely, whereas Bach was published hardly at all (see *Music Publisher*).

Telemann's productivity was of staggering proportions, even measured against Bach's enormous output. This prolific composer was said to have produced twelve complete cycles of church music, forty operas, and over six hundred instrumental pieces. Robert Schumann once quoted Telemann as claiming, "A proper composer should be able to set a placard to music."

Given the nature of Telemann's creations, one may wonder if Bach could truly find inspiration in that vast corpus. Yet there are indications that Telemann's compositions held strong interest for Bach. The Leipzig cantor seems to have included some of his colleague's work in his study library of compositions. When Telemann's flute quartets were published in Paris in 1738, Bach's name appeared among the subscribers.

But Telemann clearly returned Bach's esteem and respect, holding the Leipzig cantor in high regard. He paid Bach a touching and poetic tribute at his death.

> *Then sleep! The candle of thy fame ne'er low will burn;*
> *The pupils thou hast trained, and those they train in turn*
> *Prepare thy future crown of glory brightly glowing.*

In this same poem, however, Telemann's prophetic powers went a bit astray. He predicted that the master's "true worth" would be revealed to future generations through the work of his "worthy son"— referring to Carl Philipp Emanuel. Within a century, of course, the grandeur of the Leipzig cantor's rediscovered corpus of work would almost totally eclipse the former glory both of his son and of his friend and eulogizer, Georg Philipp Telemann.

Theory and Practice

Bach was totally committed to his craft as both a performer and a composer: he was a practitioner, not a theorist. His near-total involvement with the practice of music left him little time to set down in writing (or to discuss with others) the basic tenets that guided his work. Nevertheless, the absence of a stated aesthetic should not lead us to believe that his work lacked a coherent theoretical basis.

Henry James once observed that while "the successful application of art is a delightful spectacle... there has never been a genuine success that has not had a latent core of conviction." Bach scholars have diligently studied the Leipzig cantor's incredible *oeuvre* in search of the master's "latent core of conviction"—those principles that give his works their unique logic, decisive structure, and instant recognizability (see *Rhetorician*). Is it possible, however, to reduce to dry theory the genius that infused Bach's music with its transcendant grandeur?

One may well ask why Bach aficionados should concern themselves with the principles that guided his pen. Why not just give oneself over to the joy and edification that listening to Bach's music provides? Yet there are distinct benefits to be gained by an insight into Bach's creative methodology. Knowledge of the goals he set for himself might lead to a deeper appreciation of the miracles he wrought. Freud wisely noted that our enjoyment of art can be greatly enhanced by a knowledge of *why* we enjoy it.

In the composition of the mighty works that Bach gave to the world, he did not draw only upon the amplitude of his inner wellsprings of creativity. Bach, like every artist, was also a man of his times, highly conscious of the cultural and intellectual currents of his day. This was an era that speculated endlessly about the nature of music, as it speculated about everything else, true to its proud boast of being the Age of Reason. Most of the contemporary theoreticians looked at music as an art serving practical purposes and performing a useful function in the life of the community. A typical tome on musical aesthetics appeared in 1690, when Bach was just fifteen years old: Wolfgang Kaspar Printz's *The Noble Art of Song and Sound*. This book devoted a mere three pages to the spiritual mission of music, but dedicated twenty-one to its indispensable role in the performance of horse ballet—a musical mentality very far removed from that of Bach.

Bach *was*, however, a transitional artist. In his driving inner force, he was one of the last artistic representatives of the Age of Faith, a man whose Lutheran zeal was fundamental and pure. But he also had a lively intellectual curiosity. Though not trained as a scholar, Bach was endowed with a scholar's inquiring mind, and he was no doubt familiar with the theories of music prevailing at his time.

One of Bach's faithful followers, Johann Philipp Kirnberger, made this comment on the master's failure to produce a treatise on music: "It is to be regretted that this great man never wrote anything theoretical about music and that his teachings have reached posterity only through his students." However, one shrewd commentator, writing shortly after Bach's death, had an apt riposte: "Our lately departed Bach did not go for deep theoretical speculations on music, but was all the stronger in the practice of the art."

Universality

B ach is a unique, perhaps even an overwhelming, phenomenon because of the innovative energy that he applied to all forms of music prevalent at his time. Both his predecessors and contemporaries, while highly productive, generally focused their efforts on one field: Palestrina excelled in church music; Lully was noted for opera and ballet; Corelli mostly cultivated chamber music and the violin; and Domenico Scarlatti was the harpsichord's supreme master.

In contrast, as the new *Grove Dictionary* observes, "Bach opened up new dimensions in virtually every department of music to which he turned—with the exception of opera, though even in this area his secular cantatas exhibit features that qualify them as harbingers of the genre's future." In each period of Bach's life, he seemed to bring his creative genius to bear on a different area of music, often urged on of course by varying professional assignments. After concentrating with great energy on composing works for one instrument or genre, he would move to another. Rarely did he return with quite the same intensity to a field he had previously explored in depth.

During Bach's Weimar years (1708–1717), he produced music which enormously expanded the range of what had been and could be accomplished on the organ, even though he was stuck with a rather inferior instrument. While at Prince Leopold's court in Cöthen (see *Anhalt-Cöthen*), clavier and chamber music moved to the center of Bach's attention. The result was an almost incredible outpouring of masterworks, including the *Brandenburg Concertos*, the *Well-Tempered Clavier, Part I*, and the *French Suites*.

Bach's first Leipzig years (1723–1727) as cantor of the Thomaskirche were unequalled in his furious application to the cantata, dictated by the need to provide music for the weekly Sunday church service (see *Hauptmusik*). Estimates indicate that Bach wrote the bulk of his two hundred surviving cantatas during a seven-year period between 1723 and 1730—and perhaps only thirty more during the remainder of his life.

After assuming the directorship of Leipzig's Collegium Musicum in 1729, Bach spent the next decade concentrating on secular music, most of which was created for the concerts of this group at Zimmermann's Coffeehouse. (See *Collegium Musicum*.) In this period, Bach turned his attention to secular cantatas—including the *Kaffee Kantate* (see entry), his stab at what we might today call an operetta—as well as a large variety of keyboard music and concertos.

Even in the later years of his creative career, Bach continued to set himself specific tasks. Easing out of his Leipzig cantorial obligations after 1740, Bach devoted his time mostly to the great works of his last years, including the *Musical Offering* and the *Art of the Fugue* (see *Summation Works*)—the transcendent recapitulation of Bach's enormously productive career.

Vienna Bach Circle

While Bach and his music were mostly forgotten by the general public after his death, there was one place where the Bachian fires were kept aflame—in Vienna, thanks to the missionary zeal of one man, Baron Gottfried van Swieten (1733–1803). As Austrian ambassador to Berlin in 1777, this deeply musical man had made contact with loyal students of Bach who had congregated in the Prussian capital. Among them was Bach's pupil, Johann Philipp Kirnberger (1721–1783), who is reported to have given the baron harpsichord lessons. No doubt the name of Bach often came up in the conversation of these two men, for Kirnberger had always looked upon Bach with veneration and had sung Bach's praises in many of his publications.

Baron van Swieten had also encountered the name of Johann Sebastian Bach in another connection—during a visit to the Prussian court of Frederick the Great, who by then was stooped from age and endless battles. At a certain point, the talk of the two men, both music enthusiasts, turned to "old Bach." The Prussian king still remembered the Leipzig cantor's visit to Potsdam some thirty years earlier. In fact, he started to sing aloud the "royal theme" that he had intoned for Bach—a theme that he had asked his guest to develop into an elaborate fugue. It apparently had escaped the royal memory that as a result of this request Bach had later created for him—and for humanity too—a truly majestic gift, the *Musical Offering*. (See *Frederick the Great*).

When Baron van Swieten left his Berlin post in 1777 and returned to Vienna, he must have been greatly inspired by the spirit of Bach, and was ready to spread the gospel. The salon he held every

GERARDUS LIB.BAR. VAN SWIETEN, ord. Sanct. Reg. Stephani Commend, August. Imperat. & Imperatric. a Consilus Archiat. Natus 7 Maji 1700. Obiit 18 Junii 1772.

Mozart, in a portrait made shortly after his arrival from Salzburg, became a member of Baron van Swieten's salon, "where nothing but Bach and Handl [sic] is played."

Baron Gottfried van Swieten, a one-time Austrian ambassador to the court of Frederick the Great, was a devotee of Bach's music. Through Sunday musicales with Mozart and Beethoven as soloists at his home in Vienna, the baron spread the gospel of Bach to the town's cultural elite.

Sunday in Vienna soon attracted the city's most important composers, among them Mozart and later the young Beethoven. In a letter of 1782, Mozart reported to his father on the Sunday musical matinées at the baron's home, where, he noted, nothing was played "but Handl [sic] and Bach." Though it was worlds away from his own style, Mozart must have been inspired by Bach's fugal masterpieces which he performed at the baron's matinees. When he went home, he started to write some fugues himself. Strangely, Mozart's wife, Constanze—by all records a rather trivial young lady—was very fond of the sturdy Bachian counterpoint. "She fell in love with fugues—thought them most artistic," Mozart reported. "She craved them the way a pregnant woman craves food."

More important, Mozart's visits to the van Swieten mansion were to have a decided influence upon his own work. Apparently as an exercise, he began to study some preludes and fugues from the *Well-Tempered Clavier*, turning some of them into trio and string quartet versions. Van Swieten must have given Mozart a handwritten copy of this Bach masterwork—a copy that he in turn had probably secured from his friend Carl Philipp Emanuel Bach. (No complete printed copies of this work were available until 1803.)

In 1789, Mozart attended a live performance of the Bach motet

Singet dem Herrn (Sing to the Lord a New Song) at the Thomaskirche in Leipzig—and was deeply stirred. "His whole soul seemed to be in his ears," a contemporary eyewitness reported. "This is something from which one can learn," Mozart exclaimed. Johann Friedrich Doles— who at the time was the Thomaskirche cantor—happened to be one of the rare Bach fans to be found among church musicians and supplied his famous guest with the vocal parts of this motet. Spreading out the manuscripts, Mozart studied them with great fascination.

Tragically, Mozart had but two more years to live, dying in 1791. Still, in his last and in some ways most profound musical pronouncement, *The Magic Flute*, he evoked a dithyramb to music that was very much in the spirit of Bach:

> *To music's power*
> *We pass gleefully*
> *Through death's gloomy night.*

Van Swieten, who survived Mozart by a dozen years, continued his musical soirées. After Mozart, a new star had risen. Ludwig van Beethoven had been reputed since his youth to be an outstanding performer of Bach's *Well-Tempered Clavier*. Indeed, his performances of this work in his native Bonn had started him upon his musical career. Once Beethoven was settled in Vienna in 1792, Haydn took him in tow, and Baron van Swieten warmly welcomed the young genius into his circle. In fact, Beethoven became the baron's star performer. As Anton Schindler reported in his *Biography of Ludwig van Beethoven* (Münster, 1840), the young genius had to play

Beethoven was already renowned as a performer of Bach's *Well-Tempered Clavier* when he settled in Vienna in 1792. He became a star performer at the salon of Baron van Swieten, often playing Bach's music long into the night.

long into the night to satisfy the old gentleman's "insatiable appetite for music." As a grand finale, Beethoven would be asked to add a half-dozen Bach fugues "by way of a final prayer." Beethoven dedicated his first symphony in 1800 to his great friend and fellow Bach aficionado, Gottfried van Swieten, who died in the same year.

Violinist

Most music-lovers would today identify Bach as the master composer for keyboard instruments, especially the organ and the harpsichord. Indeed, Charles Rosen, distinguished both as a virtuoso and a music historian, once stated, "Bach's clavier works reveal, with the greatest directness, the movement of his thoughts."

Yet, in Bach's work, the violin is in no way relegated to playing second fiddle. As a youth, Sebastian's musical training seems to have begun on the violin, and he remained a lover and player of this instrument all through his life. Bach's father, Ambrosius, was a town musician, which suggests that he had to be proficient on the violin, and probably on the trumpet as well (see *Hometown*). As was the custom of the Bach clan, young Sebastian would have received his first music lessons from his father, almost certainly on the violin.

There is no indication that Sebastian ever received any training from his father on the keyboard instruments. Indeed, the Bach household in Eisenach was sparse in its resources and strained to provide for the needs of eight children, of whom Sebastian was the youngest. It is unlikely that the family could have afforded a harpsichord. The present Bach House and Museum in Eisenach has made up for this lack with an impressive display of keyboard instruments.

Sebastian's training at the keyboard probably did not begin until after the death of his parents, when he had found refuge in the Ohrdruf home of his older brother, Johann Christoph (see *Education*). While Sebastian's studies in his brother's house emphasized the harpsichord, he had no doubt continued to cultivate the violin—perhaps self-taught—and had mastered the instrument by the time he was eighteen. It was then that he acquired his first professional position, as a court musician in Weimar, a post that required proficiency as a violin player.

Six years after Bach returned to Weimar in 1708 as court organist for Duke Wilhelm Ernst, he was also appointed concertmaster of the court orchestra, a position he hardly could have filled without marked skills on the violin. His growing interest in this instrument while in Weimar is also evidenced by his intense study of Vivaldi, the violin master *extraordinaire*.

A court violinist of Bach's day. While capellmeister at the court of Prince Leopold of Anthalt-Cöthen, Bach composed for visiting virtuosi a series of violin solos—bravura pieces such as the world-famous chaconne from the *Partita in D Minor*. *Courtesy of Archiv für Kunst und Geschichte*

Bach's next assignment—as court cappellmeister to Prince Leopold at Anhalt-Cöthen (see *Anhalt-Cöthen*)—yielded a rich harvest of concertos and solo works for strings. These were surely inspired in part by his patron's skill and pleasure at performing on the viola da gamba. But Bach played the violin and viola himself, which made him a more integral part of his orchestra. Leading his instrumentalists in this manner was surely more "participatory," the conductor physically joining his men rather than conducting from the harpsichord (the more conventional method of his day).

Aside from composing and conducting violin concertos in Cöthen, Bach was also engaged in exploring, and infinitely expanding, the range of works for solo violin. One motive for creating these latter works was undoubtedly the desire to provide suitable music for the virtuosi who regularly visited the culturally rich court of Prince Leopold. One of these was Bach's good friend Johann Georg Pisendel (1687–1755), a former student of Vivaldi. Stationed at the Dresden court, Pisendel visited Cöthen in 1719, ready to put his artistry on display—undoubtedly making use of music Bach had prepared for the occasion.

Violin works to this date were intended to display the violin's potential for evoking melodic beauty. Bach extended the instrument's range in a series of three sonatas and three partitas for solo violin, which he completed in 1720. The *Chaconne* of his second partita (in D minor)—made up of twenty-nine variations—is universally acknowledged as one of Bach's greatest, most imaginative works. To this day, it remains the ultimate test of violinistic virtuosity. Essentially, the violin was designed to produce simple, single-toned melodies, imitative of the human voice. Within the course of the *Chaconne*, however, the violinist finds himself confronted with intricate three- and four-note chords, in complex chordal passages that vastly extend the range of this instrument.

For the violinist of Bach's time—such as Pisendel—Bach's innovations did not, perhaps, present an unsurmountable problem. The violin bow then in use was curved and loosely strung, enabling the performer to touch the instrument's four strings simultaneously. Today, a straight and tightly strung bow permits the player to intone the notes only successively, creating an arpeggio effect.

The melodic and contrapuntal ingenuity embodied in Bach's

Chaconne has provided both a challenge and a creative stimulus for many later composers. Mendelssohn wrote piano accompaniments to Bach's solo violin sonatas. Brahms transposed the *Chaconne* into a piano exercise piece for the left hand alone—an artistic work with almost mystical overtones. After Brahms had sent the "left-handed" *Chaconne* to his dear friend the acclaimed piano virtuoso Clara Schumann, he learned that she had injured her right hand and had craved the opportunity to keep her left hand active. Leopold Stokowski was perhaps the most ambitious of all, transcribing the *Chaconne* (which Bach had conceived as a monophonic piece) into a showpiece for full orchestra, a daring deed much applauded, but also much criticized as not true to the spirit of Bach.

In his *Chaconne*, Bach created not only a compositional phenomenon but a deeply moving musical miracle. Paul Henry Lang sums it up well in this observation: "In his *Chaconne*, Bach waves aside all restrictions and all conventions, unloosens all ties to the rational and empirical, plunging us, with the aid of a little wooden box with four strings on it, and a thin rod with horsehair stretched from end to end, into the irrational and timeless."

Virtuoso

The world around him knew little of Bach the composer during his lifetime, but as a performer on the organ and harpsichord he enjoyed a wide reputation. One of his contemporaries, Constantin Bellermann, a composer himself, commented on Bach's organ-playing: "Like Handel among the English, he deserves to be called the miracle of Leipzig. . . . For if it pleases him, he can by the use of his feet alone . . . achieve such a rapid concord of sounds on the organ that others would seem unable to imitate it even with their fingers."

It is a mystery how Bach managed to acquire this fabled mastery, already evident to his contemporaries when he was still very young. Bach was hardly eighteen years old when he was chosen in 1703 by the consistory of Arnstadt's Neuekirche to supervise the building of a new organ. Testing this organ shortly before its completion, Bach played the instrument with such impressive skill that the congregation was moved to hire him on the spot, notwithstanding the fact that the church already employed an old organist, Andreas Börner. Apparently, the consistory found it worthwhile to pension off Börner and install Bach as their organist. Their later experiences with this young firebrand were, however, less pleasant (see *Abendmusik*).

In the Germany of Bach's day, superior ability as an organist provided the assurance of a lasting livelihood; it was a talent in demand not only among the church communities, but also in the numerous princely courts. Indeed, Bach (then twenty-three) would leave Mühlhausen in 1708 to become court organist for Duke Wilhelm Ernst of Weimar. It was while employed there, in 1714, that his virtuosic talents earned him a touching, and valuable, tribute. During a guest appearance in the small principality of Kassel, the reigning prince (later the king of Sweden) "was so overcome by Bach's playing that he drew from his finger a ring set with precious stones and presented it to Bach as soon as the music had died away."

While he still was court organist in Weimar in 1717—approaching thirty years of age and clearly at the height of his powers—a rival harpsichord virtuoso unintentionally paid Bach the performer a great compliment. Louis Marchand (1669–1732) was, like Bach, a composer and court musician, a virtuoso on both the organ and harpsichord. Unlike the self-effacing Leipzig cantor, Marchand, who was employed at the royal court in Paris, was also well known as a musician "full of vanity, pride and petty caprice." When he was divorced by his wife, and the king decreed that he pay her half of his income, he is supposed to have snapped: "Sir, if my wife gets half of my salary, let her play half of the service."

Both Bach and the arrogant Frenchman chanced to be in Dresden at the same time, in September 1717. Taking advantage of the situation, Bach's friend, Jean-Baptiste Volumier, a local concertmaster who disliked Marchand, arranged one of the earliest recorded "piano competitions" between the two virtuosi. A contemporary source reported the event:

> Curiosity and excitement rose to a high pitch, as a large and brilliant assembly of both sexes had met. Bach and the umpires were punctual, but Marchand came not. The company waited a while; then the count sent to remind Marchand of his appointment, and received in reply the news that Marchand had set out that very morning by fast coach, and had disappeared from Dresden.

Bach's competitor had abandoned the field, leaving Bach to play alone. It may be supposed that Marchand had earlier heard Bach perform and must have convinced himself that the Weimar organist was infinitely his superior in both invention and technique.

Famed French harpsichordist Jean Louis Marchand was to take part in a 1717 piano competition with Bach, at the court of Dresden. But Marchand was said to have fled town, fearing that he would lose. Bach was declared the winner by default, a victory that was said to have been indicative of Germany's ascendancy over France in clavier music.

While the Dresden competition became one of music history's great nonevents, it was not at all odd that Marchand should have originally been considered a good match for Bach, especially on the clavier. It was the general opinion in the music circles of the time that the French school had the advantage and preference in clavier music, having produced great composers for this instrument, ranging from Jean-Baptiste Lully to François Couperin. Certainly, French clavier music *had* reached a high state of sophistication. But then Johann Sebastian Bach appeared on the scene, which shifted the balance decisively toward Germany. The unrealized Bach–Marchand keyboard competition—with Bach winning by default—furnished resounding proof of his and Germany's ascendancy in the art of the clavier.

Vivaldi

Aclose Bach contemporary, Antonio Vivaldi (1678–1741), has of late undergone a remarkable revival. There are few lovers of the Baroque today who do not possess in their CD libraries a recording of his classic work *The Seasons*, which has amassed nearly one hundred listings in the most recent *Schwann Catalogue*. Vivaldi's immense prodigality, some five hundred concertos, is akin to Bach's. But, similar to Telemann's (see entry), his facile talent too often sacrificed depth for speed of composition. It was said of him that he could grind out concertos endlessly, effortlessly— "like spaghetti." In no way do his works attain the richness of Bach's solid fugal construction.

Antonio Vivaldi as portrayed in a sketch by P. L. Ghezzi (1723). Vivaldi was one of the great violin virtuosi of his day, and the composer of more than four hundred concertos for this instrument. Bach was a great admirer of his Italian contemporary and created clavier and harpsichord works adapted from Vivaldi violin concertos.

As with so many composers of the Baroque era, and even beyond, Vivaldi's vast corpus was dictated by the nature of his employment. A composer and conductor, he was required to produce music for the numerous concerts of the conservatory of the Ospedale della Pietà in Venice, an orphanage for girls. The inmates received such excellent instruction in ensemble playing that they were able to form an orchestra of European repute.

During his lifetime, Vivaldi enjoyed international fame. And yet, just as in the case of Bach, his reputation collapsed after his death. It wasn't even discovered until 1938 that he died in 1741 and had been buried in Vienna, an unknown.

Bach very much admired Vivaldi's work. As early as his Weimar days, Bach had greatly profited from the study of Vivaldi's music, particularly in matters of form and structure. Vivaldi set a fine example for Bach with his light and pleasing melodic inventions, born under Italy's blue sky, an influence that tended to ease somewhat Bach's "heavier," more serious Germanic style.

However, merely to note that Bach "copied" Vivaldi's works would be a decided understatement. As was usually the case when he copied works of his contemporaries or predecessors, Bach always enriched and vitalized them, thanks to the inventive powers of his own mind (see *Recycling*). His adaptation of Vivaldi's work was no exception. A typical example is Bach's *Concerto in D Major* for harpsichord, which he fashioned after Vivaldi's violin concerto of the same key. As Gerald Herz, a prominent Bach expert, observed, "Bach here almost chuckles over Vivaldi's naiveté, his melodic and rhythmic simplicity, and builds a crackling fire of Baroque vitality under Vivaldi's melodically simplistic ditties."

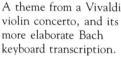

A theme from a Vivaldi violin concerto, and its more elaborate Bach keyboard transcription.

Perhaps the most telling example of Bach's imaginative reworking of Vivaldi's music occurred when the master made use of some of the Italian's violin concertos as the basis of a series of concertos for one, two, three, or even four harpsichords. These clavier concertos were no doubt premiered by Bach himself, joined by other keyboard players—perhaps among them his young sons, Wilhelm Friedemann and Carl Philipp Emanuel—in performances of Leipzig's Collegium Musicum (see entry). The *Concerto in A Minor* for four harpsichords has been hailed as the most brilliant elaboration, and elevation, of Vivaldi's nimble violin concertos. It is glorious Bach throughout, and its use of four claviers is a unique phenomenon in the musical literature.

Of course, it must be admitted with regret that not everybody likes Bach, Vivaldi-inspired or not. Hector Berlioz, an avid Bach-hater, once witnessed a memorable performance of this A-minor concerto by a group of outstanding young pianists that included Frédéric Chopin and Franz Liszt. Berlioz commented sourly: "It was heart-rending, I assure you, to see such admirable talents, full of fire, brilliant in youthful vitality, united in a bundle to reproduce this ridiculous and stupid psalmody." Notwithstanding Berlioz's harsh judgment, Bach's quadruple concerto has survived as an ever-exciting selection in today's concert programs.

Bach and Vivaldi—two men too easily forgotten in the eighteenth-century rejection of the Baroque (see *Zeitgeist*)—are today integral parts of our musical heritage. Obviously, Bach's star shines more brightly today than that of the agile, charming Italian composer. Vivaldi biographer Marc Pincherle put the two talents into proper perspective when he observed: "Far be it from me to equate Vivaldi with Bach. But to stand comparison with him—even for a moment—is quite a handsome claim to glory."

Wanderlust

Musicians tended to be venturesome travelers in Bach's time. Perhaps the prototype of the peripatetic German musician-composer was the noted organist Johann Jacob Froberger. A student of Girolamo Frescobaldi, he held positions in Vienna, London, Paris, and Brussels, and even survived a shipwreck. Handel and Johann Christian Bach, Sebastian's youngest son, also offer fine examples of musicians whose globe-trotting propensities yielded both fame and fortune. The miracle is that Bach—the very paradigm of a provincial cantor who never traveled far from home—would, in posthumous fame, outdistance all of these well-traveled cosmopolitans.

Although Bach's trips were as a rule limited in geographic range and of brief duration, he traveled often and derived obvious pleasure

Bach was a frequent traveler, starting in early youth when he had to make his way by foot. In his later years, he traveled by coach through Saxony and its neighboring German states to inspect and dedicate new organs. But in all his life he seems never to have ventured beyond a radius of about two hundred miles.

209

from his peregrinations. He was indeed a tireless trudger, restless from earliest youth and always in search of opportunities to improve his art and station. On March 15, 1700, shortly before his fifteenth birthday, he left his brother's house in Ohrdruf to walk two hundred miles north to Lüneburg, where he had been promised a position as a paid chorister in the town's Michaeliskirche. Penniless, he slept in haylofts or sheds, picking up some pin money here and there by playing the fiddle in taverns. Lüneburg was a most fortunate destination for the young Bach, offering a superb music library as well as the nearby princely court of Celle. At Celle, the peripatetic young man was first exposed to the charm of French music, which would exert a decisive influence upon his later work (see *Education*).

Within five years, Bach lived in four cities—Sangerhausen, Weimar, Arnstadt, and Mühlhausen—then returned to Weimar at the age of twenty-three, where he settled in for eight years as court organist for Duke Wilhelm Ernst. After this, only two assignments followed: Cöthen, where during his thirties, he spent six very happy and productive years, from 1717 to 1723; and Leipzig, where he stayed—not very happily on the whole—until his death in 1750 (see *Leipzig Ordeal*).

In these later periods of his life, Bach traveled frequently, usually prompted by his reputation as an organ expert. Many congregations called upon him to evaluate their newly built instruments (see *Keyboard Expert*). These invitations became in time a welcome source of income for Bach—and a relief from his crowded local routine.

Memorable in this respect was his visit to Halle during his last year in Weimar (1716). Bach was invited to inspect the new organ at Halle's Liebfrauenkirche in the company of Johann Kuhnau, whom he was to succeed in Leipzig seven years later. The community apparently treated the visit of the two noted musicians as the occasion for a gala celebration. Civic accounts reveal that elaborate preparations were made to provide for the comfort and appetites of the two judges. A staff of servants and coachmen were put at their disposal. According to contemporary reports, guests were invited to join the distinguished organists for a luxury dinner, sharing with them a generous fare that included "eggs boiled in brine, cold meats and ox tongue—all washed down with Franconian wine and beer."

Two months earlier, Bach had traveled with his master, Duke Wilhelm Ernst of Weimar, to neighboring Weissenfels, to join in the birthday celebration of the region's young Duke Christian. This petty potentate doesn't seem to have been a great intellectual light, but was fanatically devoted to hunting, a sport in which he had achieved great prowess. Bach was prepared. He had composed for this occasion his first secular cantata, the *Hunting Cantata*—"The Hunt Is My Delight." It was probably performed in the ducal park, thus earning Bach the title of Weissenfels's "open-air court conductor," a title he proudly used in his signature until the duke's death on June 23, 1730, though he had no further relationship with the court.

Bach's earliest travels were clearly undertaken in the hope of broadening his musical horizons. His peregrination from Arnstadt to Lübeck in order to hear the music of Dietrich Buxtehude (see *Abendmusik*) was a prime example. In later life, he traveled mostly to seek patronage or to pick up "freelance" assignments. The most important of these was of course the last of his professional trips, to the Potsdam court of Frederick the Great (see entry) in 1747, undertaken when Bach had reached the relatively advanced age of sixty-two. It was this visit that produced his tribute to the famed monarch—the *Musical Offering*—an immortal composition worthy of both the Prussian king and the genius of the restless Leipzig cantor.

Ye Trumpets Resound

A sprightly secular cantata that Bach wrote in 1733 is entitled *Tönet, ihr Pauken! Erschallet Trompeten!* (Resound Ye Tympanies! Let Trumpets Blare!). This stirring trumpet cantata reminds us once again that Bach's musical vocabulary extended far beyond the range of only the keyboard instruments—the organ, harpsichord, and clavichord. (See *Violinist* for another example.)

Bach again proved himself a pioneer in the uses to which he put the trumpet and a variety of other wind instruments. Even when Bach came on the scene, there were still some social taboos that stood in the way of using trumpets in church services. Wind instruments were till then heard almost exclusively in aristocratic circles. Only the mighty of the world were permitted to let fanfares resound in their festive pageantry (e.g., to announce the arrival of some august dignitary) or to have a trumpeter blare forth with a hunting horn both to initiate and to bring to an end the royal chase. The use of wind instruments remained almost exclusively a princely privilege for most of the seventeenth century. If, for example, a rich burgher—possessed by delusions of grandeur—wanted to have trumpets mark the wedding of his daughter, he could do so only with the permission of the reigning lord.

This association of trumpet music with aristocratic and wealthy patrons contributed to the elevated social and financial status of the trumpeting fraternity. In army bands, trumpeters formed an exclusive group having the rank of officers. In town bands, the trumpeters could demand pay double that of other instrumentalists.

So we can see that when the thirty-six-year-old Bach, then a widower, remarried in 1721, he made a match that was both socially

WALDHORN

Horn players were part of a prince's retinue. They signaled the beginning and end of a hunting party. *Courtesy of Archiv für Kunst und Geschichte*

acceptable and musically congenial. For he then took as his wife Anna Magdalena, the daughter of a trumpet virtuoso, Johann Kaspar Wülcken—court and field trumpeter for his Highness, the prince of Saxe-Weissenfels. Anna Magdalena was not only socially distinguished, she was also reputed to be a talented singer and a serious devotée of the musical arts (see *Helpmate*).

Trumpeter blasts forth to announce the beginning of a military campaign. The penetrating, assertive sound of this instrument and the kettle drum *(opposite page)* were believed to inspire the assembled soldiers with courage. Bach daringly used the two instruments in some of his cantatas and in the Christmas Oratorio heralding the triumphal arrival of the Saviour.

TROMPETTE

By the time of Bach's second marriage, the trumpet had lost a bit of its privileged status. It became more widely used in ceremonies staged by town authorities to mark festive occasions. Since Bach had been appointed not only cantor of the Thomasschule but also Leipzig's municipal music director (*Director Musice Lipsiensis*), he was often called upon to create secular cantatas—celebratory music to welcome

PAUCKE

dignitaries who were visiting the town. For these occasions, Bach employed brass instruments prominently (see *Pageantry*).

Whatever instrument Bach turned to—organ, harpsichord, violin, and last but not least the trumpet—he was urged on by the hope of expanding its tonal range. But his attempts to achieve this in the field of brass instruments were perhaps the most frustrating for him, because there just weren't very many capable trumpeters around. Here, as elsewhere, Bach had to adjust to the instrumental (and vocal) talents available to him—their competence, as a rule, far below his standards.

The playing of Bach's trumpet parts has remained a problem—even after Bach's death—despite the continued progress of instrument technology. But even the presence of technically advanced instruments (trumpets provided with keys) did not prevent leading musicians from concluding that Bach's trumpet parts were "almost unplayable." This belief prompted the German cornet player Julius Kosleck to construct a special Bach trumpet of extended length. This lead to a further Bach revival—of his trumpet music—though the artistry required to play this unusual instrument didn't favor its long survival.

The trumpet section of an orchestra is still to this day a conductor's anguished concern. The brasses can create glorious high points in a symphonic performance, but they are also apt to become a source of vexation, given the scarcity of trumpet players with truly virtuoso talent. Luckily, the situation may now be changing. Of late, Bach's trumpet music has seen a remarkable revival—through the performances and recordings of the young virtuoso Wynton Marsalis, as well as those of the Canadian Brass and similar groups.

Zeitgeist

How can it be explained that when Bach died, so much that he had achieved seemed to vanish from public consciousness? And yet, not quite a century later, his music was to return to the world in triumph. In 1738, twelve years *before* his death, Johann Adolf Scheibe, a respected music critic, had dismissed Bach's work as "bombastic and confused" (see *Detractors*). Less than a century later, Rossini would exult: "If Beethoven is a prodigy among men... Bach is a miracle of God."

During his astounding career, Bach had perfected the fugal art. But even before his death in 1750, at the age of sixty-five, complex polyphony was giving way to a simpler, more melodic style of music, a style in which even his own sons, Carl Philipp Emanuel and Johann Christian, were gaining fame (see *Art Galant*). The public's taste had shifted from chorale to song, from suite to sonata, from concerto grosso to symphony. Indeed, this change in musical taste was but one manifestation of a profound change, throughout Europe, in the *Zeitgeist*: The dominant cultural spirit was that of the Age of Enlightenment.

While Bach was still an infant, Isaac Newton had fired the opening shot of this new age. His *Principia Mathematica* (1687) had revealed God's universe to be governed by comprehensible, immutable laws. Three years later, in 1690, John Locke argued, in his *Essay Concerning Human Understanding*, that human beings were rational creatures who continuously learned from their experience and were perfectible, rather than being corrupted from birth by "original sin." John Toland's *Christianity Not Mysterious* (1696) attacked the power of the organized church and condemned all religious dogma that contra-dicted reason or common sense.

During the eighteenth century, these trends of thought seriously undermined the base upon which Christianity's strong fortress had stood. It was in 1751, one year after Bach's death, that the Enlighten-ment reached its peak with the appearance of the first volume of the "dictionary of reason"—the great French *Encyclopédie* edited by d'Alembert and Diderot.

However, the abrupt neglect of Bach after his death cannot be explained entirely by a cultural antipathy toward religion and religous music. After all, there was considerably more to Bach than the Protestant churchman that he appeared to be in the eyes of most of his contemporaries. Seemingly endless in number were the secular works he had created for his princely masters, his students, and the rising class of musical dilettantes.

The new *Zeitgeist* was to pass by these secular Bach works just as it had all of his deeply religious creations. In part, this was because his secular works were as fully expressive of his inimitable fugal style as his sacred works. But it must also be acknowledged that very few works out of Bach's vast corpus were even known to the cultured public after his death. Since no more than a dozen of his works had been printed during his lifetime, the world (with the exception of his faithful students) had little awareness of the musical giant that had passed (see *Music Publisher*).

Hence, it is perhaps not entirely correct to say that Bach, as a composer of both sacred and secular music, was "forgotten" *after* his death. In truth, many of the treasures he had created were not even known *during* his lifetime. Thus, when the new *Zeitgeist* of the "High Enlightenment" brought with it the taste for lighter and more melodic music, there were only a few Bachians among the mass of cultured men and women (who determined the *Zeitgeist*) that could champion the cause of the great Baroque polyphonist, the Leipzig cantor.

It remained for the Age of Romanticism, through one of its finest representatives, Felix Mendelssohn, to open the door to the Bachian treasures that had been inadvertently closed in his own time (see *Revival*). As Gerhard Herz, one of the highly respected specialists in this field, once remarked, "The secular Age of Enlightenment had buried Bach; the Romantic era, with its newly awakened sense of history, revived him."

It is ironic that in our own most secular age, Bach's sacred works have established as firm a hold on the music world as his more worldly compositions. As Arnold Schönberg observed, "Bach survives eternal."

F I N I S.

Acknowledgments

A Bach book should be written in a center of musicological research. Fate has moved me, retired from my former New York beat, far from Manhattan's rich musical and biographical resources. I was fortunate therefore—upon my arrival at Florida's Gold Coast—to become curator of rare books at Florida Atlantic University's Wimberly Library. Its director, Dr. William Miller, who truly has taken Wimberly into the computer age, extended to me every possible courtesy. Always cooperative has been the staff of its various departments—especially the one to which I was assigned. The Systems Development and Archives Department is ably directed by Zita Cael, and her associates Gloria Bock, Margaret VanHoff, and Karen Heinich. I owe a special debt to Wimberly's Inter-Library Loan Department under the guidance of Nancy Wynen. It tracked down for me Bach sources remote in origin.

The task of compiling an accurate and appropriate bibliography for a book such as this—with extensive and farflung sources—was considerably eased for me by the assistance of Lana Thompson. She herself is attached to the subject of Bach *con amore* and is a master of computer technology, a subject of which I must confess profound ignorance.

While David Gottlieb plows other fields than those of musicology—with education his main interest—he is a researcher of rare talent. Time and again he lightened my authorial burden.

The Bettmann Archive in New York is now BETTMANN, a highly computerized international picture source. Its staff has been unsparing in making its vast resources available to me. My special thanks go out to the director of the firm's new publishing division, David Greenstein, and the head of the BETTMANN researchers, Katherine Bang, a leading force in the publication of the new *Bettmann Portable Archive*.

Perhaps this book would never have seen the light (and the world would have had to limp along without it) had it not been for the advice of Dr. Faith Berry—once a colleague of mine at FAU—now professor of Afro-American literature at the University of California, Santa Barbara. It was Professor Berry who suggested that—in view of the unusual nature of my Bach biography (topicality replacing chronology)—I try to interest a publisher known for sponsoring unconventional projects: namely, the Carol Publishing Group in New York. And, indeed, I found at Carol acceptance of my idea and ever-ready support from its editor-in-chief, Hillel Black.

Bibliography

Note: The books and articles devoted to the life and music of Johann Sebastian Bach are overwhelming in number. Much of this literature has been created by Bach specialists *for* Bach specialists. A great many of these complex musicological studies may be somewhat intimidating to the layman. Within the vast library of books and monographs there are, however, some works which tower above the others in scope and scholarship. Even those Bach lovers who are more interested in listening to the Master's works than reading about them would profit from a knowledge of those books that form the core of Bach literature.

The biographies by Philipp Spitta and Albert Schweitzer remain unsurpassed, even in the face of the great strides made in Bach research since their appearance a century ago. Acknowledged at present as the leading authority in the field is Harvard professor Christoph Wolff, whose penetrating studies and discovery of previously unknown Bach works have added greatly to our knowledge of both Bach's music and the world he lived in. Dr. Wolff's articles have been assembled in his monumental volume *Bach: Essays on His Life and Music.* Another work to be recommended is Robert L. Marshall's recent study, *The Music of Johann Sebastian Bach,* which permits us to see Bach at work and to gain an appreciation of the master's thinking while he created his masterworks.

Among the literally thousands of references in my personal card file devoted to Bach, one work stands out as essential to any Bach enthusiast—a book which has been endlessly helpful to my efforts in producing this present volume: *The Bach Reader* by Hans T. David and Arthur Mendel. First published in 1945, it is to this day a staple in the music department of serious bookshops and libraries. It offers a rich overview of Bach—the man, the virtuoso, and the composer—as revealed in the words of Bach himself and those of his contemporaries.

Following is a list of many of the works from which I have profited in my long study of Bach and his world—and from whose texts I have quoted in this book.

Ackerman, Diane. *A Natural History of Love.* New York: Random House, 1994.

Balanchine, George. *Balanchine's Complete Stories of the Great Ballets.* Garden City, N.Y.: Doubleday, 1977.

223

Bettmann, Otto. "Bach in Potsdam." *American Scholar*, Winter 1982–83. pp. 81–87.

————. "Bach the Rhetorician." *American Scholar*, Winter 1985–86. pp. 113–18.

————. *Bettmann: The Picture Man*. Gainesville: University of Florida Press, 1977.

Bookspan, Martin. *101 Masterpieces of Music and Their Composers*. Garden City, N.Y.: Doubleday, 1968.

Boyd, Malcolm. *Bach*. New York: Vintage Books, 1987.

Brockway, Wallace, and Herbert Weinstock. *Men and Music: Their Lives, Times and Achievements*. New York: Simon and Schuster, 1958.

Bukofzer, Manfred F. *Music in the Baroque Era*. New York: W. W. Norton, 1947.

Butler, George. "Fugue and Rhetoric." *Journal of Music Theory*, 1977.

Chiapusso, Jan. *Bach's World*. Westport, Conn.: Greenwood Press, 1980.

Cox, Howard, ed. *The Calov Bible of Bach*. Ann Arbor, Mich: UMI Research Press, 1985.

Critchley, McDonald, ed. *Music and the Brain*. London: Heineman Medical Books, 1977.

David, Hans Theodore. *J. S. Bach's Musical Offering: History, Interpretation and Analysis*. New York: Dover Publications, 1972.

————, and A. Mendel, eds., *The Bach Reader: A Life of Johann Sebastian Bach in Letters and Documents*. New York: W. W. Norton, 1972.

Dreyfus, Laurence. *Bach's Continuo Group: Players and Practice*. Cambridge, Mass: Harvard University Press, 1987.

Drinker, Henry, S. *Index and Concordance to the English Texts of the Complete Choral Works of Johann Sebastian Bach*. New York: Association of American Colleges, 1942.

Dürr, Alfred. *Die Kantaten von Johannn Sebastian Bach*, vols. 1 and 2. Kassel: Bärenreiter-Verlag, 1979.

Edel, Leon. *Writing Lives. Principia Biographia*. New York: W. W. Norton, 1984.

Ehrenzweig, Anton. *The Psychoanalysis of Artistic Vision and Hearing*, 2nd ed. London: Sheldon Press, 1975.

Einstein, Alfred. *Essays on Music*. New York: W. W. Norton, 1962.

Fauchier-Magnon, Adrian. *The Small German Courts in the Eighteenth Century*. London: Methuen, 1947.

Felix, Werner. *Johann Sebastian Bach*. New York: W. W. Norton, 1985.

Forkel, Johann Nikolaus. *Johann Sebastian Bach: His Life, Art and Work*. Notes and appendixes by Charles Sanford Terry. New York: Da Capo Press, 1970.

Friedrich, Otto. *Glenn Gould: A Life and Variations*. New York: Random House, 1989.

Geiringer, Karl. *The Bach Family: Seven Generations of Creative Genius*. New York: Oxford University Press, 1954.

_____, and Irene Geiringer. *Johann Sebastian Bach: The Culmination of an Era*. New York: Oxford University Press, 1966.

Gelatt, Roland, *Music Makers: Some Outstanding Musical Performers of the Day*. New York: Da Capo Press, 1972.

Grout, Donald Jay, and Claude V. Palisca. *A History of Western Music*. New York: W. W. Norton, 1988.

Grunfeld, Frederic V. "Johann Sebastian Bach." *Horizon*, Winter 1971, vol. xiii, no. 1. New York: American Heritage, pp. 58–65.

Grew, Eva Mary, and Sydney. *Bach: The Master Musicians*. New York: McGraw Hill, 1972.

Hamburger, Michael, ed. *Beethoven: Letters, Journals and Conversations*. New York: Thames and Hudson, 1984.

Helm, Ernst Eugen. *Music at the Court of Frederick the Great*. Norman: Oklahoma University Press, 1960.

Herz, Gerhard. *Bach Sources in America*. Kassel: Bärenreiter Verlag, 1984.

_____. *Essays on J. S. Bach*. Ann Arbor, Mich.: UMI Research Press, 1985.

Highet, Gilbert. *Talents and Geniuses: The Pleasures of Appreciation*. New York: Oxford University Press, 1957.

Hofstadter, Douglas R. *Gödel, Escher, Bach: An Eternal Golden Braid*. New York: Basic Books, 1979.

James, Jamie. *The Music of the Spheres*. New York: Grove/Atlantic Monthly Press, 1993.

Kahn, Albert E. *Joys and Sorrows: The Memoirs of Pablo Casals*. New York: Simon and Schuster, 1970.

Kenney, Sylvia W., ed. *Catalog of the Emilie and Karl Riemenschneider Memorial Bach Library*. New York: Columbia University Press, 1960.

LaGrange, Henri Louis. *Mahler*. Garden City, N.Y.: Doubleday, 1973.

Landowska, Wanda. *Landowska on Music*, ed. Denis Restout. New York: Stein and Day, 1964.

Lang, Paul Henry. *Music in Western Civilization*. New York: W. W. Norton, 1941.

Lang, Paul Henry, and Otto L. Bettmann. *Pictorial History of Music*. New York: W. W. Norton, 1960.

Lebrecht, Norman. *The Book of Musical Anecdotes*. New York: Free Press, 1985.

Marshall, Robert Lewis. *The Music of Johann Sebastian Bach: The Sources, the Style, the Significance*. New York: Schirmer Books, 1989.

————. *The Compositional Process of J. S. Bach: A Study of the Autograph Scores of the Vocal Works*. Princeton Studies in Music no. 4. Princeton, N.J.: Princeton University Press, 1972.

Mellers, Wilfrid. *Bach and the Dance of God*. New York: Oxford University Press, 1981.

Mendel, Arthur. *Some Aspects of Musicology: Three Essays*. New York: Bobbs-Merrill, 1957.

Meynell, Esther. *Bach*. New York: A. A. Wyn, 1949.

Neumann, Werner, *Auf den Lebenwegen Johann Sebastian Bach*. Berlin: Verlag der Nation, 1957.

————. *Pictorial Documents of the Life of Johann Sebastian Bach*. Kassel: Bärenreiter Verlag, 1979.

New Grove Dictionary of Music and Musicians. London: Macmillan, 1980.

Oldroyd, Georg. *The Technique and Spirit of Fugue: An Historical Study*. Westport, Conn.: Greenwood Press, 1986.

Pachter, Mac. *Telling Lives*. New York: Simon and Schuster, 1979.

Parry, C. Hubert. *Johann Sebastian Bach: The Story of the Development of a Great Personality*, rev. ed. St. Clair Shores, Mich: Scholarly Press, 1977.

Pirro, André. *Johann Sebastian Bach: The Organist and His World*. New York: AMS Press, 1978.

Rosen, Charles. *The Classical Style: Hayden, Mozart, Beethoven.* New York: W. W. Norton, 1972.

Scheide, William H. *Johann Sebastian Bach as Biblical Interpreter.* Princeton, N.J.: Princeton Pamphlets, 1952.

Schindler, Anton. *Beethoven as I Knew Him.* Chapel Hill: University of North Carolina Press, 1966.

Schmieder, Wolfgang. *Themastisches Systematisches Verzeichnis der Musikalischen Werke von Johann Sebastian Bach.* Wiesbaden: Breitkopf & Härtel, 1950.

Schulze, Hans-Joachim, and Christopher Wolff. *Bach Compendium: Analytisch-repertorium der Werke Johann Sebastian Bach.* Frankfort; C. F. Peters, 1985.

Schweitzer, Albert. *J. S. Bach,* trans. Ernest Newman. New York: Macmillan, 1950.

_____. *Out of My Life and Thought: An Autobiography.* New York: Henry Holt, 1990.

Schwendowius, Barbara, and Wolfgang Dömling, eds. *Johann Sebastian Bach: Life, Times, Influence.* New Haven: Yale University Press, 1984.

Spitta, Philipp. *Johann Sebastian Bach: His Work and Influence on the Music of Germany.* New York: Dover Books, 1951.

Terry, Charles Sanford. *Bach: A Biography.* St. Clair Shores, Mich.: Scholarly Press, 1972.

_____. *Bach's Orchestra.* London: Oxford University Press, 1961.

_____. *The Music of Bach: An Introduction.* New York: Dover Books, 1963.

Thomas, Lewis. *The Lives of a Cell: Notes of a Biology Watcher.* New York: Viking Press, 1974.

Tovey, Sir Donald Francis. *A Companion to "The Art of Fugue."* London: Oxford University Press, 1960.

Trautman, Christoph. "Bach's Bible," in Leaver, Robin. *Bach's Theologische bibliothek.* Stuttgart: Hanssler-Verlag, 1983.

Weaver, Robert, ed. *Essays on the Music of J. S. Bach and Other Diverse Subjects: A Tribute to Gerhard Herz.* Louisville, Ky.: University of Louisville Press, 1981.

Weaver, W., and M. Chudis, eds. "The Naïveté of Verdi," in *The Verdi Companion.* New York: W. W. Norton, 1979.

Wolff, Christoph, ed. *BACH, Essays on His Life and Music.* Cambridge, Mass.: Harvard University Press, 1991.

Wolff, Christoph. *The New Grove Bach Family.* New York: W. W. Norton, 1983.

Young, Percy Marshall. *The Bachs, 1500–1850.* New York: T. Y. Crowell, 1970.

Zuckerkandl, Victor. *Man the Musician.* Bollingen Series XLIV.2 Princeton, N.J.: Princeton University Press, 1973.

Index